A Dictionary of
Chinese Symbols

The Author

Wolfram Eberhard is Professor at the University of Berkeley, California. Born in Potsdam, he has long been interested in the symbolic language of the Chinese, and in 1934–5 was 'lecteur' at Peking National University. He later became director of the East Asian collections in the Museum of Folk History in Leipzig. In 1937 he was appointed Professor at the University of Ankara, and since 1948 he has been at Berkeley. His other publications include *A History of China* (Routledge & Kegan Paul; 4th edition, 1977).

A DICTIONARY OF CHINESE SYMBOLS

Hidden Symbols in Chinese Life and Thought

WOLFRAM EBERHARD

Translated from the German by G. L. Campbell

Routledge

London and New York

First published in German as Lexikon chinesischer Symbole
by Eugen Diederichs Verlag, Cologne, in 1983
© 1983 Eugen Diederichs Verlag

This edition first published in 1986
by Routledge & Kegan Paul Ltd

Reprinted in 1988 and 1989
by Routledge
11 New Fetter Lane, London EC4P 4EE
29 West 35th Street, New York, NY 10001

Set in Linotron Times Roman
by Input Typesetting Ltd, London
and printed in Great Britain
by St Edmundsbury Press Ltd
Bury St Edmunds, Suffolk

This translation © Routledge & Kegan Paul 1986

Library of Congress Cataloging in Publication Data
Eberhard, Wolfram, 1909–

A dictionary of Chinese symbols.
Translation of: Lexikon chinesischer Symbole.
Bibliography: p.
1. China—Civilization—Dictionaries.   2. Symbolism
in art—China—Dictionaries.   I. Title   ·
DS721.E32613   1986   951'.003'21   85–8187

British Library CIP data available
ISBN 0-415-00228-1 (pbk.)

Contents

The Symbolic Language of the Chinese

i

European notions about China and the Chinese have changed more than once over the centuries. In antiquity, China was a mysterious place about which little was or could be known. Through the Middle Ages and up to the end of the 18th century, it was known as a huge country with a stable administration and refined customs and manners: a country which one might well admire. In China, wrote Leibniz, even the peasants behave with a dignity and a reserve which in Europe we find only among the nobility; and they never lose their temper.

There followed a period in which China's military weakness made her an easy prey for the colonialist powers. The Qing rulers and administration were vicious and corrupt, and sought to keep themselves in power by means of drastic, indeed savage, laws. It was around the turn of the century that individual Europeans began to realise that if we in the West are to understand China, knowledge of the Chinese language, and especially of Chinese literature with its rich legacy of poetry and prose, is indispensable. Thus it was that Richard Wilhelm, who began his career as pastor and missionary in the German colony of Kiaochow, was able, thanks to his translations and his original writings, to transform the German view of China within two decades. He was convinced, and he succeeded in convincing others, that we in the West could learn much from Oriental ways of life and thought. He saw himself as a mediator between two cultures. Now, fifty years after his death, the question still remains open: are Chinese thought processes different from ours? Several scholars in this field think that they are, and adduce the Chinese language itself in evidence. Chinese has no declensions or conjugations, in our sense of these words. Basically, a Chinese 'word' consists of one immutable phoneme: and there are some 400 of these basic phonemes. Two or more phonemes may, however, be combined to form new 'words'; and, as North Chinese has four tones (i.e. each base phoneme can be pronounced in four different tones, with consequent change of meaning) this gives a four-fold extension of the available phonemes. Even allowing for all of this, however, the number of homonyms remains very high. On the other hand, Chinese exhibits a certain economy in comparison with Western languages equipped with an elaborate morphological apparatus. Why is it necessary to say 'three books' when the word 'three' already indicates the plural? And why should we have to say 'I *was* at the theatre yesterday' when the word 'yesterday' makes it clear that we are speaking of a past event? And why should languages have to express grammatical gender?

Of course, grammatical brevity has its own drawbacks. Taken out of context, a Chinese utterance can be very difficult to understand. And yet, it may even add to the charm of a love poem if we do not know whether a man is addressing a woman or another man.

From what we have said, it follows that Chinese words cannot be 'spelled'. If a Chinese sees that a word he has used in conversation has not been understood he will write the character he means on one hand with the index finger of the other. All Chinese characters are essentially pictures, and appeal therefore to the eye. In comparison, Westerners are 'people of the ear' rather than of the eye. Only a very small proportion of Chinese characters – some 200, perhaps – are simple representations of natural objects; all the others (and an educated Chinese will use up to 8,000 characters) are composite signs. Each sign is, broadly speaking, divisible into two components: a graphic component (representing a man, a woman, a tree, a fish, etc.) and a phonetic component, giving some indication as to how the character should be pronounced. This phonetic element is provided by a sign whose pronunciation is well known, and whose own inherent meaning can be disregarded in so far as the sign is playing a purely phonetic role in the composite character. To take an example: as soon as I see a particular Chinese character I can tell two things: first, from the graphic element (the root) I can see that the character denotes a plant of some kind, i.e. not a tree, a person or anything else; secondly, from the phonetic component I can make a guess as to the pronunciation.

All this is true of Chinese writing as used up to modern times. The latest script reform, however, has introduced radical changes. Abbreviation of characters means that many of the familiar graphic elements – the 'pictures' – are no longer recognisable, and far more characters have to be learnt off by heart. Let me emphasise once again, however, that Chinese are 'people of the eye': to them, the characters are *symbols*, not ways of notating *sounds*, which is the usual function of writing. Until quite recently, the Chinese had no separate word for 'symbol', for which they used the word *xiang*, meaning 'picture'. But what is a symbol? Instead of a long-winded discussion on a conceptual level, let us content ourselves with C. G. Jung's short definition: 'A word or a picture is symbolic if it contains more than can be grasped at first glance . . .' (*Man and His Symbols*, London, 1964). The symbols we shall be concerned with in this book express more or less realistically, but always *indirectly*, something which could be directly expressed but which, for certain reasons, cannot be put into words.

It is almost fifty years since Ferdinand Lessing spoke of the 'symbolic language' of the Chinese as a second form of language which penetrates all communication in Chinese; which is, as it were, a second-tier communication level, of greater potency than ordinary language, richer in nuances and shades of meaning. It is this second tier of communication that the present book seeks to elucidate.

In some respects, I am also taking my cue from Emil Preetorius, who assembled one of the finest collections of Far Eastern art. As he puts it: 'All Oriental paintings are meant to be viewed as symbols, and their characteristic themes – rocks, water, clouds, animals, trees, grass – betoken not only themselves, but also something beyond themselves: they *mean* something. There is virtually nothing in the whole of nature, organic or inorganic, no artefact, which the Oriental artist does not see as imbued with symbolic meaning, in so far as it can be represented and interpreted in one sense or another.' He adds: 'picture and script resonate with each other in form and content so much that often they inter-penetrate each other completely' (*Catalogue of the Preetorius Collection*, Munich, 1958).

ii

Preetorius would seem to be suggesting that learning to write in China is intimately connected with learning to paint. No doubt this is true up to a point; but there is a fundamental difference between the two, when we consider them as modes of communication. Writing conveys information which the reader is expected to understand or, at least, to try to understand. But when the educated Chinese sends a picture or a piece of calligraphy to a friend, the 'message' contained therein will not be expressed in so many words: often it will take the form of a quotation from classical literature – that is to say, the message is retrievable only if the recipient knows the source of the quotation and what it refers to. We may say that the picture contains a symbol, or that the symbol takes graphic form: in either case, the picture can be 'read' in two ways – as a work of art which is intended to give aesthetic pleasure to the beholder, or as an expression of good wishes concerning the recipient's longevity, progeny, etc. The picture as a whole, and the symbolical detail, are both designed to give a third party pleasure and to transmit a message to him, albeit in cryptic form.

The cryptic nature of the communication has much to do with the Chinese attitude to the human body and to sex. In all sexual matters the Chinese have always been extraordinarily prudish. It is true that recently texts dating from before 200 BC have been unearthed in which sexual behaviour is discussed in simple words and in a very down-to-earth manner. In later texts, however, anything of a sexual nature is expressed in terms of innuendo and elaborate metaphor, and all Chinese governments down to the present have been at pains to suppress and eradicate what they invariably see as 'pornography'. Confucius in his wisdom took a positive attitude to sex, though even he saw it primarily in terms of marriage, and best confined to the intimacy, the secrecy indeed, of the connubial chamber. Later Confucianism went so far as to advise husbands to avoid, as far as possible, physical contact with their wives. We may well doubt whether such advice was ever honoured in practice; but it remains true that the open display of love and eroticism was something deeply offensive to the Chinese in that it offended against propriety, against good behaviour. In literature as in art, if erotic matters had to be mentioned, this was done in periphrastic fashion and with the greatest subtlety, through an arcane secondary use of symbols, which the recipient might well understand but to which he would never explicitly refer. For the sender of the message, it was always a particular pleasure to see whether or not the recipient had understood the hidden meaning. The interplay of erotic symbols is accompanied by a kind of counterpoint of puns – something particularly easy to do in Chinese with its plethora of homonyms. To take an example: the utterance '*you yu*' can mean 'he has an abundance of . . .', 'he has . . . in abundance' (e.g. riches) or 'there is/are fish'. Hence a picture showing a fish is a pun, and the recipient of such a picture knows at once that the sender is wishing him 'abundance of wealth'. In most languages, the notion of 'abundance' would have to be derived from such considerations as 'fish occur in shoals' or 'fish lay vast quantities of eggs'; in Chinese, it is generated by simple phonetic equivalence.

Puns like this appeal to the Chinese ear, though they may also, and often do, appeal to the eye. Puns which depend not on Mandarin (High Chinese, or the language of the officials) but on a dialect pronunciation are often difficult to understand. For this reason, the Chinese prefer their puns to be eye-catching rather than ear-tickling.

The art of portrait painting has never been developed in China. This is of great significance, not only because of the contrast vis-à-vis Western practice. In part, the absence of portraiture in China has to do with the fact that in ancient times when a person of high rank died a painter was brought in to provide an image of the deceased. The painter arrived with a ready-made picture of a man in official garb or of a lady in court dress, and all he had to do was add a few lineaments of the deceased's face to complete the picture. There were virtually no likenesses of living persons, if we disregard emperors, and a few famous philosophers. Whether of living or dead persons, however, these likenesses eschew anything that smacks of eroticism. Men and women alike are always depicted clothed. What a contrast with the West, where even in religious iconography nude men and women, and infants being suckled at the naked breast, are the order of the day.

For the Chinese, nakedness is a mark of barbarism; and even where some attempt is made to produce 'pornography', the scenes are – in stark contrast to Japanese erotic art – of an almost juvenile innocence. Shame and virtue are as indissolubly linked in the modern Chinese mind as they were in the days of Confucius. Sexual matters can be referred to in symbolic form or in oblique metaphor, and in no other way.

iii

How is this reticence to be explained? Why this reluctance to do or say what one wants to do or say? In this connection I would like to point to one factor which seems to me to be of great significance. Already in the days of Confucius (*c.* 500 BC) we find the Chinese living huddled together in cramped quarters and in crowded villages. In these villages the houses were as close to each other as possible so as to leave the maximum amount of land for agricultural purposes. In the towns the houses were just as closely crowded together (as in European towns in the Middle Ages) so as to keep the defensive radius to a minimum: the shorter the town walls, the easier they were to defend.

The huts of the poorest people were made of straw and twigs; a better-class house had clay walls and a tiled roof. Until fairly recently, the windows were simply openings in the walls, covered perhaps with paper if one could afford it. Indoors, the rooms were divided by thin walls – again, often of paper. Every word spoken in such a room was audible in the rest of the house. There was no question of separate rooms for individual members of the family, so no one had any privacy. The people next door could also hear every word that was spoken.

For many centuries, no less than five families were held legally responsible for any crime or offence committed in their immediate surroundings; and they had to account for themselves to the state police in every detail: *they could never plead ignorance.* So, it is not difficult to see why it was held advisable to say as little as possible and to avoid anything that might lead to dissension within the family or in its immediate neighbourhood. In the same way, in art, overt statement of eroticism was avoided, lest others come to harm. For these reasons too, landscape was preferred to portrait or genre painting. Through adroit use of symbols, social content could be infused into landscape painting: some beholders would miss the point, others would understand and smile inwardly. Landscape appears as a cosmos, ordered and harmonious: life was a question of give and take, and if you wanted consideration from others, you had to show them consideration. It is small wonder that the European travellers and missionaries who visited China in the 16th, 17th and 18th centuries described the Chinese as an 'old' people – tranquil and serene in their wisdom, no doubt, but *lifeless.*

What the European travellers saw as 'lifelessness' was, in fact, reticence: extreme reticence, as the Chinese always had to bear in mind how others would react to any attitude they might adopt or any opinion they might utter. Thus they came to form a society which used symbolical forms and modes of expression, reinforced by ritual, to integrate the individual with public order and morality.

It is significant that until very recently there was no word in Chinese for what we call 'freedom', either in the political or in the philosophic sense. The word *zi-you*, which is still used for 'freedom', really means 'to be on one's own', 'to be left alone' – i.e. it has a negative connotation. Similarly, there was no word for 'individualism' and no word for 'equality of rights'. As the Chinese saw it, no man is equal to another: he is older or younger than another, superior to women in that he is male, or more highly placed in the state hierarchy. 'Brotherliness', as it was grasped in early Christianity, did not exist in China, for the individual saw himself as a member of a family, and not obliged to do anything for someone who had no family of his own. The Confucian ethic which ruled society prescribed man's duties but had little to say about his rights. The permanent guide-line of education was to regulate behaviour so that it should never offend against *li* – good custom and propriety.

Life, whether of the individual or of society, proceeds in cycles. From the cradle to the grave, a man goes through a number of eight-year cycles, a woman through cycles of seven years. The year comprises four periods (in some cosmologies, five). 'The year is articulated by festivals, experience is ordered by custom' (Richard Wilhelm, *Die Seele Chinas*). The purpose of the great seasonal festivals is to renew and reinforce the harmonious understanding between man and nature.

Among the cycles which generate order or symbolise order are the year with its 2×6 months or 24 divisions, the month with its 4×7 days, the five celestial directions (the fifth being the middle) and the five planets or the three degrees of the cosmos – heaven, earth and, in the centre, man. The gods themselves are part of this ordered world: formerly they too were men who, by virtue of their good deeds, were elevated to the highest degree. Below them are placed ordinary mortals, and, right at the bottom, the dead who can turn into evil demons or who stew in purgatory until their sins are purged away. All three worlds are ontologically of equal status, and differ from each other only in rank.

iv

If we try to classify the objects which the Chinese use as symbols into various groups, some interesting results emerge. The most important object, central to the whole taxonomy, turns out to be man: man in his bodily existence and in his social setting, and with him his artefacts, the things that he makes. This corresponds very well with the basic principle of the Chinese *Weltanschauung*: man as the cardinal being in this world. To man are subordinated and subjected the animals and the plants, even heaven and earth (a way of looking at things which is not far removed from the account of creation given in Genesis).

In the realm of animate nature, animals are more important than plants. Domestic animals, however, do not figure so often as wild animals. The same goes for the analysis of dreams in China, in which the ox, the pig and poultry rarely occur. With regard to plants, the situation is the exact opposite: almost all the trees and shrubs are of significance in everyday life, being used as sources of fruit, as raw material for perfumes, or as building material.

Such natural phenomena as clouds, rain, dew, thunder also make a deep impression on man. Animals are seen in an ambivalent light – many of them threaten him physically, or have properties which he admires or envies.

The concept of *dao* – usually rendered in English as 'principle', 'reason', – has many layers of meaning, and it is from one set of these that the Taoism propagated by Lao-zi has developed. Yet even this densely significant word goes back to simple observation of nature. After heavy rains in the clay and loess areas of North China, it was impossible to walk through the morass: only when a way (*dao*) was constructed was there 'order in the land'. Most of the symbols beloved of the Chinese relate to things that can be observed with the eye, and these we may denote as 'formal symbols'. Often, however, the Chinese word for the concept which it is desired to symbolise is phonetically equivalent or, at least, close to the word for the symbol itself (thus *fu* = good luck, and *fu* = the bat: so the bat symbolises good fortune); in such cases we can speak of 'phonetic' or 'aural' symbols.

Other symbols have to do with smell or taste. It is only recently that we have come to realise how important the sense of touch is for the Chinese. What does something *feel* like – is it cool and smooth like jade? Is it smooth, hard, malleable? This last group of symbols can be called 'qualitative symbols': certain properties are ascribed to certain objects, particularly to animals and birds (e.g. the eagle is believed to retain its strength till a ripe old age).

v

This book contains some four hundred symbols, and even a casual run-through will show how many of these are concerned with the same few basic themes. These were the things that mattered to the Chinese in their everyday lives, their heart's desires – to live a long and healthy life, to attain high civic and social rank, and to have children (i.e. to have sons).

Comparatively little attention is paid to other-worldly matters – what happens after death, the chances of rebirth, divine benevolence or the avoidance of sin. The ancient Chinese pantheon comprised literally hundreds of gods, virtually all of whom had lived as human beings on earth, and who were not deified till after death. As gods, they are more powerful than ordinary humans (with the single exception of the Emperor), but they can be manipulated, even bribed, like earthly officials. In the Chinese scheme of things, the relationship between man and god is totally different from that obtaining in Christianity, Judaism or Islam.

There were good practical grounds for desiring sons in traditional Chinese society. It was up to them, after the death of the father, to care for the mother and their younger brothers and sisters, and they had to make sure that due sacrifice was made to their dead father, who otherwise would become one of the 'hungry spirits'. The Chinese male in traditional society could imagine nothing more terrible than dying without leaving a son or sons behind. This is one reason why polygamy was allowed (until 1928);

though it was never widespread, as only rich men could afford to keep more than one wife. A simpler way out for the average man was to adopt a boy from within the extended family, perhaps a nephew. It was understood that childlessness could be due to physical causes; and such considerations are not unconnected with the mass of rules prescribing when and how marital intercourse should take place. The desire to have sons underlies the sexual connotation of many of the symbols discussed in this book.

One of the first things to strike the reader who looks at any of the older books on Chinese symbolism, e.g. those by Williams or Yetts, is the almost total absence of any reference to this sexual connotation. It seems to me that these writers either drew exclusively on classical literature or consulted Chinese scholars in the selection and interpretation of their material.

The fact is that there is an astonishing amount of sexual symbolism in the popular novels and in folk-literature, and in my book I have tried to indicate at least some of the main themes and symbols in this field. Many of these symbols are used in a harmless sense, and accordingly found their way into older works like those of Williams and Yetts. Over and above this innocuous sense, however, there may be a second, more erotic connotation which most Chinese will be aware of: they are, in fact, not so 'tranquil in their wisdom' as one used to imagine. It is only classical literature and philosophy that are serene and tranquil. Poetry on the other hand swarms with sexual innuendo, though this may be very adroitly covered up.

Study of Chinese symbolism can be enlightening in yet another field – the study of categories of Chinese thought, at present largely a virgin field but one of enormous importance for a genuine understanding of the Chinese. Let us take for example the contrastive pair *chao-ye*. *Chao* is the court of the Emperor, *ye* is the wilderness; *chao* is the court and the capital city surrounding it, *ye* includes country villages and the land whether cultivated or uncultivated. But *ye* is also used of wild animals or of a 'wild' cult – that is to say, the cult of a god who is not recognised by the Emperor. Formally, we might translate *chao-ye* as 'town and country', '*Stadt und Land*' – but the underlying concepts are totally different. Again, *shan-hai* means, literally, 'mountains and sea', but the compound really refers to what is enclosed by mountains and sea – i.e. the whole country. The compounds *shan-jing* and *hai-gui* – 'mountain-spirits' and 'sea-spirits' – refer to *all* spirits, whether more or less dangerous. The expression *shan-shui* can refer to 'flowing water and high mountains' but is usually the ordinary word for 'landscape' in painting; for such a picture will almost invariably depict a mountainous landscape with rivers or brooks.

An earthquake is expressed as *shan yao, di dong* = 'the mountains shake, the earth moves'. Many more examples could be given based on such contrastive pairs as 'pure-impure', 'high-low', etc. In all of these compounds based on antithesis the first word is felt as masculine, the second as feminine. Investigation of these semantic fields is only in its infancy.

For these reasons, it is not only symbols 'in themselves', symbols pure and simple, that have been selected for discussion; wherever it seemed necessary I have included objects which are not in themselves symbols but which crop up again and again in symbolical metaphors: e.g. the eye. In the Chinese context, the eye is not itself a symbol, in contradistinction to its role in some other countries where the 'evil eye' can be warded off by a picture of an eye. But the Chinese are fond of describing the eye in symbolic or periphrastic terms. The eyebrows, on the other hand, symbolise certain traits of character, and these will be 'legible' to someone who knows how to read the symbol.

vi

In sharp contrast to the symbols so familiar to us in European religion and art, few Chinese symbols are used in a religious sense. Their function is rather a purely social one. A visitor is expected to bring a gift: this may even be money, and the recipient will not automatically feel that he is being bribed. As we take flowers to a friend or a relative, the Chinese take a vase, a painted dish or an embroidered purse; whatever it is, it is likely to be decorated with symbols.

The symbols express what the giver could very well express in words; but in such situations the Chinese regard the use of words as too 'primitive'. The symbol is far more subtle. The recipient has to inspect and study the gift; only then will he find the two or three symbolic clues which will identify exactly what 'good wishes' are being transmitted. One starts with the wrapping-paper (if any): this must be red if the occasion is a birthday or a wedding, but red would be a frightful *faux pas* if the visit and the present are to express sympathy over a bereavement. Often, wrapping-paper is not just red or green but is covered with a pattern which the European might well ignore, but which is also there to transmit a message – to express the wish for long life, for a happy married life, etc. Thus even the primary colours have symbolic significance.

The same goes for behaviour in society. Regardless of whether the person I speak to is older or younger than I am, I address myself to him as to a superior. (Though here we must point out that in the course of the 20th century the old forms of polite and ceremonial address have tended to become obsolescent.) It is not done to tell someone he should be ashamed of himself, in so many words. But a slight gesture with the index finger on the lower part of the cheek will convey this message to the culprit, without bystanders being aware of it. Thus the culprit is not *publicly* shamed, he does not lose face; after all, perhaps I was just scratching an itchy spot . . .

There is always a certain amount of tension in the use of symbols in everyday life – is the other person astute enough to grasp the meaning of the symbols I have chosen, or is his understanding of them only partial?

vii

The genesis of this book goes back to the studies which my teacher, Ferdinand Lessing, published in the periodical *Sinica* in 1934–5. To him also I owe my first introduction to modern colloquial Chinese. For the lexical material in my book I have drawn to some extent on Western and Japanese specialist literature, in so far as it was available to me, but the main source has, of course, been Chinese literature itself, the novels, the theatre and, on occasion, the erotica. I have also learned much from paintings and frescoes, from folk-art and from popular beliefs. It is impossible to list all my sources: they would add unacceptably to the book's length, and in any case, most of these sources are accessible only to sinologists.

My selection of symbols is limited to those which are still in active use today, or which are, at least, still understood. The symbolism used in ancient China – i.e. the China of some two thousand years ago – differed quite widely from that described in my book; and in the absence of elucidatory source material, the meaning of this ancient symbolism must remain doubtful. Attempts have of course been made to decode it: it is enough to mention the names of Carl Hentze and Anneliese Bulling. In very many cases, however, the researcher is left with nothing more to go on but his own more or less inspired guesswork; and the Chinese experts to whom appeal is often made rarely have anything better to offer. As an example, see the article in this book on *Tao-tie* – an extremely frequent symbol in ancient China, for whose use no satisfactory explanation has been found in the intervening two thousand years.

Furthermore, my book is concerned only with those symbols which were and are familiar to all Chinese. Specifically Buddhist and Taoist symbols are only occasionally mentioned. There are indeed many of these special symbols, but they are familiar only to a restricted circle of adepts and specialists. Such an avowedly specialist work on symbolism as that by Erwin Rousselle, breaking as it does completely fresh ground, deserves very special praise.

I have not attempted to deal with the corpus of symbols developed and used by carpenters, masons and smiths in the course of their work. My book is intended to be no more than an introduction to the subject, and much remains to be done before the treasure-trove of Chinese symbolism can be thoroughly evaluated.

It now remains for me to express my thanks to all those who have helped me in this enterprise: first and foremost, my publisher, Mr Ulf Diederichs, who not only improved the text stylistically but also provided many quotations from scholarly works in the sinological field. My thanks are also due to my friend and colleague, Professor Alvin Cohen, to Mrs Hwei-lee Chang for the Chinese calligraphy in each article, and to the Ostasiatisches Museum in Cologne for help in providing the illustrations.

Wolfram Eberhard

A

Amber
hu-po 琥珀

As far back as the Middle Ages, the Chinese knew that amber was ancient pine resin and that the remains of insects could sometimes be found in it. Amber was imported from what is now Burma, and from parts of Central Asia. It symbolised 'courage', and its Chinese name *hu-po* means 'tiger soul', the → tiger being known as a courageous animal. In early times, it was believed that at death the tiger's spirit entered the earth and became amber.

Amulet
hufu 護符

Amulets and talismans are referred to in the oldest Chinese texts. All sorts of materials were used to fashion them; in later times, however, they were made principally from paper, on which a message to the evil → spirits was written, adjuring them not to harm the bearer of the amulet. Since this message was addressed not to men but to spirits, it was written in 'ghost script', a form of writing whose characters bear a certain similarity to ordinary Chinese characters, but which is fully accessible only to Taoist adepts. Some Taoists claim that a handwritten amulet warding off fire can be understood by the spirits in the Western world as well, as one and the same 'ghost script' is uniformly used and understood all over the world. The script is in fact very old. The work known as *Bao-po ze* by Go Hung (AD 281–361) contains a dictionary of it.

The ancient Chinese regarded the → calendar as enormously influential and, in practice, indispensable; so the paper of a calendar that had served its turn was often used as an amulet. For example, old calendars

An amulet bearing the eight trigrams and the all-purpose benediction '(May you have) good fortune like the Eastern Ocean and long life like the mountain of the South!'

were hung up over pigsties, or they were burned and the ashes mixed into the swill as a tried and proven specific against diseases.

Ancestral Tablet
zu

祖

The memorial tablet is a small wooden board, often lacquered; it is about 10–20 cm broad and at least twice as high. On it are inscribed the name and often the title of the deceased, whose soul, it is popularly believed, lingers on the tablet, especially during sacrifices when it has been 'revived' by means of a little chicken blood. In well-to-do families the tablet is placed in a special temple dedicated to the ancestors in which all the members of the clan are assembled together. Poor families make do with a small table placed against the north wall of the living room and surrounded by incense burners and other objects. The tablets are arranged according to position in the family hierarchy; and the tablet in memory of a man is usually flanked by that of his principal wife. Homage is paid to ancestors on certain days of the year, and people turn to them for help and advice. Family pride in its ancestral line can be measured by the number of memorial tablets displayed.

In the case of a → married daughter, her memorial tablet after death will be placed next to that of her husband if he has pre-deceased her. However, a tablet referring to an unmarried daughter cannot be placed among those belonging to her own family. In such cases there are two possibilities: a so-called 'nominal marriage' (*ming hun*) can be arranged – i.e. asking a family whose son has died before marriage to agree to a retrospective marriage with the dead girl; alternatively, a living man can be asked to marry her. He is then, in a certain sense, a widower and can take another daughter of the family to wife. In these circumstances, the normal wedding gifts for the bride's family are dispensed with – on the contrary, the bridegroom is financially rewarded for his help in a difficult situation.

There was a third possibility: the tablet could be placed in an area specially designated for this purpose in a Buddhist temple, a procedure involving considerable financial outlay. In the People's Republic of China the ancestor cult in temples has been vetoed, and it is being discouraged in private dwellings. Politically, this is a question of strengthening state solidarity vis-à-vis family solidarity.

A stroke of luck for the angler

yi, which appeared in the early 17th century.

Angler
yu-fu

When the first → Emperor of the Zhōu Dynasty (*c*. 1050 BC) was looking around for a wise counsellor, he noticed, so the legend has it, an old man dressed in very simple clothes fishing on a river bank. This was Jiang Ze-ya (also known as Jiang Tai-gung) and it is in this form that he is always represented. The Emperor-to-be 'fished' the old man in: that is to say, he made him his chief strategist in his fight against the decadent Shang Dynasty. The story is told in the novel *Feng-shen yan-*

Animals
shou

The Chinese divided animals up into five classes, each of which had its representative: the feathered creatures were represented by the → phoenix, the furry creatures by the → unicorn, naked creatures by → man, scaly creatures by the → dragon, and creatures with shells by the → tortoise.

When a woman was granted an audience at court, she wore a skirt embellished with a design showing the *qi-lin* (the unicorn) receiving the obeisance of the other classes of animal – though man himself was absent from the group.

Phoenix, dragon, unicorn and tortoise, the representatives of their animal kinds; they are also symbols of the four directions

Five or six kinds of domestic animal were distinguished – horse, ox, sheep, pig, dog and hen (see separate entries). All of these were regarded as edible, though horse-flesh was only eaten on ceremonial occasions.

The five noxious creatures are the → snake, the → centipede, the scorpion, the lizard or → gecko and the → toad. On the 5th day of the 5th month, magical means were invoked to rid human settlements of these creatures. → Zhong-kui is the god mainly charged with operations against them, and he is helped by the → cock.

Ant
ma-yi

The second component of the Chinese word for 'ant' – *yi* – is phonetically close to the word *yi* meaning 'virtue' (the words differ only in tone), and this is probably the reason why the ant figures as a symbol of right conduct and of patriotism. It also symbolises self-interest.

In the Shanghai hinterland, the village broker with a finger in every business deal is called an 'ant', a reference no doubt to his unfailing attention to his own interests. In general, however, the ant plays no great part in Chinese symbolism.

Ao
Ao

The *Ao* is usually said to be an enormous sea turtle, though another tradition describes it as a giant fish. Once upon a time, so it is said, the goddess → Nü-gua repaired one of the four pillars which bear the earth with one of the turtle's legs. Again, it was widely believed that the earth itself rested on the back of the huge turtle. There was a long-lasting belief among the Chinese that they could make the ground they stood on firmer and more secure (i.e. against earthquakes) if they fashioned → tortoises out of → stone, and placed heavy slabs on their backs. In this way, it was believed, heaven and earth were more securely bound to each other.

The *Ao-shan*, i.e. the Ao mountain, lies in the 'Islands of the Blessed', the paradise → islands in the Eastern Ocean. It was the practice from the 12th century onwards to mark the → New Year Feast by building large figures consisting of lanterns and models, representing the Ao mountain.

The man who came first in the final and most demanding literary examination was known as 'Ao-head'. The wish to excel at something is represented as a woman bearing a staff, who holds a → peach in her hand: at her feet, a child is reaching for an Ao. This group symbolises the wish to be supremely successful in the state examination.

The Ao is also sometimes represented as an animal which eats → fire. Accordingly, it is often shown as a roof finial fending fire away from the roof ridge.

Apple
ping-guo   蘋 果

The best apples used to come from Korea and Japan; the Chinese apple was not so tasty. Even today, apples are relatively dear, and therefore an acceptable gift, especially since the apple (*ping*) can stand as a symbol for 'peace' (*ping*). On the other hand, one should not give apples to an invalid, since the Chinese word for 'illness' – *bing* – is very similar in sound to the word for apple. Apple blossom, however, symbolises female → beauty.

In North China, the wild apple blossoms in → spring, and is therefore a symbol for this season of the year. The wild apple (*hai-tang*) may also symbolise the → hall of a house (*tang*): a picture showing wild apple blossom and → magnolias (*yu-lan*) in such a room can be interpreted as meaning 'May (*yu*) your house be rich and honoured!'

The celebrated beauty Yang Guifei, the concubine of one of the Tang emperors, was known as 'Paradise-apple Girl' (*hai-tang nü*).

Apricot
xing   杏

The apricot stands symbolically for the second month of the old Chinese calendar (corresponding roughly to our March). It is also a symbol for → a beautiful woman; a red apricot stands for a married woman who is having an affair with a lover.

The apricot may also be called *bai-guo-z* (= white fruit) or *bai-guo zhi* (= hundred fruit branch). It then symbolises the wish to have a hundred sons (*bai-ge zi*). Apricot stones are sometimes compared to the → eyes of a beautiful woman.

Arrow
shi   矢

From the very earliest times arrows have been in use in China in various forms – e.g. as a kind of harpoon, and, fitted with a pipe-like gadget at the point, as a 'singing arrow' which was used in signalling.

Breaking an arrow in half signalled confirmation of a deal. Very well known in China – and elsewhere – is the story of the old → father who summons his sons and gives each of them an arrow which he asks them to break. This they do without difficulty. Then he gives each of them a bundle of arrows with the same command. But none of them is able to break the bundle. Thus are the sons taught that only in unity can they be strong.

In a modern Chinese film, a → girl who is looking for a man shoots an arrow, saying, 'No arrow comes by itself: if it comes, it comes from the bowstring', by which she means that she will marry the man who finds the arrow: a profoundly erotic metaphor.

Ashes
hui

Since ashes are a darkish grey, like the so-called 'raven's gold' (a mixture of gold and copper), they symbolise riches. They are also used to keep → spirits and ghosts away, especially spirits of dead people. The expression 'to scrape ashes' refers to incest between father-in-law and daughter-in-law.

Astrology
zhan xing xue 占星學

Chinese astrology is very closely bound up with Chinese natural science and philosophy. '→ Heaven, → earth and → man are the three forces in nature, and it is man whose task it is to bring the other two – heaven, the creative power of the historical process, and earth, the receptive power of spatial extension – into harmony. "The configurations are shadowed forth by heaven; it is for the adept to realise them," says the "Book of Changes", which is based upon the realisation that ulti-

A professional astrologer casts a horoscope for a proposed marriage: are the pair well matched?

mate reality is not to be found in static conditions of existence but in the spiritual laws from which everything that happens draws its meaning and its impulse towards lasting effect' (Richard Wilhelm).

The *Yi-jing* ('Book of Changes') is the best-known of the Chinese → oracle books. About two thousand years ago it acquired canonical status and was used as a sort of handbook in the identification and interpretation of the reciprocal relations between the heavenly and the earthly powers. Transgression of the moral law on earth is followed by unnatural manifestations in the heavens. If the → Emperor was immoderately influenced by the Empress, the (male) → sun was darkened, or even eclipsed.

To the 'Twelve Stellar Stations' or the 'Twenty-eight Lunar Stations' there corresponded on earth twelve or twenty-eight regions – parts of China, or, in earlier times, tributary states under Chinese sovereignty. A display of shooting stars in one of these regions was interpreted as meaning that the people were no longer loyal to a ruler (or an → official) who was negligent in the discharge of his duty.

To the twelve stellar stations, Chinese astronomers gave names derived from the → Twelve Branch cycle, consisting of symbols which have so far not been explained. The twelve stations are not related in any way to the → zodiac of Western astronomy, although this was well known to Chinese astronomers from the Middle Ages onwards.

Irregularities – i.e. geocentric anomalies – in the movement of the

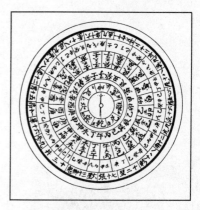

A compass as used by astrologers and geomancers (baked clay)

→ planets were precisely observed and explained.

Many → Immortals were imagined as 'emanations' of stars; but, in general, the → constellations were not thought to have any direct influence on individual lives. The amalgamation of the 'Ten Celestial Stems' (i.e. the → Five Changes in their positive and their negative aspects) with the 'Twelve Branches' (or stellar stations) gives rise to cycles of → sixty years which are of basic importance in Chinese astrology. A horoscope always consists of eight symbols – two each for the year, the month, the day and the hour of birth.

Over the centuries the astrological way of thought gradually spread to virtually every area of Chinese culture. Before concluding a → marriage under the old system, it was especially necessary to have horoscopes cast, in order to see whether they were in harmony or otherwise. In this respect, the Twelve Branch cycle was used in its other form as a cycle of twelve

The Duke of Zhou, who is supposed to have invented the astrological calendar 3,100 years ago

symbolical creatures. Could a man born under the sign of the Cock expect to live harmoniously with a woman born under the sign of the Dragon? Would he perhaps not do better to seek a partner born under the sign of the Rat? Statistical investigation has shown that 'favourable' and 'unfavourable' combinations came up in about equal proportion. An unfavourable combination meant that the proposed marriage could be called off without further ado; nor would the family of the rejected suitor feel in any way insulted.

Aubergine
qiez   茄 子

The Chinese aubergine is long and unrounded. Together with its calyx it looks like a man wearing a → hat, and so in the popular mind it came to symbolise the → official with his cap of office. Its presence in a picture expresses the sender's wish that the recipient may soon be rewarded with an official post. In Taiwan the aubergine is eaten particularly towards the end of the year; it is then supposed to make the lips red.

Its phallic form has led to its being used as a symbol for the penis in the whole of East Asia, especially in China, Korea and Japan.

Axe
fu

The axe is one of the twelve → insignia of the imperial power. At the same time, it symbolises Lu Ban, the patron saint of carpenters, and also the village broker or male or female go-between.

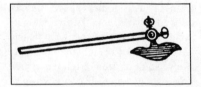

Buddhist axe

Azalea 杜鵑花
du-juan-hua

A → beautiful woman is often compared to an azalea, which is also known as the 'cuckoo flower'. The Chinese cuckoo (*du-juan*) plays a very big part in the folklore of Sichuan. They say that the cuckoo sings all night through until its throat is bloody; and whoever hears its first cry in the morning is about to be separated from his sweetheart. The azalea is very common in Sichuan, and it is probable that it gets its Chinese name from its resemblance to the → red colour of the cuckoo's throat.

B

Back-scratcher
sao-zhang 搔杖

Many folklore museums have examples of this object. Usually it consists of a bamboo handle to which the

Vase with back-scratcher and staff of office: '(May you have) the peace you desire!'

scratcher itself – shaped like a claw or a hand – is fastened. The instrument seems to have another function as well: that of 'talk-stick' (*tan zhu*, literally 'talk-help'). Often this was no more than a pine twig, sometimes a → sceptre, which the teacher placed before him: a student wishing to initiate a discussion picked it up and began to speak. It seems likely that this usage came with Buddhism from India at an early date.

The back-scratcher plays a part in the legends associated with the goddess → Ma-gu.

Badger
huan 獾

The badger is not an animal that has appealed to the Chinese imagination. In Japan, on the other hand, the *tanuki*, the badger, plays a part equivalent in importance to that of

Badger and magpie: 'Joy from heaven – joy on earth'

the → fox in China. They differ very much, however, in character. Thus, the fox likes to turn into a seductive girl or an enticing woman, while the badger prefers to masquerade as a fat-bellied abbot or a ragged mendicant monk:

The badger is out of his mind with
   excitement,
Beating on his stomach.
That's what he likes to do –
Otherwise . . . he doesn't think of
   much else. (Shikitei Samba)

The Chinese word for 'badger' is phonetically identical with the word meaning 'to enjoy oneself, to be glad' (*huan*). Hence, badger and magpie are shown together to symbolise the wish 'may you experience great happiness'.

Bald Head
tu

'Baldy' or 'Bald-headed Ass' is a rude way of referring to Buddhist monks, who all have to shave their heads. But the word *tu* may also mean 'penis'.

Even as novices, young monks have to have their heads shaved. At a later stage, when they have vowed to take the way of → Buddha, they have to prove their steadfastness by undergoing various forms of self-inflicted mortification of the flesh. The usual way is for a piece of charcoal which has been dipped in a certain fruit sap to be placed on the bald head and set alight. It is allowed to burn itself out and the deep scars thus obtained are exhibited with pride thereafter.

Two bald-headed monks

Ball
qiu

球

A ball made from red material or from feathers plays a very big part in the Chinese opera and in many popular traditions. In South China it was customary for a girl, on reaching marriageable age, to invite suitors to present themselves before her balcony on a given day: she then threw down a ball, and the man who caught it became her husband. The favourite day for this ceremony was the 15th day of the 8th month – that is to say, the day of the 'Mid-autumn Festival' (a sort of harvest thanksgiving) and also a lunar Festival (→ moon). In many parts of Central China, a red ball was fastened to the roof of the litter which bore the bride to the home of her bridegroom.

At the 'Dragon-lamp Festival', held on the 15th day of the 1st month, the → dragons (made from cloth and paper) played with an 'embroidered ball'. This was a fertility festival marking the end of

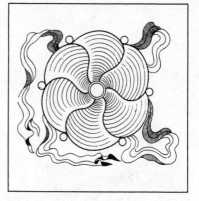

An embroidered ball

the long-drawn-out → New Year Feast, and the dragons symbolised the rain-bearing clouds of spring. A ball is often found in association with the group of two stone lions which guard temple gates against demons. The eastern lion rolls the magic sphere under his left paw, while the western one suckles its cub (according to popular tradition) with the right paw. Like an egg, the magic sphere contains the lion cub; rolling the ball helps the cub to hatch out. It is also said that the hairs torn out during love-play between the lions form the magic ball. So, here again, the ball serves as a symbol of fertility.

Two lions play with a ball

Bamboo
zhu

竹

The bamboo is one of China's most important natural products. It provides building material for houses and scaffolding, and raw material for paper. There is a saying: 'May his

The bamboo – model and guide-line in Chinese calligraphy

cacy, → wine is spiced with bamboo leaves, bamboo discs were sometimes used for money, and the Chinese counterpart of the hobby horse has always been made from bamboo (*zhuma*): it symbolises youth. In addition to its practical uses, the bamboo is a motif in many Chinese poems. Su Dong-po writes, 'One can manage without eating flesh; but one cannot manage without the bamboo'; and Bo Ju-yi, 'Everyone has worries in time of drought: for my part, when it is dry, I am anxious about pine trees and bamboos.'

name be preserved on bamboo and silk' – a reference to the handle of the calligrapher's brush and to the brownish paper which is made from bamboo. Bamboo shoots are a deli-

The leaves of the bamboo droop because its inside (its 'heart') is empty. But an empty heart is equivalent to modesty, so the bamboo symbolises this virtue. On the other hand, the bamboo is evergreen and immutable, and hence a symbol of old age – in addition, it is gaunt like an old man. When the wind blows, the bamboo bends 'in laughter'; and the character for 'bamboo' looks

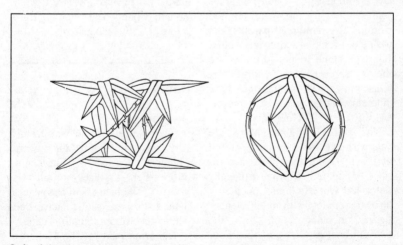

Stylised bamboo leaves: something that does not die in winter

very much like an abbreviation of the character for 'to laugh'. An underlay of bamboo which is put under the legs in bed during hot weather, in order to keep them cool, is called 'bamboo-wife' (*zhu-fu-ren*).

Fireworks used to be made from bamboo, which explodes with a loud bang when put into a fire. It was supposed to ward off demons, and its use in fireworks at → New Year and other festive occasions was for this purpose. With the departure of the demons, peace and contentment are supposed to enter, and so it is fitting that the Chinese words for 'bamboo' and for 'to wish, pray' are homonyms, as are the words for 'to explode' and for 'to herald, announce' (*bao*). A picture showing children letting off bamboo fireworks can be interpreted by the recipient as meaning 'We wish that there may be peace.' To make the good wishes even clearer, a → vase may be added: for a vase (*ping*) symbolises peace and quiet (*ping-an*). Bamboos and → plums together represent man and wife: if the picture also contains parents the wish is for → married bliss. Bamboos, pine trees and plums are the → 'Three Friends in winter'. A bamboo twig or branch is one of the emblems of the goddess of mercy, the white-clad → Guan-yin.

The young bamboo shoots are yellowish like asparagus and pointed at the tips, and they were accordingly compared to the artificially deformed feet of Chinese women – also sometimes with their slender figures. In paintings of plants, the conventional grouping of the 'Four Noble (plants)' – plum-blossom, chrysanthemum, orchid and bamboo – plays a big part. A celebrated saying has it that the artist must himself become a bamboo before he can begin to paint one. As Roger Goepper has said, 'for Oriental painting, conceived as it is in terms of calligraphy, the bamboo is both model and guide-line'.

Banana
ba-jiao　　芭蕉

In Japan, poets make much of the banana, which is – thanks largely to Bashō's influence – understood in a symbolic sense. In China on the other hand, it is little more than a symbol for self-discipline. The banana figures in the head-hunting ritual on Taiwan. The banana leaf is regarded as one of the fourteen → precious things of the scholar. It is noteworthy that in China the emphasis is always on the leaves of the plant – never on the fruit, which alone has symbolical value for Europeans (and the Japanese).

Banner
qi　　旗

Banners were used in war from a very early time. From 1205 onwards Chinggiz Khan used a white banner into which a black moon was inserted. The banners of the government troops are said to have been white, according to another text.

The armies led by Zhu Hong-wu, the founder of the Ming Dynasty

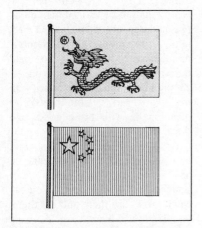

The Imperial Flag (up to 1912) and the flag of the People's Republic of China

(1368–1644), had red banners; when Zhu was proclaimed Emperor, these were replaced by yellow banners. Subsequently, yellow became the colour symbolising the → Emperor.

On the Chinese stage, generals carry banners on their backs. These are richly decorated and their number indicates the size of the armies under the generals' command.

The flag of Imperial China had a five-clawed → dragon and a red sun or a pearl on a yellow background. Since 1949, the flag of the People's Republic has had a large yellow star flanked by four smaller stars which stand for the four classes – workers, peasants, petty bourgeois and 'patriotic capitalists'.

Bao

This word has a wide variety of meanings. It may mean 'retribution',

in the sense of taking revenge. But we often come across such an expression as 'recompensing the favour shown by the state' (often, i.e., the ruler of the state). Underlying this is the idea that each citizen receives so much bounty from the state in the shape of admission to the state examinations, appointment, etc., that he must in due course repay these favours, if necessary with his death. In this case, 'the loyal heart' is praised of the man who is 'making recompense' to the state.

A newspaper reported on the case of a blind widow who had sold lottery tickets to raise money in order to see her son through his schooling. On qualifying, the son had to excuse himself: he was not yet in a position to repay his mother for her bounty and kindness which was as deep as the sea. Another newspaper report concerned an adulterous union between a man well on in years and a woman who was no younger: 'above, hot steam was rising; down below was just recompense'.

Basket
lan

A decorated basket of fruit or → flowers symbolises → Lan Cai-he, one of the eight → Immortals. The contents of the basket represent riches and the motif is therefore a popular one in New Year pictures: a young man stands before an older one to whom he presents flowers in a basket.

A basket or box is also an attribute of one of the Heavenly Twins → He-he. Here, the written character *he* = basket may be used, which also means 'agreement'.

Bat
pian-fu　　蝙蝠

In European folklore the bat is a sinister creature, associated with evil and the powers of darkness. In China, on the other hand, it has few rivals as a symbol of good luck and happiness. Again, the reason for this must be sought in a phonetic parallel: the word for 'bat' (*fu*) is identical in sound with the word for 'good fortune' (*fu*). Very often, five bats are shown together to represent the Five Blessings – a long life, riches, health, love of virtue and a natural death. Another way of expressing this wish is to depict a magician with a jar from which five bats are emerging. In another representation of this motif, one or two children are trying to put bats into a → vase (*ping*: phonetic parallel with *ping* = peace and quiet). Even a picture showing → Zhong-kui striking bats down with his sword can be interpreted as meaning he will 'bring good luck down to you'.

According to a medieval source, bats which are a thousand years old are white and hang from their boughs head downwards. If you can catch them, dry them and eat them, you will live to a great age. A → red bat is a harbinger of especially good fortune, not only because red is the colour which wards off demons, but also because the Chinese word for 'red' (*hong*) sounds the same as the word for 'enormous'.

An interesting folk-tale relates how all the birds came to the → phoenix's birthday party, but the bat did not come, on the grounds that it was not a bird but a quadruped. Later, however, it also failed to appear when the → unicorn was

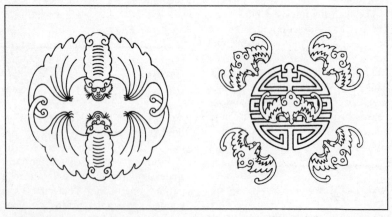

Left: Two bats – redoubled good fortune. Right: the Five Gifts and the symbol of longevity

Five bats are caught: 'May every sort of joy come your way'

giving its party – claiming, this time, that since it had wings and flew, it was not a quadruped but a bird. All the phoenix and the unicorn could do was admire its cunning.

Bath
xi-zao 洗澡

It is principally the South Chinese who make a fetish of cleanliness, taking a bath every day or at least pouring water over themselves. They also do a lot of bathing in the sea and in rivers. Men and women bath together, and the South Chinese see nothing improper in this; but we find North Chinese criticism of this 'southern' fashion in very early texts. Well-to-do families had their own bath-houses from very early times;

public bath-houses began to spread in about AD 1000.

The bath 'purifies' in a symbolic sense as well. A woman bathed before entering a nunnery. It is customary to → wash oneself before

Bath-house scenes (late 18th century)

going on pilgrimage; and both bride and bridegroom take a bath on the eve of the wedding. In the Middle Ages, statues of Buddha in temples were washed on the 8th day of the 12th month; and the bath-houses in monasteries were open for public use on the same day – the day when, according to tradition, Prince Gautama became the Buddha. It was also the eve of the great annual rite of exorcism, when the city was washed clean of evil.

Bathing had particular symbolical value at key moments in a person's life. It was also connected with fertility; and the Amazons who appear in Chinese myths became pregnant when they bathed.

Bean
dou 豆

Its protein content makes the soya bean one of the most important items in Chinese food. From it are made the bean curd (*dou-fu*) and the liquid extract which looks like milk and is a popular breakfast drink. 'Eating bean-curd' is a metaphor for sexual intercourse. At weddings in Taiwan, the mother-in-law gives her new daughter-in-law a cake made from dried bean-curd (*dou-gan*) symbolising the wish that one day her sons will be high → officials (*da-guan*). (In the Taiwan dialect, *dou-gan* and *da-guan* sound very similar.)

Bear
xiong 熊

The bear symbolises → man, just as the → snake symbolises woman. The bear stands for strength and courage. The birth of a → son is presaged by dreaming of a bear. 'The Great Yu', the mythical hero who diverted the great flood which his father had been unable to stem, was – like his father – a bear.

The constellation of the Great Bear (*bei dou*) is of special interest and significance. The literal translation of *bei dou* is 'Northern Dipper', but the word *dou* = dipper refers also to an altar vessel used in religious ceremonies. Its handle corresponds to the shaft in our 'Great Wain'. This part of the constellation of Ursa Major is also known as the 'Cloud Dipper', and symbolises the penis in the marriage ceremony. In Chinese astronomy the constellation consists of these seven stars, and it is consequently referred to as the 'Group of Seven (stars)'.

Panda in bamboos

The constellation is regarded as the seat of Shang-di, the supreme god in Chinese popular religious belief. When it is portrayed as an emblem on ships, it symbolises the goddess Tian-hou, the Empress of Heaven who protects seafarers. A square tile bearing the character for 'good fortune' symbolises the 'Northern Dipper', and is often set into an inner wall of a house.

In the ideological quarrel between the People's Republic of China and the Soviet Union, the Russian bear has come to symbolise the aggressor. Mao Ze-dong referred to it as a 'polar bear'. In Chinese versions of the Little Red Riding Hood story, the wicked bear replaces the wolf.

Beard
hu-z

A beard is a sign of supernatural power or of bravery, especially when it is red or purple. Headhunters in the borderlands between Burma and China were particularly on the look-out for men with flowing beards. It is several hundred years since a writer pointed out that while distinguished Chinese are very deficient in the matter of beards, painters always portray them with a manly growth. On the Chinese stage as well, it is customary for important male characters to have long beards.

Beauty
rangmao

Female beauty was a subject of considerable interest to the Chinese from the earliest times, and there was even a special handbook specifying the qualities a young woman had to have if she was to be considered for the imperial harem. As in medieval Europe, the catalogue of female attractions begins at the head and works downwards: thus, → eyes, → eyebrows, → face, → hair, → nose, ears, thence to hands and fingers . . . and so on.

The observations arrived at by the aesthetician Li Yu (or Li Li-weng) (17th century) are, in part at least, still valid. Colour of hair plays little part here, as all Chinese have strong, straight, black, smooth hair, in so far as it is not lightened to a reddish hue by reason of malnutrition and vitamin deficiency. 'Cloud hair', i.e. hair that seems to float lightly on the head, is particularly admired. A high brow is also considered beautiful, so many women still pluck their hair-line – a process which has to be repeated every two weeks. The face should be egg-shaped, not round: the eyebrows should be lightly curved like the leaves of the willow-tree.

According to Li Yu, the most beautiful women come from two cities, Suzhou and Hangzhou, and the women of Hunan province were renowned for their romantic ardour. Good wishes addressed to a man can be expressed in a picture showing three beautiful women, bringing →

bamboo, a basket with → flowers and a basket of → fruit as gifts. Another popular picture, suitable as a gift for a man, shows eighteen celebrated beauties of antiquity.

The plant and animal world is drawn on very heavily for comparative purposes: a woman is beautiful if her mouth is as small as that of a → fish, and her eyes are like the fruit of a → lichee, or like → flowers. 'Dove's eyes' indicate intelligence and charm: 'mussel-eyes' or red eyes are regarded as ugly, while blue eyes find no admirers. The → nose is compared with the stalk of an onion; a snub nose (known as 'lion-nose') does not make a woman attractive, but might bring her luck. The ears should be like tree fungus (*mu er*), neither too thick nor too thin, and slightly lustrous; a 'rat-ear' is too small, and an 'earth-god-ear' far too long.

The mouth and lips should resemble a cherry, that is to say, small and not protruding; women have always been expected to improve on nature here with the help of make-up. Teeth must be white and even, like the seeds in a → pomegranate. Small, uneven teeth are known as 'rat's teeth'. Protruding teeth are considered as particularly hideous, and they are compared to the little chips of wood which used to be used instead of toilet-paper. 'Fragrance' is a word that crops up a great deal in Chinese descriptions of the female body (→ odour).

The 'red face' of a beautiful woman, as lauded by the great Tang poet Li Tai-bo, has given rise to the adage 'Red face – short life': i.e. a beautiful woman lures a man into sexual intercourse too frequently, so that he soon dies. In general, female nakedness is still taboo. The small ivory figures of naked women which one sometimes finds, date from a time when no male doctor could examine a woman, whether married or unmarried. The sick woman was supposed to show the doctor where she felt pain by pointing to the place on the little figure: the doctor could then take her pulse (often by indirect methods also) and make a diagnosis.

Nowadays, small silver figures of naked women have appeared on the Chinese art market. These were, it seems, to serve the dead as servants.

While the paragon of the clothed female beauty has remained constant, ideas of female attractiveness have changed quite considerably over the centuries. In Tang times (618–906), a woman had to be rather plump to rate as attractive; a hundred years later, in the 11th century, the slim line was all the rage. Until the beginning of the 20th century, women's feet were supposed to turn men on when they had been shrunken 'to three inches': they were then known as 'golden lotus' or 'golden lily'. Originally this was an upper-class affectation only, which started in about the 7th century. By the ·19th century the custom was widespread among middle- and lower-class women as well. Today, it has vanished completely, and so, of course, has the 'fetishism of the foot' associated with it.

The whole body of a beautiful woman should look like a → willow-tree: slim, supple and curved, with only a suggestion of hips. Standards are set even for → pubic hair: every woman should have some, it should not be overlong, nor should it be yellowish – as was apparently the case with the hated Empress Wu.

Ideals of male beauty have been largely ignored by Chinese aestheticians, both in general and in particular. Remarkable features of certain emperors were praised by comparing them to mythical ancestors: the optimum was to have eyebrows like Yao's, eyes like Shun's, a back as straight as Yu's and shoulders like Tang's.

It was desirable that a → scholar should have feminine traits in his appearance. However, fat men in general – military men and wrestlers, for example – have never been regarded as handsome: even → Fat-belly Buddha stands for merriment, not for beauty. In the erotic 'Spring pictures', male breasts often outdo those of the ladies.

Flowers and a bee: like girls with a young man

Bee
mi-feng

South Chinese tribes used to hunt for bees' nests in old trees and smoke them out to get at the honey. Bee-keeping proper is scarcely attested. On the whole, the bee does not play a very important role in Chinese symbolism. However, as the word for 'bee' (*feng*) is phonetically close to the word for preferment to a noble rank (*feng*), a picture showing a → monkey and a bee together can be taken as meaning 'preferment to noble rank' (the monkey – *hou* –

symbolising 'award of a fief' – *hou*). As in the West, the bee may also stand for industriousness and thrift. Like the → butterfly, the bee also represents a young man in love, and the → peony on which it sits, or round which it flies, represents the girl he loves. The expression 'to call the bee and bring the butterfly' refers to an extramarital affair: successful conclusion of such an affair is described as 'the bee rolls up, the butterfly picks'.

A South Chinese legend, which is known also in Japan, tells how a bee helps a young man to choose the right bride for himself out of a whole row of beautiful girls.

Bells
zhong　鐘

Bronze bells have been found dating from very early periods of Chinese history. They were originally used, it seems, as musical instruments. In later times they came to be associated with Buddhist temples, where they are mainly used today. In early times, bells used to be consecrated with the blood of a sacrificial animal, and then struck with a wooden staff. There are several reports of bells being cast from weapons which had been taken by force or confiscated in order to nip a rebellion in the bud.

A bronze bell of the Zhou Dynasty

It is a Buddhist custom to sound a temple bell at midnight and on the occasion of the death of a high → official. No two bells sound exactly alike: some are harbingers of good fortune, some of bad.

There are many legends involving bells. Some fly through the air to the place where they are to be hung; holy men can lie under a heated bell without coming to any harm; evil monks put a man under a bell so that he starves to death, etc. Bells sound particularly sweet-toned if a young girl has jumped or been thrown into the molten metal.

Ceremonial chariots in ancient China were adorned with small bells; and little bells were attached to birds, so that people might be entertained by their musical flight. 'Burmese bells' (*mian ling*) are tiny silver bells containing tiny gold beads or grains of sand, which are inserted in the vagina or the foreskin as sexual excitants.

Another Chinese character pronounced *zhong* means 'to bring something off', 'to hit the mark', 'to obtain a degree'; hence, a picture showing a bell is to be understood as good wishes in this sense.

Betel
bin-lang　檳榔

Outside of South-east Asia, the betel tree is found only in South China and in Japan. The kernel is ground down, mixed into a ball with shell lime, and chewed. Long-term chewing makes the teeth black. The juice when spat out looks like blood.

Betel-chewing makes the ears hot and the face red: the eyes swim and a giddy sensation like drunkenness is induced – or, at least, so it is claimed in the Chinese texts. Betel is supposed to be a cure for malaria. Among the minority peoples in the South it is given as a wedding present. Boxes made specially from silver or tin are available for this purpose. These have three compartments, one each for the lime, the leaves and the betel.

Bird
niao

'White-headed Birds' and peony

Particular symbolic significance attaches to the following birds: crane, eagle, magpie, oriole, pheasant, quail and swallow (see separate entries). The 'White-headed Bird' symbolises great age, and a pair of them is sometimes shown on a → peony: expressing the wish that the recipient of the picture may have 'riches and honour till the close of life'.

Chief of the feathered creatures was the mythical → phoenix. There are many tales about men who could understand the language of the birds and who used this knowledge to get themselves out of danger or to amass great riches. Another popular motif is that of people who change into birds. Bird-song is sometimes explained along these lines. For example, there is the story of the wicked step-mother who gave her own son good seed-corn, but to her step-son corn that had been cooked. Both sons were supposed to come back only when the grain had sprouted, but they never came, and the step-mother was turned into a bird which continually bewails its fate.

Birds are also said to keep the grave of the primeval Emperor Yu clean; they bear earth to the burial places of pious men, and use their feathers to cover their corpses.

Good people may be rewarded in some way by the birds. But there are also bird-demons and one must be on one's guard against them: it is particularly important to make sure that birds' droppings do not fall on children's clothes.

Both in China and in Korea the word *niao* is a term for 'penis', and it is often used as an expletive.

Birthday
sheng-ri   生 日

As far back as the 5th century AD, it was customary among the upper classes to celebrate birthdays, at least those of → sons. The new-born child was given a red shirt on the first day of his life, and nine red eggs were sent to the mother's parents in token of the glad tidings. If the child was a boy, it was up to the father to acquaint his ancestors of the event; in the special 'Hall of Ancestors' in the case of rich families, at the domestic altar-table in ordinary homes (→ ancestral tablet). 'The spirits of the ancestors are less interested in girl children, as in due course they will → marry and leave the family' (Richard Wilhelm).

The follow-up customs to be observed differed according to the sex of the child. In the case of a boy, a bow made from a mulberry branch and four arrows made from the wood of the jujube tree were hung up at the door of the house. On the hundredth day after the birth, presents poured in from all quarters: 'Bangles, bells, necklaces with clasps engraved with good wishes for the child in its encounter with life, are handed over, along with gifts which correspond to those given by god-parents in the West. The boy is placed on a table, on which books, swords, official insignia and money are laid: whatever he takes hold of first is a pointer to his future career.

Birthday picture for women

Birthday picture for men

Girls were confronted with scissors and tape-measure, powder and rouge, jewellery and money' (Richard Wilhelm). Additionally, a → tortoise and writing brush might be offered to a boy, a knife to a girl.

On their first birthday, children normally received their first → names. This ceremony was deliberately low-key, the names chosen in inconspicuous fashion, lest the attention of demons be attracted. If a son died in infancy, the next son to be born was given a girl's name: this was to fool the demons long enough for the boy to gain strength and be safe from them.

Marriages were celebrated in the 'Hall of Ancestors' or in the reception room, the main room of the ordinary house, and here too the 'great' birthdays of the parents – especially the sixtieth, seventieth and eightieth – were celebrated. The birthday was known as the 'Feast of the Thousand Autumns' – that is, 'May you (whose birthday it is) live a thousand years.'

From the 8th century onwards, there are many accounts of imperial birthdays. From 907 on, officials were given special leave on their birthdays if these fell on the days preceding and following the Emperor's birthday.

Birthmark
zhi (chi)

Given the Chinese obsession for seeing everything in a symbolical light, it is not surprising that the birthmark should be invested with significance. If the birthmark is on the sole of the foot, is black and looks like a → tortoise's shell, one can rest assured that the person so marked will attain to high office.

If a woman has a birthmark on her lip, spectators will assume she has a matching one on her genitals. Similarly, a birthmark on the cheek suggests a counterpart on the → breast.

Bi-section

The round section of → jade, whose outer diameter is double the width of the circular hole in the middle, is taken to be a simple symbol of → heaven. It was formerly part of the ceremonial apparatus used in earth worship. Some sinologists think that it also had an astronomical purpose.

'Intact ring' (*wan bi*) signifies, *inter alia*, 'virginity'.

Black
hei

When Shi Huang-di, the first → Emperor of China, had defeated the red Zhou Dynasty he chose black as the colour of his dynasty, since water (associated with black) puts out fire (red). His successors in the Former Han Dynasty (from 206 BC) let all of a hundred years elapse before they opted for red again.

According to the ancient teaching of the five permutations of the → elements, black was associated with → water, the North and a salty taste, and its representative domestic animal was the → pig. Black was chosen by later historians as the symbolic colour of the first of the three ancient dynasties – Xia; the second – Shang – was symbolised by white.

As a symbol, black stands for darkness, death, honour. In the Chinese theatre eight heroes with blackened faces represent men who are honourable, if rough and ready: the Chinese Solomon, Bao-gong, is one of them.

Blood
xue

In Chinese, a distinction is made between two kinds of blood: fresh, red blood, the kind that flows from wounds, is a symbol of life, while the dark blood of → menstruation is unclean; contact with it brings illness or unhappiness. Red blood is the seat of the → soul, and any object smeared with this blood acquires magical powers thereby.

If a demon can be successfully smeared with blood, it is forced to assume its true form. When pictures of gods or goddesses are being consecrated, the eyes are painted over with blood, and in this way the picture or statue is animated or given a soul. Several stories tell of a painter who paints a picture of a dragon which is then criticised by a customer or recipient because the eyes have not been painted over: when the painter makes the omission good, the picture turns into a real dragon and flies away.

In other stories we read of a child retrieving the bones of its parents from foreign parts, a widow who seeks out the mortal remains of her late husband. They then prick their flesh and let the blood drip out. The blood will enter the bones only of their dead relatives, which can then be gathered together and buried at home.

Blood was also used in a test to establish chastity. A woman whose chastity was in question only had to prick her cheek and let the blood run into some water: if the blood did not mix with the water but remained suspended like a pearly globule her case was proven. A virgin's blood was always red, never black.

Male semen is transformed blood, and if too much semen is expended, the man's health suffers. A mother's milk is also blood in a different form; it was said that if a bowl of human milk was left out in the dew it would have turned into blood by morning. A nightmare about 'blood on the bed' indicates the wife's unchastity.

Blue
lan

One should never wear light or dark blue flowers or ribbons in the hair: it is unlucky. Blue may also be a harbinger of high office and social preferment – with added worries and difficulties. Blue eyes are regarded as ugly; as a rule, blue eyes were found only among non-Han minorities in Central Asia, e.g. among the Hunza.

'Blue Faces': Kui-xing, the god of literature, was originally a → scholar, who was frustrated in his ambitions and committed suicide. He is often represented with a blue face. Jian-zhai, one of the demon kings, is also often shown with a blue face and red hair; 49 days after a death, a paper figure of Jian-zhai is folded and set upright at the memorial sacrifice. In many traditions, a man with a blue face is a → ghost or a bad character.

The word *lan* is not found in the older literature. It is derived from the name of the indigo plant, until recently the most important source of dyes for the clothes of ordinary people. The older word for 'blue' is *qing* which covers all shades from dark grey through blue to green. *Qing* can be used of the blue of the sky or of the sea.

Qing also symbolises the study carried out by the scholar who goes on working into the night by the light of the 'blue lamp'. 'The way of the blue clouds' is a metaphor for progress from one examination to another. Formerly, a 'blue tent' used to be erected at marriage ceremonies; and the nomadic tent in Mongolia is similarly described.

'To sow jade in the blue field' means 'to be pregnant' (→ bridge). 'Blue Dragon' is a metaphor for the penis. The 'blue bird' is a messenger from → Xi-wang-mu: hence, any messenger.

Boat
chuan

船

A picture showing two children pulling behind them a wooden boat on wheels containing a cap of office, an official's sash and a pomegranate, is a pictorial riddle. The → hat (*guan*) symbolises an → official (*guan*), as does the → sash (*dai*); the boat (*chuan*) means 'from generation to generation' (*chuan*), while the → pomegranate (*liu*) means 'to flow, transmit' (*liu*). Thus, the riddle

'The ruler is the boat, the people are the water. It is the water that bears the boat; it is also the water that can make the boat capsize' (Xun-zi, 3rd century BC)

expresses the wish that the recipient of this picture may receive the cap and sash of an official: that is, attain an official post, and that the same state of affairs may be extended to his progeny.

On the 5th day of the 5th month, a boat race using long narrow boats is held in South China and in the Ryukyu Islands. It is a fertility ritual: quite often one or another of the participants is drowned, and thus the Water-god, who confers fertility, is not deprived of a sacrificial offering. The government or the local authorities have apparently tried to ban the race, but, at least until very recently, without success.

It was the practice of the South Chinese coast and in Taiwan, on certain days of the year, to fashion large boats out of paper and thin boards, which were set on fire and pushed out to sea. These were supposed to carry plague away with them. A seaworthy boat carrying a picture of the Plague-god (Wang-gong) was launched: at the point where it made landfall, a temple was built to the god.

A 'dry-boat' (*han-chuan*) is the frame of a boat without a bottom, which one or two men can carry along, so that it looks as though it is being rowed. This was a popular game in North China at the → New Year festivities.

Bodhi
pu-ti

菩 提

The → Buddha himself does not record that he received enlighten-ment under the Bodhi-tree (*Ficus religiosa*). Nevertheless, there are some grounds for believing that when Siddhartha Gautama became a Buddha one night in 528 BC, not far from the site of the present-day Mahabodhi Temple of Bodh-Gaya, he was sitting under a tree which can be identified as a Bodhi tree by reason of its heart-shaped leaves with their long divergent points. In China, the pearls in a → rosary are called *pu-ti-zi* because they can lead to enlightenment when used in prayer. 'Pu-ti-water' is a metaphor for semen.

Book
shu

The book is one of the → eight symbols of the → scholar; it represents his learning. Until quite recently, parents used to lay out various objects before a son on his first birthday – → money, silver, → a tortoise, a banana and a book. If the baby tried to grasp the book, it was a sign that he would be studious.

For more than two thousand years, the literary topos of the handing down of a book from super-natural powers has figured 'not only in the initiation but also as a harbinger of a new age: a concept which has struck particularly deep roots in the Dao-inspired secret societies' (Wolfgang Bauer).

Chinese ways of thought have always been based on certain books – whether 'the five' classics, or 'the four books' of Confucianism. In the *Tai-ping-jing* ('Way of Supreme heaven and earth, and match *yin* and *yang* so that natural catastrophes and inauspicious signs vanish, rulers live long and the government enters upon the stage of "Supreme Peace"?'

Tradition says that there was a 'Burning of the Books' in the 2nd century BC – to be precise, in 213 BC, when Li Si, the all-powerful Chancellor of Qin, is said to have forbidden the private ownership of certain books – including the *Shi-jing* (the 'Book of Odes') and the *Shu-jing* (the 'Book of Documents') – on pain of death: all copies were to be handed over for destruction by the authorities. The ban applied to all the works of the philosophical schools, and all of the historical literature, apart from the annals of Qin and certain books of use in everyday life.

Books and a spray of almond blossom: 'May you pass your examination and achieve high official rank'

Peace'), a Taoist work of the 2nd century AD, we find this theme dealt with in a teacher's answer to disciples who have asked him what, in the long run, is the real use, if any, of Taoist literature like the *Tai-ping-jing*: 'You really are too stupid! Are you really asking whether my Dao can be weighed in some sort of scales? Yes? You are asking me to put a price on all I have told you, all I have done to enlighten you and give you insight into the world of the divine Dao? If, instead, I had given you 1,000 pounds of gold to be used in the service of the state – would you then be in a position to place a cheerful heart at the service of

Bo-shi

In modern Chinese, *bo-shi* means 'Professor', 'Doctor', 'scholar'. In the old language it simply referred to a scholar versed in the classics, who had passed the state examinations. By the Middle Ages, men who worked in the corn mills were called 'mill professors'. And similarly, employees in wine-shops were known as 'tea professors'.

Bottle-gourd
hu-lu

The bottle-gourd is a typical part of the magician's or the Taoist's para-

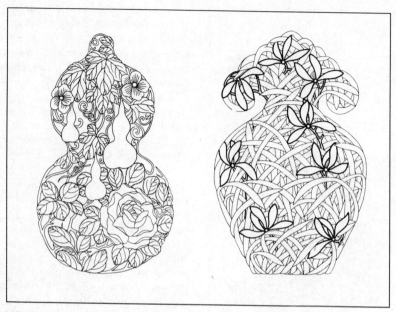

Left: Three pumpkins and hedge-roses in a bottle-gourd. Right: orchids in a bottle-gourd, signifying friendly relations

phernalia. It contains his magic potions and so forth. The story about a Taoist who goes inside a bottle-gourd is well-known; his voice can be heard outside before he emerges.

The bottle-gourd is a miniature replica of → heaven and → earth: in its shape it unites the two. When it is opened, a sort of cloud comes out which can be used to trap demons. Temple paintings depicting the battles between good and evil gods (scenes based usually on the celebrated early 17th-century novel 'The Metamorphoses of the Gods') show the bottle-gourd as an active protagonist on the side of the good, helping them to victory over their evil opponents. A bottle-gourd embellished with arabesques expresses the wish for → 'Ten thou-

sand generations of sons and grand-sons'. A bottle-gourd decorated with arabesques and roses signifies the wish that 'Spring may last for ten thousand generations' – i.e. that the recipient family may last for ever.

On the feast of the summer solstice (the 5th day of the 5th month) a bottle-gourd made of paper is hung up at the gateway into the house. This is a symbol of → Li Tie-guai, one of the eight → Immortals.

Bow
gong 弓

As early as in the 2nd millennium BC, the typical Chinese war bow was

BOX   47

compound, a refinement which did not appear in Europe till the 2nd century AD. The South Chinese minorities, on the other hand, were still using the simple bow at a much later date. Bow and arrow together symbolise the arrival of a male baby. In ancient China it was the custom on the third day after the → birth to shoot arrows made from Artemisia (→ yarrow) into the air from a bow of mulberry wood, in order to drive away evil spirits. It was also the custom every night to scare away nocturnal birds of ill omen by means of the 'sun-rescuing bow with the moon-rescuing arrows'; and until quite recently, during solar and lunar eclipses, arrows were shot upwards in an attempt to scare away the supposed monster.

The Homeric motif of Odysseus' bow which no one else can draw, can be found in a Chinese text dating from the 3rd century BC, according to which none of the courtiers could draw a certain king's bow: a story which the text rather spoils by suggesting that this was only because they were too polite to offend him! A later text has it that the youthful → Buddha alone could draw the bow of his ancestors. As a reward, he is supposed to have been given a wife. In the medieval play 'The Story of the Iron Bow', it is the successful suitor of the heroine alone who can draw the bow.

Closely connected with the longbow is the crossbow whose use was widespread among the inhabitants of the southern provinces at a very early date. It was often used to launch ball-shaped missiles instead of arrows.

A picture of a man surrounded by children shooting an arrow into the air represents the West Chinese god Zhang-xian, and expresses a wish to have many sons.

Archery is an ancient art in China. To win a contest, one had to be in possession of 'perfect virtue' (*de*): that is, one had to have achieved a harmonious balance of all inner and outer forces.

Bowl
pen

The bowl is one of the → eight Buddhist precious things: it represents the stomach of the → Buddha. It may also represent the urn into which the bones of the dead are put. A 'speaking bowl' plays a decisive role in helping Bao-gong, judge turned detective, to solve a murder mystery. The play in which this occurs is still frequently staged, and provided the plot for the first film made in China.

Box
he

The Chinese for 'box' – *he* – is phonetically identical with the word for 'concord, harmony'. A box with → lotus-leaves (*he*) hanging out of it, and a sceptre near-by, means 'May everything turn out as (you) wish, in concord and harmony.'

The Chinese 'Heavenly Twins' → He-he (often followed by *er-xian* = the two holy ones) were formerly worshipped in Peking on the 19th day of the 1st month. Each carried in his hands a box and a lotus. In popular belief they were linked with the 'Blue Dragon' (*qing long*) and the 'White Tiger' (*bai-hu*) and were revered by traders and merchants as the gods guarding the door of the house.

Boxwood
huang-yang　　黄楊

Boxwood was used for the characteristic → sash toggles, which every scholar once possessed, and which can now be studied (outside China) in a large collection in Santa Fé. Boxwood was peculiarly suitable for this purpose since it is evergreen and grows very slowly: hence, it was a symbol for → longevity.

Breast
xiong　　胸

In popular art it is the male breast that is strongly emphasised, not the female. The ancient Chinese believed that for a man to have a well-developed bust was a sign of good fortune. Indeed, the founder of the Zhou Dynasty had no less than four breasts, which was considered a peculiarly auspicious omen. In ancient times, women wore a broad sash across the breasts so that they were not visible. Nowadays, the female bust is called the 'jade mountain' or 'the two moun-

tains'. It is also known as *man-tou* = dumpling, steamed bread.

The nipple is compared to a grape, or to the seed of the → lotus. Women belonging to the lower classes, we are assured, have red nipples the size of dates. A woman with small nipples may bear children who will rise in society; a woman with large nipples, on the other hand, bears children who stay in or sink to the lower classes.

The cleavage between the breasts is compared to a ravine between two mountains.

Bridge
qiao　　橋

A bridge connects things which are separated: therefore, the dead must cross the narrow bridge that leads from this world to the next, and sinners who do not deserve to reach the other side, fall down into the foul waters full of blood and pus. According to legend, Xiuan-cang went on a pilgrimage from Tang China to India to fetch Buddhist texts so that the Emperor should no longer be haunted by the spirits of the many people he had killed. On the journey he had to cross a bridge which consisted of nothing more than a tree trunk: he and his companions 'lost their bodies', i.e. they became → immortal.

A scene from the novel 'The Chronicle of the Three Kingdoms' is often depicted: it shows General Zhang Fei on horseback fighting his enemies on the bridge known as the 'bridge of the long boards'.

Close to Chang-an on the river Wei is the celebrated → Blue Bridge, at which wives and friends said good-bye to those who were being sent to take up posts in remote provinces. This bridge is under the protection of its own goddess – the 'Person of the Blue Bridge' – who is none other than the Moon-goddess.

The young Lord Wei once arranged to meet his sweetheart under the Blue Bridge, but the water of the Wei river rose higher and higher, and he was drowned. This tale of extreme devotion is very popular in Taiwan, where it is told of two friends who thereupon became local divinities. According to another version of the legend, Lord Pei Hang met his sweetheart Yun-ying in a haunted cave near the bridge and both acquired divine status.

There is also a god of bridges who does not allow evil demons to bring their ills and sicknesses across. In many parts of China, people cross three bridges on the 16th day of the 1st month, in order to avoid the pestilential demons. One of the most popular Chinese legends tells how a pair of young lovers (a cowherd and a spinning damsel) who were so besotted with each other that they could not work properly, were parted by a river (the Milky Way) with the result that they could meet only once a year (on the 7th day of the 7th month, or in some parts of China on the 6th day of the same month). It is on this day that the → magpies build a bridge so that the cowherd can hasten to his beloved → spinning damsel. A bridge built by sea-creatures, by means of which

The bridge in the flower bay

a hero is able to save his life, appears in Chinese, Korean and Japanese legend.

In erotic literature, the bridge stands for the area between the anus and the vagina. Pictures showing a man hurrying towards a bridge over a stream between two high mountains have erotic implications.

Broom
sao

The broom often symbolises wisdom and insight. It must never be left in the room where someone is dying, however, as otherwise the dead person will turn into a spirit with long hair. Nor should it stand behind participants in a game of chance, as it may well sweep luck out of the window. The goddess Sao-qing niang-niang (i.e. 'the woman who

Shi-de with his broom

every word he uttered and every breath he drew were in agreement with the Dao.'

Brush/Writing Brush
bi

Traditionally, Chinese is written with a brush: and the brush is therefore seen as the tool of the scholar. The Chinese word for 'certain(ly)' is pronounced *bi*, so inclusion of a brush in a painting may suggest certainty, particularly when the brush is shown transfixing a wheel: this can then be interpreted as 'he will strike the centre', i.e. he will certainly pass the state examination. The wheel may also refer to the Buddhist 'Wheel of the Law'. Together with a → money-bar (*ding*) and a → sceptre (*ru-yi*) the writing brush forms a rebus whose meaning is: 'May (you) certainly (*bi ding*) get all you want (*tu-yi*).' The brush may also symbolise the penis.

sweeps everything clean') is often represented as a woman with a broom; she is the goddess of fair weather, as she sweeps away clouds and rain. She is especially venerated at the New Year festivities.

The 'foundling' Shi-de, friend and confidant of the poet Han Shan, is also often shown holding a broom and laughing, as he has just been sweeping out the monastery kitchen. Of this 'saint' it is told that 'he shouted and ranted and annoyed people. Then again he would stare into space and laugh wildly. But

Bucket
tong

Buckets made of wood used to be common articles in every household, used for washing the baby, feet, clothes, etc., and also as chamber-pots. A folk-print shows five men standing round three buckets: this symbolises the three basic social relationships between people (*gang*, which is phonetically identical with another word for a jar or crock – *gang*): namely, between ruler and subject, father and son, and husband and wife. They are also tasting wine: the word *chang* = to taste being close to *gang* = basic bonds.

Buddha
fo   佛

Tradition has it that the Buddha was born in 621 BC and entered Nirvana in 543 BC. Recent research goes to suggest, however, that he lived at a somewhat later date: 563–483 BC. His teaching is supposed to have reached China in the first century AD, but there are indications that, centuries before this, Buddhist ideas had come in via the Silk Road, carried by traders from India and Central Asia. Indeed, from the 2nd century BC onwards, Buddhist communities are attested in several regions of China. Scholars were hostile to the new religion; in the first place because it seemed to them impious – after all, Buddha had deserted his family, and all monks who followed him were expected to do the same; and secondly Buddha himself appeared in the guise of a 'barbarian', i.e. traditionally clad with one shoulder bare and with no form of decoration. There was a theological difficulty into the bargain, not unlike the dispute that developed much later in Christianity: was the → Emperor to bow down before the image of Buddha? Or were Buddhist disciples to kneel before the Emperor?

As time went on, non-Chinese missionaries translated, with Chinese assistance, the main texts of

the Pali canon into Chinese. Later, Chinese were allowed to become monks, and began to translate Buddhist texts from Prakrit into Chinese. The result was the emergence of several schools, which were described, not quite accurately, as 'sects'. The difference between these schools reduced essentially to individual preference on the part of teachers for certain texts to the exclusion of others. Disciples had to learn their master's favourite texts off by heart, and pass them on to their own pupils. It was over the first five centuries AD that these schools took shape.

Today, as far as ordinary people are concerned, Buddhism is largely a way of understanding and coping with death; and this means that it is usually the elderly who take any interest in it. Monks conduct services for the dead and coffins are often kept for years in Buddhist temples, as are the family plaques of those who have died young. The skeletons of unknown people and of foreigners are kept in special chambers near the temple. Formerly, the corpses of practising Buddhists were burned rather than buried, and the present government has opted for cremation, though for reasons unconnected with Buddhism.

The birth of Buddha is celebrated in China on the 8th day of the 2nd month according to the old calendar, which corresponds to the 8th day of the 4th month by current reckoning. Many texts give this date as that of Buddha's conception.

The → eight Buddhist symbols (*ba-ji-xiang*) are derived from the very oldest stratum of Indian royal ceremony: the mussel symbolises the call to the sermon, which is itself symbolised by the wheel; the → canopy protects all living beings, the → umbrella shades all medicinal herbs, the → lotus is the symbol of purity, the → vase that of perfect wisdom; the → goldfish symbolise release, and the → knot symbolises eternal life.

In Buddhist art, the Buddha is sometimes shown surrounded by → children at play: this symbolises the 'good fortune that comes down from heaven'. When the Buddha is shown standing on a lotus bloom in the water, together with a woman clothed in red who rides on a fish, this is a reference to the play 'The White Snake' (*Bai she zhuan*).

See also Bodhi, Fat-belly Buddha, Finger-lemon.

Butterfly
hu-die

蝴蝶

For no better reason than phonetic similarity, the butterfly may symbolise a man in his seventies (*die*); more frequently and more reasonably, however, it is also the emblem of a lover sipping nectar from the calyx of a flower (a female symbol). In one of the oracle texts we read: 'The colourful butterfly dances among the flowers, the yellow → oriole sings on the willow tree': here, oriole and willow are female symbols. A deceased wife may appear to her husband as a butterfly, and there is a very well-known love story in which the soul of the dead girl comes from the grave in the guise of a butterfly. Sexual intercourse is described as 'love-crazed butterfly and wild bee'. One also speaks of 'letting free a butterfly that seeks the fragrance (i.e. the woman)'.

Butterflies and → plum-blossom together in a picture symbolise long life and immaculate → beauty. The butterfly and the → cat (*mao*) together express a reduplicated wish that the recipient of the picture may reach the age of 70 or even 80.

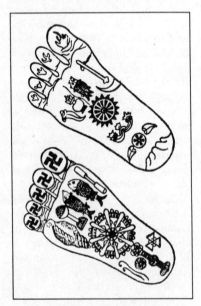

Footprints of the Buddha on stone, with the emblems of Buddhism

Butterflies on an embroidered handbag

C

Cakes
gao

Gao is one of several kinds of cakes which are specially eaten at New Year festivities because *nian-gao* = 'year-cake' can also mean 'May you rise in rank (*gao*) every year!'

At lunar festivals it is customary to eat → gourd cakes.

Such cakes are made at home, unless there is mourning in the family. This means that it is only to friends who are in mourning that cakes may be sent as gifts.

Calendar
li

Geared as it is to the revolution of the earth round the → sun, the Western calendar is a purely solar calendar. The old Chinese calendar, on the other hand, was basically related to the movements of the moon, but regulated when necessary with reference to the sun. The calendar 'year' had 12 months of 29 or 30 days each, amounting in all to 354 days: but as this did not fit in with the solar period, an intercalary → thirteenth had to be inserted seven times in a 19-year cycle (cf. the metonic cycle of the ancient Greeks).

A lunar calendar of this kind has certain advantages. For one thing, it is always possible to tell what day of the month it is from the phase of the moon. Every month begins with the new moon. Chinese seasonal → feast-days and holidays are all connected with phases of the moon, especially full moon as then the nights are brighter. From the farmer's point of view, however, the lunar calendar is not so attractive, as it does not correspond accurately to the seasons: indeed, the discrepancy can be as much as two weeks. The farmer's needs are met in special 'almanacs' which give the days in both notations – the Chinese and the modern European – plus all the information he needs for his work, and a great deal more besides. Thus, along with useful tips – for example, that autumn is the best time for felling trees, repairing the house and doing other things for which there was no time in the busy season – there are chapters on → medicines and cures for sickness, ringing in the ears, twitching of the eye, interpretation of dreams, good and bad omens. From such an almanac we can learn on which day we should get a hair-cut or do the washing, get married or buried, or go on a journey. These almanacs enjoy great popularity in Taiwan. On some days, the roads are full of wedding processions; on other days one meets only funerals; on others again, everybody's washing is hanging out to dry. This is in spite of the fact that it is now fifty years since the Western calendar was officially introduced.

Callings, The Four
shi-nong-gong-shang

士 農 工 商

In popular Chinese belief, the woodcutter who makes use of the mountains, the → fisherman who exploits the waters, the peasant who causes the earth to bring forth fruits, and the → scholar who can read the heavens and the signs – these four represent the main callings of mankind. In popular prints the four are shown together crossing a →

bridge. The four are not identical with the recognised four social classes of ancient China: the scholar (*shi*), peasant (*nong*), craftsman (*gong*) and trader (*shang*).

Camel
luo-tuo

The two-humped camel – the 'true' camel – came to China from Central Asia, and was used until modern times as a beast of burden, especially of salt. For expeditions such as that of Sven Hedin, across the Gobi Desert in the 1920s, it was indispensable.

The Chinese regard the camel as a lazy beast, though one of great endurance. Art of the Tang Dynasty (618–906) is especially rich in representations of the camel, sometimes with, and sometimes without humans. One of the best-known pictures (a painting on silk by Wu Dao-zi, *c.* AD 750) shows the dying Buddha Sakyamuni under the sala trees, with the camel, → water buffalo, → elephant, → tiger and other animals grieving round him.

Camellia
shan-cha

In translations from Chinese into Western languages, one sometimes comes across the expression 'wild tea' or its equivalent: literally translated, the two Chinese characters given above mean 'mountain tea'. This is actually the Chinese name of the camellia. The flower plays a rather minor role in Chinese literature. Among the Hakka, a minority people in South China who live mainly in mountain areas and grow a lot of tea, the words *shan-cha hua* = 'mountain-tea-flower' are used to describe a fresh, young → girl.

Candles
la-zhu

Wax candles have been in use in China for over two thousand years. An 8th-century text mentions 'coloured candles' being used in marriage ceremonies. 'Lighting the wax candles' is a metaphor for defloration of a virgin. The candle was also used, like the incense stick, as a means of measuring a set period. One story tells how an Emperor kept a → scholar up so long one night that a whole wax candle burnt down. But the grateful Emperor rewarded the scholar with a gold lotus candle. In the 5th century candles of wax were, it seems, still very expensive, because an Emperor of the Southern Dynasty gave the Emperor of the Toba ten candles as an imperial gift. 'Hanging wax candles upside down' is a symbolic expression for a form of sexual intercourse.

Cannon
pao

In China, as in medieval Europe, cannon developed from catapults and similar engines of warfare. In the middle of the 13th century the Chinese were firing 'small bamboo canes' filled with explosives at the Mongols. In the 16th century the Fu-lang-ji (the 'Franks', i.e. the Spaniards) introduced more powerful cannon into China, and these were promptly used against the non-Han peoples of South China. 'Cannon' is a common metaphor for 'penis'.

Canopy
gai

According to old and fragmentary traditions, the Chinese imagined the cosmos as an imperial chariot: and they compared the world to a carriage with a cover or canopy over it. This canopy is round in shape and symbolises the → heavens. The driver sits well forward, under the rim of the canopy. 'The name of this place (*xian*) corresponds to that point in the reception hall at which the lord must place himself when he is holding court. To say "The earth bears and the heaven covers" (Li-ji, Chap. *Zhong-yong*) refers as much to the house as to the carriage' (Marcel Granet).

Reliefs dating from as far back as the Han period (206 BC–AD 220) show canopies carried by servants to protect someone of noble family from the sun. Pictures of → Xi-wang-mu often show a canopy or umbrella held over her by a maidservant.

The → umbrella also goes back to the time of Confucius: and like modern umbrellas it could even be folded when not in use. The canopy tended to become more and more a purely Buddhist symbol. It is one of the → eight Buddhist symbols, and represents the lung of the deity.

Cao Guo-jiu 曹 國 舅

One of the eight Immortals. He is always shown in court dress, and often he is holding an official sceptre or castanets. The *guo-jiu* part of the name indicates that he was 'maternal uncle of the Emperor'. The legend tells us: 'From early childhood onwards, he loved the secret way of things (*dao*). To him, riches and honours were as dust' (tr. Richard Wilhelm).

Cao Guo-jiu is the patron saint of actors and actresses.

Cao Guo-jiu with castanets

Carp 鯉
li

The Chinese words for 'carp' and 'advantage' (*li*) are phonetically identical (apart from the difference in tones): so the carp symbolises a wish for benefit or advantage in business. It is also said that on its journey upstream this → fish can jump the rapids in the upper course of the Yellow River (at the Dragon Gate). This feat is compared to success in the state examinations, and is frequently shown in pictures: the carp, surrounded by shoals of smaller fish (those who don't pass!), is in the act of making its powerful

Carp, a child and a lotus: 'May you have something over (to keep) every year!'

leap. As this is no easy feat and requires long preparation, the carp is also a symbol of patience and steadfastness. Its → beard is in itself a token of its supernatural powers.

In other pictures a fisherman is seen selling a carp to a woman with a child. He is wishing her a good income and social advancement.

A picture showing a young woman attended by her maid standing at a brook with a bucket into which a carp is trying to jump, expresses the wish that the recipient may be able to spring over the more ordinary humans in his path.

Cat
mao

A cat looking at a peony: 'May you be rich!'

Mao = cat, and *mao* = octogenarian, are phonetically close; so a picture showing cats and → butterflies expresses the wish that the recipient should live to be 70 or 80. A cat with → a plum (*mei* = plum is phonetically close to *mei* = each, every, always) and → bamboos (*zhu* = bamboo is phonetically close to *zhu* = to wish, pray) means: 'At all times we wish that you may reach a ripe old age.'

If a strange cat has her kittens in one's house this is a very bad sign: even if she only enters the house it is an omen of poverty, because the cat knows that lots of rats are going to come and eat the family out of house and home. Mothers warn children who won't go to sleep that the cat will come and get them.

Cat flesh is not eaten in North China, a prohibition which does not apply in the South. Nor was the cult of the cat known in South China, which was practised in Gansu. North Chinese cats catch mice, but in South China, especially in the Canton area, they are said to be too lazy to bestir themselves. Because of its very good eyesight, the cat can see → spirits in the dark. In the province of Zhejiang white cats are never kept, because they get on to the roof at night and steal the moonbeams: they can even turn into mischievous spirits. For this reason too dead cats should never be buried lest they turn into demons; it is safer to hang them up on trees. In Taiwan one may still occasionally see a tree festooned with dead cats.

It was believed that if a cat jumped

over a coffin, the corpse was revived and became 'undead', to haunt the area. In short, the cat has demonic powers: it has its uses as a mouse-catcher, but it can also be a very dangerous creature indeed.

A girl who dolls herself up a lot and flirts around is castigated as a 'black cat'. The 'mountain cat' is the hare. Insincerity in someone is described as 'the cat weeping over the mouse' (which it has just eaten!).

Cauldron of Oil 油鍋
you-guo

Among the things awaiting sinners in the Buddhist → hells is the cauldron of oil. In each of the ten main hells sits an infernal judge who passes sentence on the guilty. They are then sawn up, soaked in boiling oil, ground in a mortar, etc. The cauldron of oil is generally taken to be in the seventh hell. Sinners are boiled in it, then revived and boiled again, and so on. This is the punishment visited on venal → officials, on judges who have wittingly given false judgment, on clerks who have altered documents for bribes, and on ruffians who have murdered prisoners.

Cave 洞
dong

The Chinese regard caves as places where good-natured supernatural beings dwell; sometimes hermits live there too. As in West Asian legend they may also be the portals leading to another, more beautiful world. Hence the room in which a bride-groom first meets his betrothed is called the 'Cave-room'.

Centipede 蜈蚣
wu-gong

The centipede is the arch-enemy of the → snake, and many a folk-tale tells how the hero is saved by a centipede from a snake which is about to attack him. It used to be said that when people living in South China went into the mountains they took with them a sort of → rattle. This was a bamboo cane with a centipede inside it. The centipede reacted at once to the proximity of a snake by stirring, thus warning the walkers. Big centipedes (*yan-yu*) are poisonous. If their dried seed falls into what you are eating, you will die. In this sense, the centipede is one of the five → noxious creatures; attempts to expel these from human settlements are made mainly on the 5th day of the 5th month. It is also believed that they can be destroyed by the → cock.

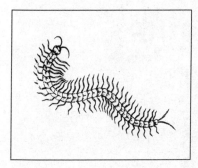

Centipede

Chang-e 嫦娥

The Moon-goddess, Chang-e, is supposed to have been the wife of the archer Hou Yi, who had received the herb of → immortality from → Xi-wang-mu. When Hou Yi was away, his wife ate the herb, achieved immortality and ascended to the → moon, where she lives to this day in the 'Palace of the Far-reaching Cold' (*guang han gong*). Hou Yi tried in vain to follow her, and thereafter took up residence in the → sun.

She is often represented as a fine lady who is looking at herself in a mirror held for her by a lady's-maid, while another maid brings tea. Beside her are two children who are admiring a → hare: this is the 'hare in the moon'. It is using a phallus-shaped pestle and a mortar to grind down the bark of the → cinnamon tree which confers immortality.

The Moon-goddess, Chang-e, returns with her beloved to the Moon Palace

Cherry
ying-tao 櫻桃

The Chinese words *ying-tao* really mean 'baby peach'. Like many other kinds of fruit, the cherry was probably brought at an early date from western Asia. As in the West, 'cherry lips' or a 'cherry mouth' are stock attributes of female → beauty. The expression 'eating cherries', however, should be used with caution in China: it means 'having sexual intercourse'.

Chess
xiang-qi 象棋

Several variants of chess are attested in China at an early period. The game known in Japan as *go* is described as a game of 'encirclement chess' (*wei-qi*). *Go* was exactly like war and was played according to the rules of military strategy. The usual game of chess, however, is said to correspond to the 'Plan of the Yellow River' (*he-tu*): and the first man to spot this, at once defeated the ruling grand master. This 'Plan' takes the form of the magic 'square'. 'Figure chess' (*xiang-qi*) is connected with astrological symbolism, and is also supposed to be an imitation of Chinese football (→ games).

Chess is one of the 'four arts'. People playing chess are often to be seen in paintings. A celebrated scene shows the two → constellation deities of the North and South Poles playing chess with each other. A boy comes along and watches for a while – when he gets home, however, he finds that many years have passed.

Chestnut
li

The so-called 'gold-leaf' chestnut is native to the eastern part of the Himalayas. It is a shrub variant of the chestnut-leaved oak. In Chinese, the word *li* = chestnut is phonetically close to *li* = propriety, good manners (only the tones differ). Another meaning of the character for *li* = chestnut is 'fearful', 'anxious' – i.e. lest one's behaviour be found wanting. At weddings, chestnuts are served together with → dates (*zao*): the implicit message is 'May they soon (*zao*) have sons (*li*).'

Children
haiz

Implicitly if not explicitly, for the Chinese, 'children' means → 'sons'. Before 1949 only a male heir could inherit the parental estate and perform the ancestral sacrifices for father and forefathers. The superior status of male issue is already evident in the → birthday and → name-giving ceremonies. The more sons a man had the better; and some

patriarchal prodigies in Chinese history who, we are told, had a hundred sons, are held up as ideal exemplars. Thus, for example, Wen-wang, the founder of the Zhou Dynasty (*c*. 1050 BC).

The preferential treatment of male issue emerges very clearly from a well-known passage in the 'Book of Odes' (No. 189). The 'Great Man' (chief diviner) is asked to interpret a dream: 'Black bears and brown-and-white bears, they are good omens of sons; snake-brood and snakes, they are omens of daughters. And so he bears sons; they lay them on a bed, they dress them in skirts, they give them as toys (*jang* jades) jade insignia; they cry shrilly; their red knee-covers will be brilliant, (they will be) rulers of hereditary houses. And so he bears daughters; they lay them on the ground, they dress them in wrappers, they give

'We are harbingers of peace'

Children flying dragon kites

them as toys spinning-whorls . . .' (Karlgren).

With the emancipation of women and their advance to equality with men in many fields, such customs have vanished. The intense concern shown by parents in the education of their sons survived much longer. 'At least the first provincial examination! Then the higher grade exams, at last the final examination in the capital! For two thousand years, that was what parents aimed at for their sons. The examinations were the steps that led to high office, to success, to respect from one's fellows and often to wealth. By taking these steps one could rise from the peasant and artisan classes, even from the merchant class to the highest class in the land – that of the officials and scholars.'

A folk-print shows a hundred children playing with → lotus flowers in a pond. The inscription is 'Wenwang loved lotus' (*lien* = lotus symbolises '*lian*' = love). A picture showing two children in adult clothing, one holding a lotus, the other holding a little box, is a representation of the Heavenly Twins, the → He-he (*he* = lotus, or concord; *he* = small box, or concord): the He-he are the gods of conjugal felicity. Two children standing smiling at each other express the wish '(May you) meet each other in joy', a metaphor for conjugal intercourse. Five children may be shown holding a placard bearing the words 'May five sons pass the examination.' One often sees a picture divided into two sections, each showing a woman with a son: one son holds a lotus in his hand, the other is mounted on a → unicorn. The picture expresses the wishes 'May the heavenly powers send you a son' and 'May the unicorn bring you a son.' The wish 'May good luck, long life and children, all be (yours) in plenty' is expressed by a picture showing twelve children with → pomegranates and → peaches. A picture showing an old man dressed as a child playing on the ground in front of an even older pair, is a reference to Lao Lai-zi, one of the 24 ideal examples of filial piety (→ xiao); he played on the ground like a child in order to convince his parents that they were still young! In Taoist literature, the child epitomises the ideal innocence of the holy sage, absorbing all that it sees. A man who still owes his father money when the latter dies will have a bad son, a son who will cost him the equivalent of the debt; conversely, a son who is owed something by his father when the latter dies will have a duly filial son of his own.

In olden times it was believed that the songs that children sang on the streets at play were manifestations of the supernatural. They were noted down and analysed and political decisions might be taken in the light of deductions therefrom.

Chopsticks
kuaiz; zhu

Paired pieces of thin wood used for eating purposes have been found in graves dating from at least 1200 BC. Today, chopsticks are made almost exclusively from bamboo or other woods, though silver, ivory and plastics are also used. The word *zhu* is taboo at New Year, because it is phonetically identical with the word meaning 'to come to a halt' (*zhu*). Chopsticks should not be lent to anyone, as they break very easily. After use, they should never be left in the bowl or on the plate, as one does when honouring one's ancestors. To do so would bring bad luck.

According to the regulations for eating laid down in the 'Book of Rites' (*Li-ji*) chopsticks should not be used for eating → rice or → millet. Of course, the 'Book of Rites' was concerned mainly with ceremonial occasions and with the eating habits of the upper class, which goes far towards explaining this prohibition.

Chrysanthemum
ju

The chrysanthemum is the flower of autumn, which it symbolises. The flower is especially associated with the 9th month of the old Chinese calendar. Its name is phonetically close to the word for 'to remain' (*ju*); and the word for 'nine' (*jiu*) is identical with the word for 'long time' (*jiu*); so the chrysanthemum is also the symbol of long life and of duration. It is best to pick chrysanthemums on the 9th day of the 9th month. Alternatively, a form of tea can be prepared on this day from dried chrysanthemums. The flowering of the chrysanthemum is also celebrated by adding the flowers

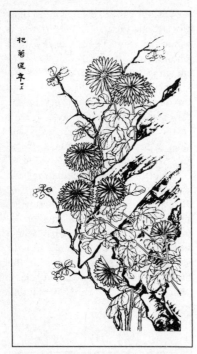

Chrysanthemum growing on the rocks

Good wishes expressed by a cicada and a chrysanthemum: 'May you be an official occupying the highest rank'

to the previous year's rice-wine. As Tao Yuan-ming says:

> Autumn chrysanthemums have a lovely tint,
> I pluck their fresh petals so full of dew.
> Drowned in this sorrow-banishing liquor
> I leave behind a world-laden heart.
> Though I enjoy the goblet all alone . . . (Tr. Roland Fang)

And another of the great lyric poets, Tu Mu, sings of the 9th month festivities as follows:

> Put chrysanthemums in your hair! You must

be blossom-bedecked when you accompany me home.

The chrysanthemum is often depicted along with other natural symbols – e.g. the pine-tree, in the combination known as *song ju you cun*. This group expresses the wish that the recipient of the picture may have a long life. In Tao Yuan-ming's poem 'Returning Home' we find the words:

> Pine-tree and chrysanthemum outlast (all things): (may you do likewise).

A wish that the recipient of the picture may continue for a long time (*jiu*) to occupy high official rank (*guan*) is expressed by a grasshopper sitting on a chrysanthemum; in North China, the word for 'grasshopper' is pronounced *gua.r*, which makes it phonetically close to *guan*. Of similar import is a picture showing the chrysanthemum with nine quails: *jiu shi tong ju* = 'may nine generations live under one roof in peace'. The Chinese word for the quail is *an-chun*, which can be taken as a phonetic reference to *an* = peace. The word meaning 'peacefully' is suppressed in the interests of maintaining the four-character structure of the saying: the reference to 'peace' then emerges from the phonetic echo in the first syllable of the word for 'quail' alone.

The characteristic flower of the spring, the → plum-blossom, and the chrysanthemum form a contrastive pair. It is significant that two lady's-maids in a well-known novel are called 'Chrysanthemum-blossom' and 'Plum-blossom', and there are no names referring to summer or winter. These seasons – summer and winter – represent extremes: summer and man, winter and woman, form a conjugal union, but their servants must attend to both and are therefore called after the seasons which are intermediate stages between man and woman.

The expression 'Chrysanthemum Brigade' (*ju-bu*) refers to prostitutes who can sing folk-songs in 'southern style'.

Chrysanthemum with bamboos. A woodcut from the 'Manual of Painting from the Mustard-seed Garden' (1701)

Cicada 蟈 蟈 蟬
guo-guo; shan

In ancient times, the cicada symbolised → immortality, or life after death. A cicada made of → jade was laid in the mouth of the deceased. Later, a fish was used in this ceremony instead of a cicada. According to one legend, the queen of the feudal state of Qi in Eastern China turned into a cicada after her death; and for this reason, the cicada was also known as the 'girl of Qi'. Representation of a cicada on a → hat symbolises an honest man of principle.

Cicada ornamentation

Cinnabar 丹
dan

Cinnabar is a reddish mineral which contains mercury: symbolically, it is linked with the colour red. It is the basic substance of Taoist alchemy, and a component ingredient in many an elixir which was supposed to confer → longevity but which all too often cut short the lives of those who put too much trust in such things. In some quarters, it was even held that cinnabar conferred → immortality.

In the Han Dynasty, a cinnabar fleck on the forehead of a harem girl served as a sign to the Emperor that she was not available (because of → menstruation). A 'cinnabar-note' (*dan-shu*) was a certificate on red paper. In earlier times, slaves were furnished with similar documents, confirming their status.

Taoists believe that there is a 'cinnabar field' just below the navel in the human body, comparable to our 'solar plexus', which plays a big part in meditation. Finally, the inner part of the vagina is called the 'cinnabar cave'.

Cinnamon Tree 桂
gui

A mythical cinnamon tree (or cassia tree) grows in the courtyard of the Palace of the Moon. 'The cassia tree grows so luxuriantly that if it were left to grow it would overshadow all the brilliance of the → moon. So it must be cut down every thousand years' ('The Legend of the Moon-Fairy', tr. Richard Wilhelm). Another version of the tale says that every night a man tries to cut the tree down, but he cannot keep pace with its growth: however much he cuts down has grown up again by next day. This Chinese Sisyphus is variously known as Wu Gang or Wu Zhi.

The flowers of the tree (species *Osmanthus fragrans*) have a very attractive and delightful scent. The expression 'to break off a cinnamon twig' means 'to pass the state examinations' – because then one will be 'in good odour' on all sides. Similarly one speaks of 'cinnamon-sons' and 'orchid-grandsons'. However, the expression 'breaking the cinnamon (bough) and mounting the dragon' refers to sexual intercourse.

The cinnamon tree blooms in the 8th month of the old Chinese → calendar and is accordingly an autumn flower. Depicted together with → peach blossom it symbolises 'great age and limitless duration in honour (*gui*)'.

Clean/Unclean
su/hun

'Clean' (*su*) and 'unclean' (*hun*) form a contrastive pair which appears in various contexts. One of the commonest is the contrast made between 'vegetarian' (*su*) and 'non-vegetarian' (*hun*): a culinary distinction between Buddhists and non-Buddhists. → Monks must eat *su*, i.e. 'simple', not enhanced in any way. *Su* is also used for garments worn in time of mourning, which should be made of coarse, undyed material. The word *hun* is used for food which includes meat in any shape or form. In non-Buddhist contexts, the distinction is between 'clear' (here, *su* = *qing*) and 'dull', 'cloudy'.

Before 1949 it was customary for a Chinese to use disparaging expressions when referring to his wife, in token of modesty and that sense of propriety which required that one should denigrate one's own possessions and speak respectfully of anything belonging to the addressee, or to a third party. Thus a man could refer to his wife as *hun-jia* = the turbid or confused one, without, however, meaning the words to be taken literally.

Clouds
yun

Clouds symbolise good fortune and happiness, especially when they have more than one colour; and clouds with five colours (*wu-se-yun*) are emblems of five-fold happiness. Auspicious clouds such as these are also harbingers of peace. Clouds are correlated with the West. They arise from a union of the two main principles → *yin* and → *yang*. Stylised clouds are frequent in ornamentation, e.g. the 'intertwined band of cloud' which takes the form of a spiral wave; but we also find more realistic representation as well. 'Cloud mountains', i.e. far-off ranges of hills, represent separation and longing. As the great poet-painter Wang Wei (Tang Dynasty) sang:

> I will walk till the water checks my
>   path,
> Then sit and watch the rising
>   clouds.

'Cloud-mother' (*yun-mu*) means 'mica'; 'fragrant clouds' is a meta-

Five bats in clouds: harbingers of good fortune

phor for beautiful hair when a woman lets it float free. 'Cloud-fog' (*yun-wu*) is an enticingly full brassière.

Perhaps the most frequent image involving clouds is *yun yu* = 'clouds and rain'. This refers to sexual union, the clouds being the blending of male with female, and rain the climax of the union. We find the 'cloud and rain game' mentioned in an ancient tale according to which a king in South China once dreamt by night on the 'magic mountain', close to the rapids of the Yangtse river, that he was making love to a → fairy. Here again, a natural image – the cloud which breaks in rain on the mountain – is combined with symbolism.

Cock
gong-ji

公雞

The cock is the tenth creature in the Chinese → zodiac. It is never eaten in China, and even at → New Year it is not to be killed. It wards off evil: a picture of a red cock will protect the house from fire (cf. the 'red cock' of German folklore). Placed on a coffin, a white cock will keep demons at bay.

There is ample textual evidence that cock-fights were being held in China in the first millennium BC. Today, although prohibited, they remain a very popular sport in South China.

There is supposed to be a cock in the → sun, though other traditions say it is a three-legged → raven. The cock is admired not only as a courageous bird but also as a beneficent

A cock with handsome comb and the herb of immortality

A cock-fight

one: he summons the hens to eat any food he finds. Again, he symbolises reliability, as he never fails to mark the passing hours. He is also a symbol of male vigour. According to Indian legend, a cock sits on a tree in the Continent of Jambudvipa: this is the 'King Cockerel' and when he crows all the cocks on earth crow.

Symbolically, a cock (*gong-ji*) crowing (*ming*) represents 'achievement and fame' (*gong-ming*). The word for 'cock's comb' (*guan*) is phonetically identical with *guan* = official; a present of a cock with a handsome comb, therefore, expresses the wish that the recipient may be rewarded with an official post. A cock with five chickens is a reminder that a father's job is to educate his five sons.

Coffin
guan

The Chinese believed that two → souls inhabited the human body; and funeral ceremonies had to take this into account.

Well-to-do people provided themselves during their life-time with coffins made of good hard wood, with an air-tight lid. In the side, a hole was left through which the *hun*-soul could pass, to stand trial in the underworld and thereafter be born again as a human being or as an animal.

The *po*-soul (or sentient-soul), on the other hand, must not be allowed to escape, as otherwise it would haunt its relatives as a → ghost. The very thought of rotting boards in the family graves was enough to give people sleepless nights.

In South China, far less attention was paid to the coffin, since the deceased had in any case to be disinterred after two years so that his bones could be 'washed' and laid in a clay urn (→ vase).

If you dream about a coffin, it means that you are going to get an official post: this is because the word for 'official' (*guan*) is a homonymic of *guan* = coffin.

Cold
leng-qi

Cold goes along with poverty. So a 'cold → scholar' is a poor scholar (or, in other contexts, a sly beggar).

On the 105th day after the winter solstice (4 April) the 'Cold Food' feast was observed. On this day, no fires were kindled, and people ate food prepared the previous day. It seems possible that this observance reached China from Western Asia where it had been originally a → spring festival in honour of the equinox (when the new year begins).

In Chinese tradition, this festival also figures as an act of remembrance for Jie-zi Tui. According to legend, this man had been invited by the Duke of the feudal state of Jin to serve him as minister. Tui refused all overtures and finally the Duke decided to take drastic measures – he ordered that the forest in which Tui dwelt should be set on fire. But Tui preferred death in the flames to serving a prince whose policies he could not endorse.

Confucius
Kong-zi 孔子

If we take deep and persistent effect on succeeding generations as our yardstick, no single person in the whole history of China can compare with Kong Qiu, or 'Master Kong' as he came to be known. He lived from 551 to 479 BC. He came from a family of minor nobility and spent his life trying to secure or retain various official posts in the service of feudal princes. Dismissal from such posts as he secured was always on the same grounds: his ideas on ethics and morals were not those of his lord and master. So, late in life, he gave himself over to wandering about with his disciples – most of whom were of noble birth – whom he inculcated with his doctrines. Tradition has it that he edited the 'Spring and Autumn Annals' (*Chun-qiu*), thereby turning what had been a purely historical work into a treatise on ethics and morals. Commentaries on the 'Book of Changes' (*Yi-jing*) and the compilation of the 'Book of Odes' (*Shi-jing*) were also ascribed to him. Music affected him deeply; on one occasion, he was so moved by the *Shao* (the music of the legendary Emperor Shun) that 'for three months he did not know the taste of meat'. He left behind no writings of his own, but his Analects (*Lun-yu*) were collected by his pupils and published after his death. Furthermore, the *Jia-yu* ('School Talks'), dating from the 3rd century BC, are at least in part attributable to him. And finally, the 'Book of Rites' (*Li-ji*) is permeated with his thought.

Confucius with his disciples studying the Yi-jing

It was not until long after his death, however, that the doctrinal system based on his thought – the body of thought known as 'Confucianism' – came into its own. Around 100 BC the rulers of the Han Dynasty were looking about for → officials, versed in the rules of propriety and able to read and write. This was the beginning of the ascendancy of Confucianism as the sole ideology of the Chinese state and its management. In the 12th century the Analects were canonised as one of the classical → 'Four Books'. Till the revolution of 1911, when the Chinese Empire was replaced by Sun Yat-sen's republic, Confucianism retained its hegemony.

Confucius himself produced nothing that could be called a systematic philosophy (as the Neo-Confucians were to attempt in the 11th and 12th centuries AD). The ontological and epistemological problems which were even then being discussed by the Pre-Socratics, were of little interest to him. What concerned him was man's life in society – life *before* death. His ideas

on morality are summed up in the doctrine of the → five virtues, or the → four 'bonds' (*si wei*). Confucius was an agnostic, but he did not deny the existence of supernatural beings. The state ceremonies involving the worship of → heaven and → earth, which play a key role in his precepts, scarcely come under the heading of 'religion'. It is significant that his tombstone in Qu-fu bears no more than the posthumously conferred honorary title 'King of Literature'.

Confucius died at the age of 72, without having had a chance to apply in practice the philosophy of life he had elaborated in theory. 'Certainly he died in the belief that he had failed; and yet no other man has ever had such a profound effect on the culture, the life and the manners of a people: an effect, moreover, which has endured for two thousand years' (Erwin Wickert). If any one thing goes to making the Chinese 'Chinese' it is the Confucian moral code (→ *xiao*). Confucian attitudes have 'penetrated their very being so completely that people are surprised if you remind them that they have just repeated an aphorism of Master

Kung's. The fact is that middle-aged Chinese and those of the younger generation know nothing about him; only now are people beginning to read him again.'

Symbolic representations of scenes from his life used to be very common. These began with his → birth, when two → dragons appeared over his parents' house and → five spirits gave their blessing, and ended up with the → 72 disciples he is supposed to have taught.

Taoists and Buddhists have tried to show that their own teachings do not conflict with the Confucian state religion, and have coined the phrase 'The → three teachings are one.'

Constellations
xing   星

The Chinese see seven stars in the constellation of the Great → Bear. These seven stars are very frequently represented in art, and play a very important part in Taoist ritual. One very attractive legend tells how the astral gods were once overcome with longing for life on earth and the pleasures of wine. So down they came to the house of a man who had been unjustly condemned to death, and began to drink. Whereupon the Astronomer Royal informed the Emperor that the Seven Stars had vanished from the heavens and that a major catastrophe was imminent. He recommended an immediate general amnesty. The Emperor took his advice, and soon the Seven Stars reappeared in their proper place.

The unjustly condemned man was thus saved from death.

According to another legend, it is the red-faced god of the 'Northern Dipper' (Bei Dou = Great Bear) who decides the hour of death for us. He plays → chess with the god of the 'Southern Dipper', and between them they determine our earthly lot. The Southern Dipper is more commonly known as the 'Immortal of the South Pole': he possesses the herb of → immortality.

Chinese astronomers (by the 2nd century AD they had counted and recorded 11,520 stars) saw the shafts of the Plough as a determining influence on the seasons, as every month they pointed in a new direction.

In Taiwan, the Dipper reappears in a funeral custom. The dead body is placed on a board in which there are seven holes representing the constellation, and laid thus in the coffin.

It often happens that only three of the seven stars are shown. This occurs in a series of 12 insignia, in which the three stars symbolise the heavens, while mountains represent the earth. The → three wishes: for long life (a man riding on a stag), for a good income (a man in a red robe) and for good luck and happiness (a man in a blue robe) are also known as the 'Three Constellations'.

The Chinese believe that each man is associated with a certain star, to which he should make sacrifice at → New Year. The stars therefore symbolise 'the people'. From his celestial journey a man brings home a star which one day flies into his wife's mouth. She becomes pregnant

Constellation deities

and gives birth to a son who turns out to be a reincarnation of a friend whom the father once helped. Shooting stars foretell the death of eminent men (see also Longevity, Planets, Spinning Damsel and Cowherd)

Copper
tong

The Chinese word *tong* covers also bronze and brass. The old Chinese coin with a square hole in the middle (often rendered as 'cash' in English) was made of copper. One thousand cash formed a 'string' – on which the coins were threaded. The real value of the coinage varied widely over the years, so that sometimes it was advantageous to melt the coins down to make household goods and weapons: at other times such copper articles would be melted down to make coins. The same sort of thing happened later when silver bars replaced the string of cash as the higher unit.

In North China it was customary to put copper bowls and shoes in the bridal bed, because *tong* = copper is phonetically identical with *tong* = together; and 'shoes' (*xie*) are always in pairs. So this was a way of expressing the wish that the couple would grow old together.

In the 8th → hell, or rather purgatory, sinners are forced to drink molten copper, as they used pernicious doctrines to make money. In the 6th hell the lascivious are attracted to a dancing partner whom they embrace – only to find too late that they are embracing a glowing hot pillar of copper. The last Emperor of the Shang Dynasty (which ended in 1050 BC), evidently a sadist, had his opponents made fast to copper pillars which were then heated. Bronze columns played a big part as boundary markers in the South Chinese border areas.

For articles made out of bronze, see also Bells, Drum.

Courtyard
ting

The open space surrounded by the main dwelling, the two side buildings and the main gateway, and which is the setting for a fair amount of family life, is known as the *ting*. A *ting* may also be a somewhat larger room used for special occasions such as festivities (cf. the → hall). Behind the main dwelling, many houses had a rear courtyard with another dwelling which was often inhabited by the parents of the householder. 'The Rear Hall' is a metaphor for the anus, and 'Flower of the Rear Hall' means anal intercourse, usually homosexual.

Crab
xia

蝦

In olden times it was believed that jade crabs existed. There is a legend about a well that had dried up round about 1600: here, a foreign merchant kindled a fire every night, and every fourteen days (the period between the full and the new moon) he got a jade crab out of the well.

In the province of Sichuan (where there are no real crabs) the jade crab is feared as a plague-bringing demon. In Shanxi and Henan, crabs are dried and hung up at the main entrance of a house, or pictures of crabs are hung up over the door. The crab looks more or less like the head of a → tiger, and this is why it can repel bad magic.

Dried crab enjoys a reputation as an aphrodisiac for men.

Two crabs

Crane
he

鶴

The crane is one of the many symbols of → longevity; and as such, it is often shown together with a → pine-tree and a → stone, two similar symbols. Variations on this theme couple a crane with a → tortoise or with a → deer. A picture showing a crane, a → phoenix, a → mandarin duck, a → heron and a wagtail is a representation of the → five relationships between people. In this setting, the crane symbolises the father–son relationship: when it sings, its young answer it.

Two cranes flying up towards the sun express the wish that the recipient of the picture may 'rise high'. Expressions like 'heavenly crane' (*tian-he*) or 'blessed crane' (*xian-he*) point to the wonderful qualities attributed to the crane in its second role – that of a symbol of

A crane on a rock, looking at the sun: a high-placed official who sees all things

Crane and peach – two symbols of longevity

wisdom. The death of a Taoist priest is said to be *yu-hua* = 'turning into a feathered (crane)'. Cranes, each with → a wooden rod in its beak, flying towards a → pavilion by the sea reflect the saying 'One more counter for the pavilion by the sea.' This is a reference to the legend of the three Taoists who counted their age not in years but in geological periods: every time the ocean turned into a mulberry plantation they laid down a counter, and they did so again when once again the land was flooded. In this legend there is a three-fold intensification of the longevity motif – the crane, the counter and the pavilion (the Taoist paradise).

The 'Boy of the White Crane' is a kind of demiurge, an attendant of the gods who lives in the palace of 'jade emptiness' in the cosmic mountains of the Kun-lun: he is an emissary of the gods and he helps heroes in their good works. His doings are recounted above all in the *Feng-shen yan-yi* ('The Metamorphoses of the Gods').

Pictures often show the 'Tower of the Yellow Crane' (*huang he lou*). This was a building in the state of Wu in the days of the Three Kingdoms: in it Liu Bei, the future Emperor of the small state of Shu-Han, was to have been slain by Zhao Yu – a celebrated episode in the 'Romance of the Three Kingdoms'.

Creator of the World
Pan-gu 盤 古

Pan-gu with the cosmic egg

The theory of creation put forward by Chinese philosophers in general, and by the Neo-Confucian rationalists of the 11th and 12th centuries in particular, allotted no role in the process to a deity. The Chinese man-in-the-street, however, has always preferred a more personal creator in the shape of Pan-gu. The myth of Pan-gu seems to have developed among the non-Han minority peoples in South China, from whom the Chinese then borrowed and transformed it. Originally, Pan-gu was a cosmic being whose limbs, when he died, turned into animals and plants and all the other manifestations of nature. In pictures he is sometimes shown, however, carving the world out of rock.

A very widespread myth relates that human beings were created by the goddess → Nü-gua from loam or clay: they then had to be dried out.

A more recent version of this myth says that she fired the clay figures in an oven. Some were overdone and came out black; others were insufficiently fired and came out white. It was only the third firing that was successful – the figures came out a nice yellow colour, and these are the Chinese. A complementary myth relates that during the drying-off process it began to rain, and some figures were spoiled – which explains why there are cripples in the world.

According to a completely different myth, the earth rests on the back of an → Ao, or → tortoise; and when the tortoise moves there is an earthquake.

It was for long held that the → heavens were round and the → earth square, which meant that there were parts of the earth which were not under the canopy of heaven. In these regions eternal darkness reigned, and they were inhabited by a race of sub-humans.

Cricket
xi-shuo

The cricket is a summer insect. It symbolises pluck and fighting spirit; and children shake them out of the trees and train them for cricket-fights. These encounters used to take place in autumn on market days, and the owner of the winning cricket got an → ox as a prize. Cricket-fights are textually attested from the 8th century onwards. Nowadays they take place, if at all, only in a few places in Central and South China, though I have often seen children picking them up from trees and keeping them in a container.

Cuckoo
bu-gu

The Chinese cuckoo is also called *du-juan*, who was, according to legend, a ruler of Sichuan (otherwise known as the 'Soul of Shu', Shu being an old name for Sichuan). In the Bon religion of Tibet, the cuckoo is regarded as a sacred creature, as it is supposed to have impregnated the ancestress of the founder of the Bon religion. It is said that the cuckoo cries until it spits blood – which is how the → azalea gets its colour. In a non-Han minority group in the province of Guizhou, people do not mourn for their dead until the cuckoo has reappeared.

The peasants in the province of Sichuan pay a lot of attention to the cuckoo, which helps them to pick the right day for starting various jobs on the farm. The local dialect has several expressions for the bird, like 'reap the wheat', 'forcing us to plough', 'watching the silkworms' or 'watching the fire'. 'Fire' here probably refers to the 'fire-star', Antares (α Scorpionis), whose appearance was a key date in the agricultural year.

Cypress
bo

Cypresses are often to be found by → graves; the tree lives to a great age, and it adds an appropriate note of permanence to the burial site. The tree is also a symbol of → longevity. In pictures, it symbolises the wish '(May you have) a hundred (*bai*) sons!' – 'sons' here in the sense of 'seed'. The word *bo* is also phonetically the same as *bo* (also read *bai*) = earl, count: the picture would then symbolise the wish that the recipient should attain to high rank.

Cypress seeds are supposed to have good curative properties; if you keep on chewing them, your hearing and eyesight will improve.

D

Date
zao

東

The Chinese date is not at all the same thing as the North African date. Properly speaking, it is the fruit of the jujube tree. In Chinese, the name of this tree is phonetically identical with the word meaning 'early' (*zao*), so we often find the idea of 'soon' or 'early' symbolised by the jujube tree. The tree is often portrayed together with → lichee fruit, and this group expresses the wish that the recipient of the picture may soon have sons. When a → cinnamon tree is coupled with a jujube, the wish expressed is that sons should soon be born who will attain to high office.

North Chinese are said to be particularly fond of eating the jujube fruit, so much so that their teeth are stained yellow. A dream in which a jujube tree figures presages an early death: this is because the character for 'jujube' looks rather like the character for 'to come' written twice, one above the other, and this is taken to mean the coming of dead spirits.

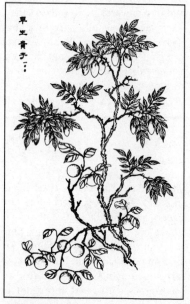

Chinese dates and longans: 'May you have not long to wait for high-ranking sons!'

The unripe fruit of the jujube is supposed to be an abortifacient.

Deer
lu

Because of the exact phonetic equivalence of *lu* = deer to *lu* = good income, the deer symbolises → riches. More frequently, however, the deer is a symbol for → longevity. The deer figures prominently in the folk-legends of North and Central Asia, and of India also, but plays little part in Chinese myth. There is one story about a deer which gives birth to a girl who is found and

Official and deer: 'May fame and riches come your way!'

brought up by a man. When she dies, her body disappears.

The story of Zhou Yan-zi, however, is very well known in China. He is always shown wearing the deer-skin which he adopted as a disguise when his blind parents wanted deer's milk as a cure. Zhou's subterfuge was successful. This is one of the best-known of the 24 examples of filial piety (→ *xiao*) still familiar to all Chinese children. It has even found its way on to Taiwanese stamps.

'Père David's deer' (*mi-lu, Elaphorus davidianus*) is popularly known as the 'Four Unlikes' as it has a deer's head, an ass's tail, a camel's back and a cow's ear.

In the popular novel 'The Metamorphoses of the Gods' this deer figures as the favourite mount of the hero, Jiang Zi-ya. If a pregnant woman sees a *mi-lu*, her child will have four eyes.

Dew
lu

Dew may symbolise the grace and bounty which flow downwards from the → Emperor to 'bedew' the people. But it may also symbolise a fleeting love affair which passes like morning dew. When one of the Song Emperors was completely captivated by the charms of a new concubine, the forsaken Empress lamented that now 'she was no more besprinkled by the gracious rain and bounteous dew'. The 'Temple of Sweet Dew' (*gan lu si*) was a building in the southern state of Wu, according to the 'Romance of the Three Kingdoms': the ruler of Wu, the southernmost of the so-called 'Three Kingdoms' (3rd century AD), hoping to marry his daughter to the ruler of the western state of Shu, had invited the latter to visit him. But first of all, while the visitor was waiting to be received, the ruler of Wu sent his mother with two lady's maids, to have a look at the prospective bridegroom and size him up. The ruler of Shu saw through the subterfuge and promptly made his departure. This scene is often depicted in temples.

Divorce
li hun 離婚

According to legislation which was in force as far back as Tang times a man could divorce his wife on any one of seven counts: if she had failed to bear him a son, if she had committed adultery, if she was too talkative (i.e. discussed family matters with the neighbours), if she was a thief or obsessively jealous, if she was 'sick' (probably this refers to venereal disease) or if she suffered from a severe illness. It was a punishable offence to reject a wife (i.e. an espoused wife, not a concubine) except on one or another of these grounds. A wife could divorce her husband if he had reviled her ancestors or had murdered a member of her own family (in the wide sense). Divorce was legalised by drawing up the requisite certificate.

Even today – and especially among the morally conservative peasantry – divorce rates as the last way out of an intolerable situation. Where domestic strife has become habitual the wife may prefer to pack her things and go home to her parents. Once she has been divorced, a certain stigma attaches to her.

Nowadays, divorces like marriages have to be registered. A childless couple can seek divorce, if both parties are in agreement. All they have to do is to go to the registrar and make the necessary declaration of intent. If there are → children in the family, attempts are made to smooth things over; but where one partner does not expressly agree to divorce, it is flatly refused.

Dog
gou 狗

The dog is the eleventh creature in the Chinese → zodiac; but that does nothing to help the average dog in China, which has on the whole a pretty poor time. Its symbolic role in the North of the country differs very widely from that in the South. In North China, paper dogs used to be thrown into the water on the 5th day of the 5th month – a feast-day – so that they should bite the evil → spirits and drive them away. The dead were also given paper dogs for their protection. Lunatics were washed with dog's dirt in order to expel the demons who had possessed the sufferer.

Symbolically, the dog was associated with the West. For this reason, in those parts of China where dog-flesh was (and still is) eaten, it was permissible to do so in autumn and winter, but not in summer. In Taiwan it is believed that dead dogs must be thrown into the water; → cats, on the other hand, should be hung up. Neither animal should be buried, as it will turn into a demon. If you dream that a dog has bitten you, it means that your ancestors want something to eat. Again, if someone is suspected of being a spirit, it is enough to sprinkle him with dog's blood – he will then appear in his real form. If a dog runs towards you, it is a good sign: riches will be yours. The dog is regarded as the companion of the god Er-lang, who purifies the world by ridding it of evil demons.

So much for the North. The dog is seen in a very different light in South and West China, especially among the minority peoples who live there. In their folk-tales it is the dog that brings → rice to mankind. Further west, towards the Tibetan border, rice is replaced in this legend by → millet. In the province of Guangdong, the story of the faithful dog is very popular. This is about a man who is said to have lived in the 3rd century. One day, while on a journey, he lies down in a meadow and falls asleep: the meadow catches fire, and the dog is unable to wake its master. So it keeps on running to the river and bringing enough water to wet the grass round him to keep it from catching fire. The master is saved – but the dog dies of exhaustion. Over his grave they put the

Woman with a dog on a lead (from an old almanac)

inscription 'The grave of a faithful dog'. Another, related story tells how a dog guards its master's belongings until it dies.

Among the Yao (another of the South Chinese minority peoples) the dog is venerated as the forefather of the race. At the root of this idea lies a legend according to which a Chinese → Emperor, after struggling in vain for a long time against his enemies, finally promised that whoever brought him the head of the rebel leader would have his daughter's hand in marriage – whereupon a dog appears bearing the head of the slain leader, and, however unwillingly, the Emperor has to honour his word. The dog takes the girl into the mountains and they marry. The Yao are the issue of this union. They still wear a 'dog-cap' (which I saw for myself in Zhejiang in 1934) and of course they do not eat dog-flesh.

Stories about dog-men, who have men's bodies and dogs' heads, are widespread in North Asia. Some Chinese reports even locate them on an island to the east of Korea.

It is striking that pet-names for dogs are very rarely mentioned in Chinese texts. At most we hear of 'the yellow dog' and so on. Nowadays, foreign names are usually given to dogs: they are never given names which could be the names of people. A 'black dog' is a man who runs after every woman he sees.

Donkey
lü

For the Chinese, the donkey is a stupid animal. In ancient times it was

'The Donkey-mill'. From the techno-logical encyclopaedia Tian-gong kai-wu *(1637), which gives a graphic description of all sides of life and work in Ming China*

ridden by the poorer people and by minor officials. Holy men also had a habit of riding on donkeys. Thus → Zhang Guo-lao, one of the eight → Immortals, rides on an ass (or on a mule) which he can fold up and stow away in a bamboo cane.

At one time, a bronze ass stood in the *dong-yue miao*, The Temple of the Eastern Mountain in Peking. Sick people used to visit this statue on New Year's Day and touch the parts of the body affected by their illness. Today, the donkey's genitals are completely rubbed away, but no sufferer is ever seen to touch them.

Ru-yi Jun (→ sceptre), one of the Empress Wu's lovers (Tang Dynasty), was, if we are to believe what we are told in one of the classical novels, a donkey reborn in human form. After his death, he was turned into the 'Ass's Head Spirit' which fought against the Tang Dynasty.

Buddhist monks are often derided as 'bald-headed asses', and in popular parlance the → bald-headed monk is often compared to a penis.

Dove
ge 鴿

In ancient India, the dove was the bird of death and the spirit world; in Rome, it was the bird of love; in China it symbolises fidelity and → longevity, probably because doves pair for life, and both sexes take a share in raising the young ones. Since Tang times, the dove has figured in the head-dress of the 'goddess who sends children' (*song zi niang niang*), so it is presumably also seen as a fertility symbol. Carrier pigeons were already in use at the same time.

Dragon
long   龍

Combining as it does all sorts of mythological and cosmological notions, the dragon is one of China's most complex and multi-tiered symbols. Indeed, the word *long* covers a variety of heterogeneous beings. In sharp contrast to Western ideas on this subject, the Chinese dragon is a good-natured and benign creature: a symbol of natural male vigour and fertility (→ *yang*). From the Han Dynasty (206 BC–AD 220) onwards, the dragon is also the symbol of the → Emperor, the Son of Heaven. It is the first of the '360 Scaly Creatures' (see the → five kinds of creature) and the 5th creature in the Chinese → zodiac. As one of the four creatures of the world directions, the dragon stands in the East, the region of sunrise, of fertility, of spring rains and of rain in general. In this guise, he is known as the 'blue-green dragon' (*qing-long*) and is contrasted with the 'white → tiger' (*bo-hu*), the ruler of the West and of death.

In this vegetative connotation, the dragon was imagined as spending the winter under the earth; on the 2nd day of the 2nd month he rose from the earth into heaven thus causing the first spring thunder and rainfall. In North China, this was the sign for a start to be made on the fields. To this day, the Chinese community in Marysville (California) hold a great dragon-feast to mark this occasion: fireworks representing the dragon are let off, and whoever finds a piece of one can look forward to a lucky year.

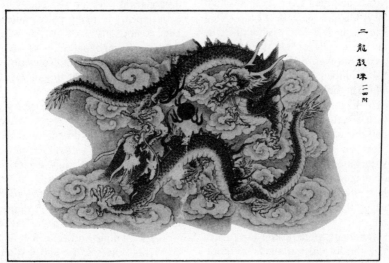

Two dragons playing with a pearl

Dragons large and small: 'May (your) children have an illustrious career!'

As a magic animal, the dragon is able to shrink to the size of a silkworm; and then again it can swell up till it fills the space between heaven and earth. It can be visible or invisible, as it chooses. On the day of its ascent into heaven it cannot be seen, being hidden in the rain clouds on which it rides. Pictures often show two dragons playing in the clouds with a ball or a pearl (= thunder) – and this causes rain to fall.

At an early date, cosmological speculation distinguished four kinds of dragon: first of all there are the heaven-dragons (*tian-long*), symbolising the regenerative power of heaven; then the spirit-dragons (*shen-long*), which cause the rain to fall; thirdly, earth-dragons (*di-long*), which rule over springs and water courses; and finally the dragons which guard treasure (*fu-cang-long*). In addition, people believed in four dragon-kings (*long-wang*), each of which ruled over one of the four seas that encompass the earth.

These 'sea-dragons' play a particularly big part in popular tradition. The sea-dragon king, it was believed, dwelt in a splendid palace full of the most beautiful and valuable things. Those on whom fortune smiles may visit him at the bottom of the sea – they may even be rewarded with one of his daughters in marriage!

At → New Year, men in North China join in a dragon-dance, and a similar dance takes place during the marriage ceremony at the moment when the young couple leave the gathering and make their way to the bridal chamber. Here the dancers enact the conjugal kiss.

The belief that a woman could give birth to one or even several dragons was widespread. The word *long* appears in many place-names, and compounds such as 'dragon-mother', 'dragon-lake', etc., are common. The town of Kowloon is the 'town of the nine dragons' (*jiu long* in Mandarin).

Since the number → nine symbolises male vigour (3 × 3) it is often associated with the dragon, and the formula *yi long jiu zi, ge zi bie* = 'the dragon has nine sons, each one different' is very commonly used when wishing a young couple good fortune. Dragons come in all shapes and sizes. In general, it is portrayed with a serpentine body plus feet and claws; its skin is scaly, and it often has horns like those of a stag (→

Dragon and phoenix – man and wife

Dragon with nine sons, all of whom are endowed in different ways: the first can carry heavy objects, the second can put out fires, the third can make a noise like a bell, the fourth is as powerful as a tiger, the fifth likes his food, the sixth likes water, the seventh is a courageous fighter, the eighth is as strong as a lion, the ninth is a keen observer

deer), though its ears are more like an → ox's.

Dragon-boats are long, narrow → boats decorated with dragon motifs. They are used in South China as racing boats in festivities which take place on the 5th day of the 5th month. If a man fell overboard and was drowned (formerly very few Chinese could swim) this was looked upon as a not unwelcome sacrifice to the dragon-god, who would there-upon be moved to increase fertility.

'Dragon-claws': ceremonial dress among the upper classes indicated the wearer's rank by the number of claws on the dragon depicted. Thus the dragon on the Emperor's robe had five claws; four claws indicated a prince, three or less an official. Together, the dragon and the → phoenix embody the male and female essences, and naturally symbolise the married state.

'Dragon-spittle' was ambergris, the very costly perfume brought from Arabia. 'Dragons' eyes' (*long-yan*) are small sweet fruits, known in English as 'longans'.

A popular play on the Chinese stage shows Emperor Tai-zong of the Tang Dynasty clad in yellow robes playing → chess with his minister Wei Zhen. The latter falls asleep, and the audience sees breath coming out of his mouth and killing a far-off dragon: this is in fact a dragon-king who had made a wager with Wei

Zhen that he would not cause rain to fall when the supreme deity ordered him to do so. Thus, we are told, are disobedient dragons punished. The story is told in the celebrated novel 'The Journey to the West' (*Xi you ji*).

Dream
meng

Dreams are regarded as experiences of the → soul, which can leave the human body during sleep. The → Immortals have no dreams, because they have no desires or wishes. Dreams may presage good or bad luck (→ mirror), and they can be interpreted in the same way as → oracles.

The professional interpreter of dreams is less in evidence nowadays, but books on the meaning of dreams are still in constant use. The favourite one is the *Zhou-gong jie meng*, which is said to have been compiled by the Duke of Zhou around 1050 BC. This work relies very heavily on the 'dialectical' or antithetic explanation of dreams – e.g. a dream about death means long life, etc.

Particularly well known is the story concerning the dream of Han-dan (in the 'Magic Pillow', a work by Shen Ji-ji of the early Tang Dynasty). The Taoist Lü Weng, an adept in the mysteries of the Immortals, meets a man called Lu in an inn in the city of Han-dan. Lu has failed in his examinations: Lü Weng lends him his pillow and causes him to dream of earthly happiness. When the dreamer awakes, Lü Weng soon talks him out of such illusory attachments. The tale has been dramatised as the 'Dream of the Yellow Millet'. See also Snake, Sword.

Drum
gu

The drum is one of the → eight musical instruments; it was much used for ceremonial purposes. In ancient times, drums gave the signal for attack in battle, and their noise was compared to the rolling of → thunder. Drums were beaten at many festive occasions – e.g. the 'Drum of the Great Peace' was beaten in Peking at the → New Year festival. Before the city gates were closed at night, and before a market shut down, a drum was beaten. Outside the court-house hung the 'complaints-drum', which was there for anyone to beat who wanted to bring a lawsuit. Every evening in Taoist temples the great drum was beaten, to be answered by the → bell.

In North-west China and also in parts of the South, drums had earthenware resonators which were enamelled in brilliant colours. The big kettle gongs of the non-Han minority peoples in the South are famous. Attempts have been made to interpret the imagery found on these instruments: frogs sitting round the outer rim, figures of men who are sailing in ships or taking part in processions. Few of these images have been satisfactorily decoded, but these big drums have been in use for more than two thousand years, and are among the most valuable possessions of these peoples.

Dryness/Drought
gan

Placed before words denoting certain relationships – e.g. father, mother, son, daughter – the word *gan* indicates adoptive status. 'Dryness' here means that adopted children, for example, have not drunk the milk of their mothers: they have gone forth 'dry'. An adopted sibling is known as a love-child.

Duck
ya

The figure of a duck is a frequent motif in peasant embroidery. In some parts of East China, the word for 'duck' (*ya*) is taboo, as it also

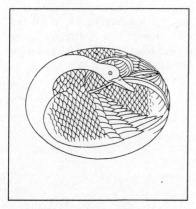

A duck in the reeds: 'May you do well in your examination'

means 'homosexual'. In the North, *ya* is one word for 'penis'. In Buddhist ritual, the duck stands for another word in the *ya* series: *ya* meaning 'to suppress' (evil). In Taiwan on New Year's Eve, a black duck is sacrificed and its blood inserted in the mouth of a paper → tiger. This paper tiger is then burned at the city gates, and this is supposed to rid the town of all evil influences.

In Taiwan in 1661, a man called Zhu Yi-gui led a major rebellion against the Chinese government. As he had been a duck-breeder, he was given the soubriquet of 'Mother-duck King'. It was because of his rebellion that duck-breeding was banned for a number of years in Central Taiwan. (Hummel says that Zhu trained ducks 'so that at his command they marched in military formation – much to the amazement of his neighbours'.)

Adherents of the sect still known as the 'Duck-egg Religion' in China and parts of Taiwan are strict vegetarians, apart from making duck-eggs their staple diet. When worshipping the goddess → Guan-yin they hold duck eggs in their hands. The cult has been accused of immoral behaviour, and is therefore banned in Taiwan.

The → mandarin duck symbolises → married bliss.

Dust
chen

Like → smoke, dust is a constant reminder of the transitory nature of things. 'Dust handle' (*chen bing*) is a Buddhist metaphor for the penis. The broom for sweeping dust seems to have come to China from India. Nowadays it is the emblem of → Zhong-li Quan, one of the eight Immortals.

Dwarfs
zhuru

In ancient texts we find mention of lands which are inhabited by dwarfs. These are lands that lie beyond Chinese ken, either in the extreme South or far to the North. Within China proper, however, there was a region (Tao-chao in what is present-day Hunan) where, it was said, many dwarfs were to be found; and this was a source for the supply of court jesters. Both Western and Chinese sources tell of dwarfs who were so small that snow-geese could swallow them. In many texts, again, it is cranes that gobble them up. The aboriginal inhabitants of Taiwan are supposed to have been dwarfs, and legends about them are still very much alive on the island. Dwarfs play an important part in the songs sung at the harvest festivals of the Saisiat tribe which holds, every two years, a sacrificial rite in honour of the dwarfs. In 1970 this took place on 13 November, and in November 1974 a three-day festival started on the 28th. There is much reference to dwarfs in the myths of the Taiwanese tribes, and Chinese anthropologists are of the opinion that these myths do not relate to the Negrito people who live in the Philippines and who are dark-skinned. The Miao or Hmong, a non-Han minority people in South China, believed that dwarfs were subterranean dwellers. The festival associated with these dwarfs is also observed in Xin-zhu and in Miao-li, where the population is now exclusively Han Chinese.

Dyeing
ran

The Chinese word *ran* has two main meanings: to dye, to apply colour; and to infect, be infected, catch a disease. An extension of this second meaning is 'to have (illicit) intercourse with' (*you ran*). Thanks to a play on words (*ran/ren*) the word *ren* = harvest, crop, is then used as a metaphor for '(illicit) sexual intercourse'.

E

Eagle
ying 鷹

The eagle figures in Chinese painting as a symbol of strength. A picture showing an eagle perched in a →

Eagle on a rock in the sea: symbol of the hero who fights alone

pine-tree is a suitable gift for an older man, wishing him the strength of the eagle and the longevity of the pine. An eagle on a rock in the sea symbolises the → hero (*ying*) who fights a lone battle.

For the Xiong-nu (the 'Huns', who moved through Central Asia in the period from the first century BC to the end of the second century AD) the eagle symbolised the ruler.

When an eagle is shown struggling with a → snake, the picture is a reference to the Indian garuda bird.

Earth
tu; di 土地

'The earth bears and the heavens cover' say ancient Chinese texts. Heaven and earth were regarded as a generative pair, and the *Yi-jing*, the 'Book of Changes', speaks of earth's condition as 'receptive abandon' (2nd Trigram: *kun* = the receptive one). And earth is given

the square (*fang*) as symbol, while →
heaven is symbolised by the circle.

According to early cosmologies,
the world resembles a chariot with
its → canopy. This canopy is round
and symbolises heaven: the
rectangular box in which the travellers are seated – or rather its floor –
corresponds to earth. Then again the
flat earth is said to be connected to
the circular contour of heaven by the
→ eight pillars, which are in their
turn correlated by means of the eight
winds with the → trigrams arranged
in an octagon. The expression
'heaven and earth' means 'the whole
world' (*tian di*). The cosmological
view of the whole earth as a square
extends to earthly divisions – square
fields, houses, villages, → town
enclosures. The basic principle of the
square persists semantically in such
expressions as *fang-wu* = the
produce of an area, *fang-bo* = the
governor of a province, and *fang-
yan* = a dialect. The earth is also
one of the five → elements, or
'generative powers'. To the earth are
allotted the → middle position, the
colour → yellow, the number → two,
the tastc 'sweet', white → millet as
product, the → ox as domestic
animal, and finally, since man is
bare-skinned, earth is correlated
with 'naked' in the five-animal
series.

In astronomy and → astrology, the
'earthly branches' (*di-zhi*) play an
important part. They are to be
distinguished from the 'heavenly
stems' (*tian-gan*), which are the signs
of the decimal cycle arranged in a
coordinate system. The *di-zhi* are
the signs of the duodecimal series
arranged in circular form. This
meaningful inversion of the two
series of symbols emphasises their
mutual interdependence and also
that of the two elemental forces,
heaven and earth (according to
Marcel Granet, *Chinese Thought*).

Eel
shan

According to one Chinese legend of
the Flood, Xiang-liu, a 'minister' of
the mythical → Emperor Gong-
gong, who called up the Flood, was
an eel. According to another myth
which has been preserved only in
part, Jiang-Shen, the god of the
Yangtse river, stopped up a leak in
a boat with an eel: an episode which
calls to mind certain variants of the
biblical legend of the Flood. If a →
snake is eating an eel, you should
wait till only the head is still visible
and cut it off; if you then carry this
head about with you, your income
will be assured and you will always
win at games.

In popular parlance, the word 'eel'
often means 'penis'. This is also
found in Japanese. 'Yellow Eel' is an
expression denoting a homosexual.

Egg
dan

In China, as in Europe, the egg is a
symbol of fertility. During wedding
festivities in Zhejiang Province, girls
used to roll eggs down the bride's
breast, so that they fell into her lap.
Painted eggs used to be used in the

ceremony of washing the bride; they are now given to wedding guests (→ marriage). After giving birth, a mother is given scrambled eggs; and eggs are given to invalids, in token of wishes for a speedy recovery. On its first birthday, a baby gets a soft-boiled egg. Eggs painted red are exchanged at → New Year: this is called 'sending happiness' (for the year to come). Only zealous Buddhists disapprove of eggs, believing that those who like to eat them will go to the hell of the 'empty city' after death.

Among the minority peoples of South China, the egg is much in use as a means of foretelling the future. A beautifully painted egg is boiled and then opened – predictions are made according to the shape taken by the yolk and the white.

Again it is in South China that most of the myths are found in which the egg plays a big part. The world is supposed to have been an egg, out of which all creation came. After the Great Flood, only a brother and sister were left alive. In due course, they come to the conclusion that incest is the only way open to them if humanity is to be saved. The woman thereupon bears an egg, from which numberless children issue forth. Founder-heroes are born from eggs which are sometimes incubated in a nine-storey tower (cosmic tower). A South Korean myth tells of someone finding an egg in which a baby is lying: the child grows up to be the leader of all the world's peoples.

Adherents of the *hun-tian* school of astronomy (e.g. Ge Hong, 254–334) believed that the cosmos was egg-shaped: the earth was inside the shell, completely covered by it, and resting like a yolk on the fluid white. It was incubated by heaven.

Eight
ba

Like all even numbers, eight is feminine, i.e. it is a *yin* number. It appears in various combinations: the eight symbols of the → scholar, for example, are → pearls, the → musical stone, the coin (→ money), the → rhombus, → books, paintings, the → rhinoceros horn and the Artemisia leaf (→ yarrow). In many pictures these symbols appear in greatly reduced form. They may be reduced in number to four or expanded to fourteen. Many see in them the eight treasures of Confucianism. The eight symbols of the → Immortals (also known as the eight Taoist saints) are: → the fan, the → sword, the → bottle-gourd, the castanets, the flower basket, the → bamboo cane, the → flute, the → lotus. These are personal emblems.

Like Confucianism and Taoism, China's third great religious system – Buddhism – also has its eight emblems: the sea-slug, the → umbrella, the → canopy, the → lotus, the → vase, the → fish, the endless → knot, the wheel of learning symbolise various aspects of Buddhism.

The eight → trigrams (*ba gua*) of the *yi-jing* give all possible combinations of a complex of three broken and unbroken lines. These trigrams appear as symbolical decorative motifs in paintings, embroidery, etc.

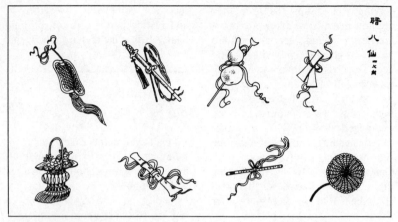

The symbols of the eight Immortals

Although eight is a *yin* number, it is connected in mystical numerology with the male, i.e. with a *yang* being: 'The life of a man is ruled by the number 8. At 8 months he gets his milk teeth, at 8 years he loses them. At 2 × 8 years of age he becomes a man, at 8 × 8 years of age he becomes incapable of procreation.' The changes in → *yang* are generated by the opposing power of → *yin*; just as, vice versa, in the case of → seven, the power of the male eight has its effect on feminine development.

The eight 'pillars of heaven' of the

The eight Immortals wish us good luck

ancient cosmology are connected with the eight directions, the eight mountains and the eight gates through which the rain clouds and the eight → winds enter. In the 'Book of Rites' (*Li-ji*) these are described as follows: 'Which are the eight winds? From the North-east comes the burning wind / From the East comes the roaring wind / From the South-east comes the cheerful wind / from the South comes the great storm / from the South-west comes the cool wind / from the West comes the wind that lasts / from the North-west comes the sharp wind / from the North comes the cold wind' (tr. Richard Wilhelm).

Elements, The Five
wu-xing　　五 行

The → five elements as specified in Chinese thought bear very little resemblance to the four elements of ancient Greek speculation or the elements recognised by the Iranians or the Indians. Indeed, sinologists cannot agree on the best translation of the word *xing*; the basic idea is one of 'changing states of being'. The elements themselves with their associated colours and directions are: wood, East, blue; → fire, South, red; → metal, West, white; → water, North, black; → earth, Centre, yellow.

These five metamorphoses or states of being form a whole: in the '*Hong fan*' chapter of the 'Book of Documents' we read: 'water is said to soak and descend; fire is said to blaze and ascend; wood is said to

curve or be straight; metal is said to obey and change; earth is said to take seeds and give crops' (tr. Karlgren).

Dozens of parallel series are correlated with the five elements: e.g. the four → seasons of the year (here, 'earth' is the odd man out, either receiving no season specifically associated with it or, at most, a few days from each of the four seasons); the five → animals (hairy, feathered, scaly, armoured, naked); the five tastes (salty, bitter, sour, sharp, sweet) etc., etc. As a whole, the system is bound up with Chinese astronomy, → astrology, → geomancy, and also with a branch of ancient Chinese → medicine.

In ancient times, ceremonial garb varied according to the season of the year. Even the administration of justice was not unaffected by the doctrine of the five elements: thus we find that criminals could only be executed in autumn, the time of year when everything dies. All human actions had to be in harmony with nature.

Elephant
xiang　　

In early times, elephants roamed all over China, even in the far North, and they were often hunted by the upper classes. They were native to South China until quite recently. From the 3rd century BC onwards, tame elephants are mentioned in texts, and in popular tales the hero often rides on an elephant. Pictures showing a man ploughing with an

An elephant bearing precious objects

A boy on an elephant, with a sceptre: 'Good omens = (what you want) you will get'

elephant refer to the mythical Emperor Shun: he was the exemplar of perfect filial piety (→ *xiao*) and lived exactly 100 years, as befitted such a paragon.

The legend of the hunter who slays a monster which kills elephants, and is thereupon taken by an elephant to a place where he finds more than 300 ivory tusks, is not later than the 10th century. We find a parallel in Sindbad's seventh journey in the *Thousand and One Nights*.

The elephant is regarded as an animal with very high moral standards. Sexual intercourse between elephants is said to take place only in water, as the elephant – like humans – appreciates privacy. It feels gratitude: as we have seen, someone who helps it may be rewarded with ivory. In addition, it symbolises strength and astuteness, and is often shown in this connection along with the → lion, the leopard and the → tiger. Riding on an elephant (*qi-xiang*) symbolises happiness (*ji-xiang*): the rider is usually a child carrying a → sceptre (*ru-yi*). The elephant cover is decorated with various motifs symbolising happiness and good fortune – e.g. a rock rising up out of the sea, while high above a pearl floats in the clouds. A deity on an elephant is Puxiau (Sanskrit: Samantabhadra).

Emperor
huang-di   皇帝

Chinese Emperors were believed to be descended from the mythical

Shang-di, the Ruler of heaven. The Emperor was the Son of Heaven, entrusted with the mission of safeguarding the harmony between → heaven and → earth. He was the ruler of the → 'Middle Kingdom' and the 'Four Directions', to each of which he made periodical journeys of inspection and in each of which he was represented at other times by his most august → officials. At the beginning of spring he guided a plough drawn by an → ox to make the → eight sacred furrows at the Temple of Husbandry in Peking: he also sowed rice and four kinds of → millet. He dwelt in a palace which faced south – the only being in China to enjoy such a privilege (→ left and right). He was symbolised by the → dragon. The → unicorn might also appear in the imperial gardens, provided that a wise ruler sat on the throne: when this happened it was a palpable manifestation of divine approval from on high.

Early Emperors did not just sit about: they could turn their hand to many things, and the legendary → Fu-xi is credited with inventing marriage as an institution, the eight → trigrams and the fish-net. The historical Emperor Yong-le (r. 1402–24) had the Great Wall and the Imperial Canal repaired: he moved the capital from Nanking to Peking, built the Temple of Heaven, and commissioned an encyclopaedia covering the entire body of knowledge then available. Even he was surpassed by Shi-huang-di, the 'First Emperor' of China who used a reign of only eleven years (221–210 BC) to lay the foundations for the Middle Kingdom that was to last for two thousand years. He introduced the system whereby 36 'commanderies' were each administered by a Military Governor and a Civil Governor, a centralisation which spelled the end of the old feudal system and the ascendancy of the → officials. He unified the Chinese script, the weights and measures, and the coinage: he opened up the land by building canals and roads, and is responsible for the two greatest edifices of his time – the Great Wall and his own mausoleum, in which there was, apart from everything

Huang-di, the Lord of the Yellow Earth; the Great Yu, the controller of the waters; the mythical Emperor Yao, regarded by the Confucians as the ideal ruler

else, room for an army of 7,000 life-sized clay warriors. The number of people who perished in the construction of these monuments cannot even be guessed at; and he is also responsible for the first burning of the → books.

Shi-huang-di made his mark in the realms of magic and cosmology also. → Fire, which had been the ruling element in the preceding Zhou Dynasty, was replaced by → water: → black became the ruling colour in the place of → red. The number → six was now to rule Chinese life: even the → hats worn by officials were to be 6 inches long and 6 inches wide. The First Emperor travelled the length and breadth of his realm and visited all its main cities; one might say he took ritual possession of the Middle Kingdom. All his life he was terrified of death, and he sent one expedition after another to search out and bring him the herb of → immortality and the miraculous mushroom of longevity.

Virtuous Confucians have always seen Shi-huang-di as the very quintessence of all that is bad. It is only now in our own times that a reassessment of him has become possible, as archaeologists gradually reveal the astonishing contents of his tomb.

See also Canopy, Insignia, Left and Right, Middle, Step of Yu, *yang*.

Excrement
fen; da-bian   大便

Faeces were supposed to be a means of keeping evil → spirits at bay. A spirit masquerading as a man could be exposed if daubed with excrement and urine.

On the other hand, it was considered lucky to dream about excrement, as this was a harbinger of fortune or riches. In one of the (recently found) earliest Chinese medical recipes a concoction made of chicken or pig faeces is mentioned as medicine against boils caused by liquid fresh lacquer or against scabies. While ordinary Chinese used toilet paper long before Europeans did, Buddhist monks are asked to use the middle and ring finger of the right hand.

Eye
yan   眼

The Chinese are visually oriented people, and accordingly a lot of attention is paid to the eye. A beautiful woman is said to have eyes like almonds or like meteors. One's mistress is described as *yan zhong ren* – 'the being in my eyes'.

Red eyes count as a bad sign: the god of the brothel has red eyes, and white eyebrows into the bargain. 'One-eye' is an expression for the penis.

There is an 'eye' in the middle of the old Chinese copper coins, that is to say, a hole so that they could be looped together in units of thousands. Many pictures show coins together with a → bat: the Chinese words for 'bat' (*fu*) and 'good luck' (*fu*) are homonyms, and the same goes for 'in front of' (*qian*) and 'money' (*qian*). Thus such a picture means 'Good luck is before your eyes' (*fu zai yan-qian*).

Eyebrow
mei

Eyebrows play an important part in Chinese ideas of physical attractiveness (→ beauty). As early as two thousand years ago, people were shaving them off and painting them in. There is a well-known tale of a man who was so much in love with his wife that he painted her eyebrows for her instead of letting her do this woman's work for herself. Well-formed eyebrows are said to resemble a moth; when they are thick and slightly curved they are said to resemble a butterfly. One of the Tang Emperors had a picture painted showing ten different kinds of eyebrows, to each of which he gave a special name. Poets often speak of 'eyebrows like far-distant hills' or of 'sad (= fine) eyebrows'.

The god who looks after prostitutes is known as the 'god with the white eyebrows' (*bai mei shen*). In appearance he resembles the god of war: he is mounted on a horse and carries a sword. On the occasion of her first assignment with a client, the girl was supposed to make sacrifice to him; according to a later tradition, the client was expected to do the same when he first visited a girl.

Eyelashes are also pointers to a person's character. A woman with very long and curved eyebrows is supposed to be temperamental.

F

Face
mian; lian 面 臉

The Chinese word *mian* means not only 'face' but also 'persona'; *lian* covers in addition 'character', 'reputation'. Both words subsume, therefore, the behaviour expected of a person in keeping with his or her social standing. The often-heard expression 'to lose face' (*diu lian*) means that by doing something or behaving in a certain way, a person has forfeited the respect of the grouping to which he or she belongs. Coming to a sympathetic understanding with someone you are talking to corresponds to your own need 'to harmonise inner and outer, interior and exterior. No one should be "put to shame", "made to appear ridiculous", and every effort should be made to avoid this. Equally, one must try not to "lose face" oneself. "Loss of face" is something essential affecting the whole person. It is noteworthy here that *lian* means both body and personality' (Richard Wilhelm, *Die Seele Chinas*).

The Chinese believe that the face provides clues to a person's character: cf. phrenology in Europe. Many books have been written on this subject.

Fairies
xian nü 仙 女

Chinese mythology has several sharply individualised fairies (goddesses) around whom many legends have been woven. We may mention: → Xi-wang-mu, the 'Queen Mother of the West', who is supposed to hold sway over a fairy realm in the Kun-lun Mountains on the Tibetan borders; → Chang-e, the Moon-goddess, → Ma-gu, the fairy with the long nails, → Ma-zu, the fairy who looks after fishermen, and

→ Nü-gua, who was both sister and wife of the mythical → Fu-xi.

These fairies and their retainers are almost always imagined as connected with the → Immortals. Their realms are usually earthly paradises, such as the eastern 'Isles of the Blessed' as described by Lie-zi: 'Day and night in innumerable swarms they flew to visit each other.' Then there was the remote island of Chang-zhou, about which we learn from the 'Sketches of the Ten Continents within the Seas': 'There are purple palace grounds there; it is a land which the celestial maidens of immortality traverse.' There is a distinction between the fairy goddesses (*shen*), who are worshipped in their own temples, and the 'sacred maidens' (*xian-nü*), who are not worshipped in any specific or organised way.

There is much reference to fairy palaces on the → moon. According to a legend about the heavenly journey of the Emperor Xuan-zong (who ruled from 713 to 751), 'the Emperor could not stop thinking about the moon fairies, and how they danced flying in the wind, with their sleeves and draperies fluttering. So he began to compose a tune to the words "Cloud-garment and Feather-cloak".'

Buddhist paradises knew nothing of such pleasures, nor did Buddhists ever imagine anything like this happening on the moon. Perhaps it is precisely because of the absence of Buddhist colouring that the Chinese fairy-stories are so full of erotic elements and a subtle → beauty. On the other hand, there is no disguising the fact that many Chinese fairy-tales, both on the literary level and still more so on the popular level, are very largely kitsch.

Fan
shan zi

Round fans and palm-leaf fans were well known in China in the first millennium BC. The folding fan appears to have been invented in Korea, and does not appear in China till the 10th century AD. It seems to have been first used by servants, as it could be so easily folded up and laid aside. In early times, round fans were very frequently made from birds' feathers; later, paper or silk was used. Folding fans for men and women differed in the number of sections; those for men had usually 16, 20 or at most 24 sections, while women's fans had never less than 30.

Occasionally, the fan symbolised the rank of an → official. → Zhong-li Quan, one of the eight → Immortals, is recognisable by the fan with which he revives the dead. Many gods have fans which they use to drive away evil. Because of phonetic similarity (*shan* = fan; *shan* = good) the fan is a symbol of 'goodness'. A fan is given as a parting present in the hope that the traveller can use it to keep himself cool! Beautifully painted fans have always been a speciality of the great Chinese artists.

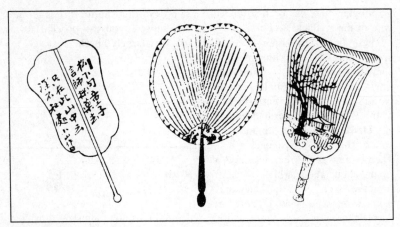

Three kinds of fan

Fang-zhang 方丈

According to tradition, Shi Huang-di, the first → Emperor of China, is supposed to have sent the wise man Xu Fu to the three mysterious islands in the Eastern Ocean, in order to find out more about them.

These three islands had the following names: Fang-zhang = 'Square Fathom'; Peng-lai = 'Profusion of Weeds'; Ying-zhou = 'Ocean Continent' (Fairyland). They were supposed to be islands of paradise in which immortals led a happy life that never ended. The Emperor was troubled by thoughts of approaching death, and part of Xu Fu's mission was to bring home the weed of → immortality.

In addition to meaning 'square' and being correlated with → earth, *fang* means 'prescription' or 'recipe'. It also means the cell of a Buddhist monk in which visitors are frequently received.

The precise meaning of *fang* – 'a fathom square' – would restrict its use to denoting a rather small, modest room: in practice, however, the space so denoted was not always so small.

Fat-belly Buddha
Mi-le fo 彌勒佛

Non-historical Buddhas proliferate in both India and China, and all of them are equipped with detailed iconographies: for example, Amitabha Buddha, the 'Buddha of the Endless Light', who lives in the 'Paradise of the West', surrounded by countless Bodhisattvas. Then there is Maitreya Buddha, 'one yet to come', who reigns in the Tuṣita Heaven; he is of noble and ascetic appearance, and he looks with unfathomable eyes into an eternal future in which the world has been redeemed (something which the historical Buddha never promised). Towards the end of the first millennium AD, Maitreya Buddha, the 'Buddha yet to come', made his appearance as the laughing 'Fatbelly Buddha'. Under the Song Dynasty (960–1280) he came into his own as one of the most popular gods in East Asia.

As a rule he is shown in a sitting posture, a corpulent man with a bare chest, holding a sack and always laughing. Often he is surrounded by children, who sometimes catch him in a net, only to set him free. He is a symbol of naive geniality. In view of its revolutionary nature, the Maitreya cult had been bloodily suppressed by earlier rulers; but good old Fat-belly drew its teeth by dismissing 'all the misery and unhappiness in the world as nothing more than illusion; a monumental trivialisation' (Wolfgang Bauer), which, no doubt, made the future quite safe for the 'Buddha yet to come'.

The 'Buddha of Pleasure' (*huanxi fo*) has nothing to do with Fatbelly; this is a euphemism for sexual intercourse.

Fate
ming　　　

Basically, the word *ming* means 'command' in the special sense of 'divine decree', 'will of God'. In a restricted sense, it is used to mean human fate or destiny. What is meant is not exactly 'predestination': we arrive at our 'destiny' if we 'go along with it'. An example may make this clearer. Suppose a sooth-

sayer tells me that I am going to die on a certain day – all he has done is to outline a 'tendency', and I can take steps to counteract it. It is particularly in connection with the death of a child that one says, 'That's fate' – a phrase which closes the subject. 'Predestination' can always be circumvented by means of prayer and sacrifice.

Another word for fate is *yun* = revolution, i.e. 'movement round', and hence 'turn of fate', 'luck'. Things move in this or that direction, and the person caught up in this 'movement' cannot really be held responsible either way. A proverb says: 'When *yun* withdraws, yellow gold loses its colour; but when the right time comes, even iron shines in splendour.' The connection here between 'fate' and 'time' is instructive: a man may be disposed to do something good, but if the time is wrong, his good intentions come to naught. The concept of the 'proper time' is fundamental in Chinese thought; everything must be done at the right time, irrespective of whether good or evil is intended.

This concept of the 'right' time is already present in the *Yi-jing*, whose whole structure it informs. This very ancient oracle text has had hundreds of imitations right down to the present day. None of them do anything more than identify the situation in which the enquirer actually finds himself, i.e. at the moment of enquiry. As regards the future, there was another method of foretelling it, a method made famous by a book which was long banned, as it foretold the fate of the Emperor in pictures accompanied by enigmatic rubrics (*tui bei tu*). Pictures in this book which have to do with past events can now be deciphered with some certainty; but some pictures refer to the future, and no regime has looked kindly upon attempts to expound them. Widely differing interpretations of the text and pictures alike are current in Taiwan, Hongkong and in various parts of China proper.

Father
fu
父

Father and → son form one of the → five human relationships. As described in Chinese literature, however, the relationship is something of an antithetical one. The father is 'strict' while the mother is

Father and son: 'May the young man attain as lofty a post as your own!'

'loving'; one does not say, 'I *love* my father'. In the old patriarchal social set-up, the father symbolised the ruler, the son symbolised the subject. Again, it is the eldest son who is permitted to accompany the father at → New Year to the family grave and the ceremonial invitation to the ancestors.

There is no shortage of pictures showing father and son in court dress, the former wearing the hat of an → official and the son wearing the head-dress which identifies the wearer as one who has come first in the highest state examination. Such a picture wished the recipient 'May your son accompany you to court!'

Feast-days and Holidays
jie-ji
節季

Most of China's great feast-days are related to the old lunar → calendar, which remained in force well into the 20th century, in spite of the official introduction of the Gregorian calendar. By the old reckoning, the year began on the second new moon after the winter solstice (21 December). This made it impracticable for agricultural purposes, as the date of the New Year could vary by as much as a month; and over a period of 19 years no less than 7 intercalary months had to be inserted.

The first annual festival was New Year, which ended with the Feast of Lanterns on the 15th day of the 1st month (full moon). The festival of the beginning of spring was formerly observed as a sacrament (→ Emperor). It was followed by the 'Spring Festival of Purity' (Qingming). This was the only festival regulated by the solar calendar, and it corresponded in some measure to our Easter. The day before, one had to fast, it was forbidden to light fires, and on the day itself eggs were boiled, coloured and eaten. It was also the feast of resurgent life, dedicated to remembering the dead. The family graves were cleared of weeds, burial mounds were repaired, and sacrificial vessels laid thereon. After the 1911 Revolution, this feast turned into a tree festival, which was observed in all schools as a mass planting of saplings.

The day of the summer solstice – the 5th day of the 5th month – was the festival known as Duan-wu. From this day on, the power of the sun is declining, and the dark → spirits are lying in wait. People tried to protect themselves by hanging talismans on doors and windows, e.g. the → bottle-gourd. This solar festival lives on in South China as the → Dragon-boat Feast. It is also known as the Festival of Swings.

The Feast of Young → Girls was held in the light of the half-moon on the 7th day of the 7th month: tales were told of the → Spinning Damsel and the Cowherd. The Moon Festival proper was held five weeks later, i.e. at full moon on the 15th day of the 8th month: people threw balls, and baked the 'moon-cakes' which are still popular. This was a mid-autumn festival: the warm days were over, and cold dew now fell in the evenings. The feast of the

Double → yang followed, on the 9th day of the 9th month.

The ninth month is the month of the → chrysanthemum, but it is only in Japan that we find a fully fledged Feast of Chrysanthemums, complete with large-scale exhibitions. The year is growing older, cold winter approaches: but already in secret the forces of the new year are stirring.

Until the end of the Empire in 1911, solemn ceremonies were held twice a year in honour of → Confucius: first of all at the Feast of Ancestors in spring, and again on the 23rd of August, the birthday of the sage.

Quite recently (1979) the birthday was honoured once again in Qu-fu, the town where Confucius died. The event seems to have been observed as was proper 'according to the ancient ritual, and accompanied by the ancient songs and dances' (Erwin Wickert).

Feelings
qing

Asked what mattered most in connection with the rites, → Confucius answered that they provided human beings with a model of moderation to aim at: 'Joy and sorrow must be in moderation (the doctrine of the mean).' If we gave way to our feelings and expressed them openly, we should be letting ourselves be guided by the standards (*dao*) of the barbarians.

The emotional life of the Chinese is held in check by traditional rituals, and is therefore to some extent standardised. It is marked by a use of conventional symbols and of obligatory → gestures. 'The superior man is above all concerned that others will not find him lacking in the right forms of expression' ('Book of Rites').

The *Huang-di Nei-qing*, that breviary of old Chinese → medicine, details the correspondences between microcosm and macrocosm. Just as the doctrine of the → five virtues ties up with our teaching on the five viscera, so do the affects correspond to the bodily orifices: eyes and anger, tongue and joy, mouth and intention, nose and sorrow, ears and fear.

Other authorities give seven affects: joy, anger, pain, fear, love, hate, desire. It is clear from their novels that the Chinese are especially gifted in the sense of touch: the texts are full of descriptions of skin, how it feels to the touch, is it soft under pressure, cool, etc.

Some insight into Chinese emotional life is afforded by two of the expressions used to denote it: *gan-qing* and *ren-qing*. The former means 'feeling', 'affect' in general, but is in practice limited to the feeling of mutual obligation between spouses. *Gan-qing* covers what we mean by 'love', including intercourse and caresses; it can be 'ruptured' by adultery or by failure to perform one's marital duty. The second expression, *ren-qing*, means 'human feelings' and is usually employed in this sense. But it can also mean 'bribery' – an extension from 'the expression of goodwill by means of presents': normally to someone in a higher position.

'Putting up with' and 'giving in' as behavioural forms are denoted by → *ren* and → *rang*.

Finger-lemon
fo-shou 佛手

This is a citrus fruit of bizarre aspect, with excrescences which look like fingers on a hand: in Chinese it is called 'Buddha-hand' (*fo-shou*). It is sweet-smelling and is therefore often kept in rooms. It is not eaten. In erotic literature it is compared to the male member; though as a rule it does not occur alone but usually in combination with other symbolic plants and animals. A picture showing children bringing an outsize → peach, a → pomegranate and a finger-lemon symbolises the wish 'May you have long life, many sons and every happiness.' Here,

'Much happiness, long life and many sons!'

'Buddha-hand' (*fo-shou*) symbolises 'happy life' (*fu shou*); the hand (*shou*) symbolises 'long life'. A Buddha-hand with a → butterfly (*die*) means 'long life' or 'life until 80' (*die*).

Fingernails
zhi-jia   指甲

Formerly there was a widespread belief that nail clippings should not be left lying around, as → owls might eat them and use them to cast evil spells. As in Latin countries, the long fingernails affected until quite recently by rich Chinese were regarded as a symbol of wealth: it was clear that such hands were not used for work! Nail guards to prevent accidental breakage of these status symbols were in use from the 7th century AD onwards. Men's nails were expected to be shorter than those of women. If a woman has fine slender fingers, these are compared to onion shoots, and in order to make them even more attractive they are coloured with sap obtained from a South Chinese plant.

Some men let the nail of the little finger grow very long, and there was a superstition that if this long nail snapped off, the man would shortly die.

Fire
huo   火

Fire is one of the five → elements or 'metamorphoses of being'. It is

The god of fire with a fan

correlated with the South, with the colour → red, with a bitter taste, and a smell of burning; its associated category in the five-creature series is 'feathered' and its domestic creature is the → hen.

In Tibetan Tantrism, fire is a male symbol, while the fireplace is female. 'Fire-walking', i.e. walking over live coals, is a → spring ritual, held on the 15th day of the 1st month. It is still practised today in Shamanistic and other purification ceremonies. Fire used to be taboo on the 105th day after the winter solstice, that is, on 4 April by the Western calendar. This was a sort of → New Year's celebration: old fire was allowed to die out and new fire was kindled by means of a fire-stick. On this day of transition from the old to the new, no fire was permitted in any house.

As a result, the feast was known as the 'Feast of Cold Food'.

The New Year festivities between the first and the fifteenth days of the new year were marked by letting off fireworks, whose bangs and crackles were supposed to scare away demons. For the same reason, fireworks could be let off at other festivities as well. The fireworks (*bao*) 'announce' (*bao*) the festivity.

The 'great fire' is the red star Antares (α Scorpionis). In ancient China, the rise and fall of Antares in the sky was used by peasants as a sort of calendar for agricultural occupations. Taoist monks when they marry form 'fire families' (*huo jia*). 'Fire-pit' is a frequently used metaphor for a brothel. Finally, the fact that the Chinese words for 'fire' (*huo*) and for 'living' (*huo*) are phonetically identical led people to light great fires on New Year's Day in honour of the god of → riches, who might thus be moved to bestow on them not only wealth but also long life.

'May there always be something left over'

Fish
yu   魚

The Chinese word for 'fish' (*yu*) is phonetically identical with the word meaning 'abundance, affluence' (*yu*): so the fish symbolises wealth. A picture showing a child with a fish means 'May you have an abundance of high-ranking sons.' Another popular grouping shows a goldfish (*jin-yu*) in a pond (*tang*) in the courtyard of a house: by the pond stands a well-to-do lady with two infants

and her attendant lady's-maid. This picture may be symbolically interpreted as meaning 'May gold (*jin*) in abundance (*yu*) fill the whole hall (*tang*) of the house.' Together with → lotus-blossom (*lian*) a fish expresses the wish 'Year after year (*lian nian*) may you live in affluence (*yu*).'

Even in the very oldest Chinese literature we find the belief attested that an abundance of fish in the waters foretold a good harvest. When the fish swam up-river in shoals, this was interpreted as 'rebellion' against the social order and as a harbinger of civil unrest.

Fish were much used in sacrifice. In Central China, fish-heads (*yu tou*) were sacrificed over a long period to the god of → riches, in the belief that they symbolised the beginning (*tou*) of wealth. Fish is a popular dish at → New Year, symbolising the wish for 'affluence year by year'. When the constellation of the Fish becomes visible in the skies, it is a sign that the time for → 'clouds and rain' has passed. That is, it is no longer auspicious for the Emperor to have sexual intercourse.

'Fish and water come together' is a metaphor for sexual intercourse, and a happily married couple may be described as having 'the pleasures of fish in water'. Thus, a pair of fishes symbolising harmony, mutual sexual pleasure and the development of the personality was a popular wedding gift.

In ancient China the word *yu* had the secondary meaning of 'penis', but today the eel has ousted the fish in this respect.

There are many tales of drunk men turning into fish, and fish-demons of this kind sometimes married women. However, they could be recognised from the fact that they had to bathe every day! Other tales tell of fish turning into birds, and there is a 1st century BC tale of a giant fish swallowing a boat. The fish is one of the eight Buddhist symbols.

Fisherman
yu fu   渔 夫

Like the woodcutter, the peasant and the scholar, the fisherman represents one of the four basic occupations. → Officials and merchants are secondary in the sense that they can only make their appearance in a political and social framework organised and developed by the primary four.

The legendary → Fu-xi is said to have been the first to introduce the Chinese to catching and eating fish, and he is also said to have shown

Goldfish in bowl: 'May gold and jewels fill your house to overflowing'

A fisherman selling carp; he hopes for a good income and social advancement

them how to make nets. Under the Han Dynasty, fishing was brought entirely under state control. The value placed on a calling which provides the Chinese with their major source of food along with rice is clear from Shao Yong's famous 'Talks on Fishermen and Woodcutters' (*c.* 1050). Shao Yong's setting is often depicted in temple paintings.

Mao Ze-dong compared the partisan leader to a fisherman who casts his net wide but holds the ends very firmly in both hands – a clever use of symbolism for political ends.

Fish Trap
gu

The legendary Emperor → Fu-xi is credited with the invention of the fish trap. It is a sort of cage made from bamboos woven together, with a large opening towards the front and a small opening behind, and is so constructed that fish can swim into it but cannot get out. It is also a metaphor and rebus for the vagina (cf. the phonetically close *ku* = hole, slit).

Five
wu

Five is one of the most important numbers in Chinese number mysticism. Being uneven, it is a 'male' number. It is associated with the Five Directions (the four points of the compass plus the → Middle), five odours, and five tastes. In →

Lao-zi we read: 'The five colours make man's eyes blind; the five notes make his ears deaf; the five tastes injure his palate' (Book I, section XII; tr. D. C. Lau, London, 1963).

One big Chinese dictionary lists twelve meanings of the character *wu* = 5, and 1,148 compounds using it. Of these, about a thousand are directly connected with the → elements or 'states of being': five customs (practices) (i.e. festive customs, funeral customs, hospitality customs, military customs, customs associated with good wishes); five → noxious creatures; five kinds of animal:

> The essence of the furry creatures is the *qi-lin* (→ unicorn); the essence of the feathered creatures is the → phoenix; the essence of the shell creatures is the → tortoise; the essence of the scaly creatures is the → dragon; the essence of the naked creatures is man.

So we read in the 'Book of Rites'. In the same book we are told of the five relationships between people: ruler and servant, father and son, man and wife, elder brother and younger brother, friend and friend. Confucian doctrine sees all of these relationships in terms of strict hierarchical ordering: even in the case of two friends, the elder is always 'above' the younger.

Traditional Chinese → medicine is based on various relationships and objects arranged in quintuples; similar combinations underlie Chinese → astrology and → geomancy.

Five men with five lucky symbols

A few combinations are worthy of special notice: the 'five signs' (*wu zheng*) are indices of female lasciviousness. The Buddhists recognise 'five prohibitions' (*wu jie*). These are:

Do not kill; do not steal; do not lust; do not drink wine; do not eat meat.

The 'five pures' are the moon, water, the pine-tree, the bamboo, and the plum-tree. The 'five Classics' (*wu jing*) are:

'Book of Documents' (*Shu-jing*)
'Book of Songs (Odes)' (*Shi-jing*)
'Book of Changes' (*Yi-jing*)
'Book of Rites' (*Li-ji*)
'Book of Ceremonies' (*Yi-li*)

The elemental spirits (i.e. the 'Five Ancients'), who appeared over the house when Confucius was being born. On the left, two dragons, symbolising the male, generative forces in nature

The 'Five Dynasties' (*wu-dai*) is the period between the Tang and Song Dynasties, i.e. from AD 907 to AD 960.

The 'Five Moral Qualities' (*wu-chang*) are: humanity, sense of duty, wisdom, reliability, ceremonial behaviour. The 'Five Gifts' are: riches, long life, peace and quiet, virtue, life without sickness. The 'Five Permutations of Being' (*wu-xing*) are: wood, fire, earth, metal and water.

'Songs of the Fifth Night-watch' (*wu-geng ge*), i.e. of the fifth double-hour of the night, are love-songs corresponding to the European *albas*. The 'Five Thunders' is a Taoist magic spell. 'Five Bushels of Rice' (*wu-dou-mi*) is the name of an early Taoist sect (3rd century AD). Its founder, Zhang Lu, always asked for payment in this form when he had healed a spirit.

Flowers
hua

花

The 'Flowers of the Four Seasons' are: for spring, the iris or the → magnolia; for summer, the → peony and the → lotus; for autumn, the → chrysanthemum; and for winter, the → plum and the → bamboo. There are also various lists of 'flowers of the twelve months'. These lists vary much from one to another, but there are some common factors: thus, all lists have the → apricot in the 2nd month (roughly corresponding to our late March), → peach-blossom in the 3rd month, → lotus in the 6th, → cinnamon blossom in the 8th, and

A branch of plum-blossom – harbinger of the spring

→ chrysanthemum in the 9th. A picture showing an orchid (*yu-lan*), a wild apple (*hai-tang*), a peony (*mu-dan*) and a cinnamon blossom (*gui-hua*) is a symbolical way of saying: 'In the hall (*tang*) of jade (*yu*) reign riches (*fu* – another word for peony) and honour (*gui*).' One may thus wish a friend well.

The slogan 'Let a hundred flowers bloom', which became celebrated in the Mao Ze-dong era, goes back to the very earliest Chinese sources. In the 'Book of Odes' we find the following description of the preparation of a bridal chamber:

I strewed lotus leaves on its roof, gladioli on the walls and mountain orchids. Pepper plants smell sweet in the courtyard, the beams are of cinnamon wood, there are mussels on the walls, the gateway is of magnolias, peonies on the roof-

Flower vases as ornaments along garden walls

ridge, many-coloured lianas are woven together to make a curtain. A carpet of basil covers the floor, the mats are weighed down with white jade. The mountain orchid spreads its fragrance, hazel twines among the lotus, mixes with iris and splendid lilies: a hundred flowers bloom in the garden.

The 'Four Friends of the Flowers' are the swallow, the oriole, the bee and the butterfly.

The physical appearance of a beautiful woman is described as 'flower-like' and she herself is a flower reborn. The two are essentially one and the same thing, says a 19th-century writer.

The 15th day of the 2nd month is the festival of the Goddess of the Hundred Flowers, Bai Hua Shen. On this occasion, young girls do obeisance to the Jade Emperor (Yu-huang-di). In pictures of the festivities, other gods are shown arriving on boats made from banana leaves, or on → clouds, and offering flowers.

A girl can be described as 'like a yellow flower' (*huang hua mu*) if she is a virgin, while a 'smoke-flower' is a prostitute, whose life, like smoke, is dissipated in the brothel. In a 'flower-list' (*hua bang*) courtesans are listed in terms of price and attractiveness, and 'flower-boats' are the floating brothels in the Hong-kong area and off the Middle China coast on which courtesans sing and play and entertain guests. Expressions such as 'to enjoy flowers and play with the moon' or 'to look for flowers and enquire of the willow' or 'to sleep among flowers and lie under willows' or 'to look for flowers and challenge grass' – all describe a man who consorts a lot with prostitutes.

In South Chinese villages, a 'battle of flowers' is held on the 5th day of the 5th Chinese month. Since the date is very close to the summer solstice when manly vigour (*yang*) is at its maximum and female influence (*yin*) is beginning its ascent, this symbolic battle is a kind of fertility rite. 'Flower-heart' is a name for the vagina. A basket of flowers carried by a young girl is the symbol of → Lan Cai-he, one of the eight → Immortals.

Flute
di; xiao

笛 簫

Many forms of flute are known in China, both vertical and transverse.

Pan-pipes and mouth-organs are also used. The type known as *di* seems to have originated in Tibet and reached China about two thousand years ago. To the Chinese ear, the *di* has a melancholy sound.

The vertical flute (*xiao*), on the other hand, is a purely Chinese instrument played mainly by women. There are five holes in the upper part and one in the lower; one end is open, the other end is closed. The flute is a symbol of the → Immortal Lan Cai-he (in other versions, of → Han Xiang-zi). Pictures showing a young woman playing a flute to a man have a sexual connotation; and the expression 'to play with → jade and blow the flute' refers to sexual practices, especially fellatio. In Korea, as in Europe, the flute may symbolise the penis.

The Immortal Han Xiang-zi with a flute

Flying
fei

Ability to fly is one of the privileges enjoyed by the → Immortals: 'Standing erect, many fly up to the → clouds, where they fly about with no beating of wings; many ride on the vapours, drawn by yoked → dragons to the footstep of heaven; many turn into animals and birds and wander through the blue → clouds . . .' (from a biography of the Chinese Methuselah → Peng-zu).

'Flying together' is a metaphor for → married bliss. In European languages, too, the notion of 'flying' is connected with sexual pleasure, but the Chinese expression is more graphic: 'The male → phoenix dances and the female flies.' A poetical way of describing orgasm is 'The soul flies away over the heavens.'

If you dream of flying, you are going to receive honour and riches. A 'flying → sword' is a short, very sharp sword which returns like a boomerang after being thrown. 'Flying money' is an old expression for paper money. Many texts refer to a 'flying head' which has become separated from its torso. These tales originate, however, among the non-Han minorities in Southern China.

Fly-whisk
fu-zi

The fly-whisk is a symbol of authority, and is thus used mainly by

Buddhists. As a rule, it is made of the white hairs from a cow's tail, fastened to a handle.

Food
yinshi

China's most distinguished thinkers and statesmen did not consider it beneath their dignity to give at least some of their attention to food and ways of cooking it. The whole of the eighth chapter of Book X of the Analects is devoted to Confucius's eating habits: it ends: 'Although his food might be coarse rice and vegetable soup, he would offer a little of it in sacrifice with a grave respectful air' (tr. Legge).

Tradition has it that the statesman Yi Yin was able to win King Tang over to his designs because he had served the king so well as cook. Yi Yin's conversation with the king is set down in the *Chun-qiu* of Lü Bu-wei (died 235 BC), and the symbolic content is plain: 'The basis for all foods is → water. There are → five tastes, → three substances, → nine ways of boiling and nine ways of roasting, where it is a question of using the different kinds of → fire. In mixing, one must correctly balance sweet, sour, bitter, spicy and salty; one must know which of these and how much is to be added first, which and how much later. The changes that take place in the food after it has been prepared and is still in the bowl, are so secret and so refined that there are no words to describe them. It is like the most subtle and artistic touches in archery and char-

iot-driving, or like the secret processes of natural growth' (tr. Richard Wilhelm). Here there is no mistaking the system of the five 'permutations' or states of being, whereby water is associated with salty, fire with bitter, etc. (→ elements).

When giving food to a guest, one should bear his particular requirements in mind. Thus, old gentlemen should be given tortoise flesh which is still hanging from the broken shell; also, → swallows' nests, as they enhance a man's sexual prowess.

Three farinaceous products have particular symbolic significance: first, → noodles made from → wheat and other things, symbolise → longevity. Then there is *man-tou*, a kind of dumpling made from flour and yeast and filled with meat or (less frequently) with sweetmeats, and steamed. The word *man-tou* means 'barbarian-head' and was first used in the province of Sichuan, where it seems to be connected with head-hunting. At all events, Zhu-ge Liang, who conquered parts of the province, is supposed to have invented them in order to use them in place of human heads at sacrificial ceremonies in time of war. Finally there is *hun-dun* (or, *wan dan*) – small meatballs lightly rolled in dough which are boiled in water and served in the soup thus prepared. The name *hun-dun* means something like 'original chaos' which holds within itself life (the filling) but is still surrounded by water.

We learn something about the significance of food in ancient China from the conversation in the 'Land of the Noble' which occurs in the highly imaginative novel *Jing-hua yuan* ('The Fate of the Flowers in the Mirror') by Li Ru-zhen (died AD 1830). The ideal of modesty is held up against the claims of a questionable luxury. To illustrate the relativity of tastes and values Li quotes the case of that Chinese delicacy, the → swallow's nest. Basically, it tastes of nothing better than wax, and it needs all sorts of additives to make it even barely acceptable. Its value rests entirely on the affectations of certain exclusive circles.

Until the 20th century, a whole galaxy of great Chinese cuisines vied with each other in pleasing the gourmet – Shandong, Henan, Sichuan, Shanghai, Canton were among the best. Connoisseurs could tell at the first mouthful where a dish came from. Now that Peking is once again capital, the Peking style of cooking has gained a lot of ground.

Forest
lin

It is fairly clear from ancient sources that China used to be heavily wooded. Over the centuries, most of the trees were cut down until such forests as remained were only to be found in thinly populated frontier areas. It is only since 1911 (the establishment of the Republic) that a reafforestation policy has been adopted, a policy endorsed by the Communist government from 1949 onwards.

Sacred forests on the slopes of holy → mountains are often mentioned, as are sacred groves. In general, however, the forest was seen as an eerie, spooky place full of dangers. In the forests of South China, the → tiger roamed, and bandits had their lairs – which is why bandits were called 'people of the greenwood'.

Forest and mountain spirits (→ *shan-xiao*) are as plentiful in China as in Japan, where as late as 1824 placards were hung up in the forests ordering the *Tengu* to vacate the Nikko Mountains for the duration of the Shogun's visit to the local temple. Both peoples also venerate 'sacred trees', i.e. very old pine-trees, firs or ginko-trees of remarkable size or shape.

Trees in Chinese pictures are always accompanied by buildings, roads and people: in other words, what is represented is 'tamed nature', not → wilderness.

Fornication
yin

In a broad sense, this word denotes any sort of sexual practice which is in contravention of good moral custom: what is obscene and licentious – in a word, excesses of whatever sort. A proverb says: 'Of the ten thousand evils, fornication is the worst', and a tract on morality lays it down that 'He who seduces others slays his own relatives for the next three generations.' As in Europe, secret religious communities were often suspected of promiscuity, although trustworthy evidence for this, in the case of China, is extremely scanty. 'Licentious/

obscene books' is a term covering not only pornography but also such renowned classics as 'The Dream of the Red Chamber' (*Hong-lou meng*) by Cao Xue-qin (1715–64). In what is probably the most famous erotic novel of all, 'Plum-blossom in a golden Vase' ('The Golden Lotus') – better known by its Chinese title, *Jin Ping Mei* – we find the man playfully addressing his beloved as 'my little wanton' – not in reproach, that is, but in admiration of her → beauty. What we might call a 'forni-kit' consisted of various instruments and devices to heighten sexual pleasure. Rakes and libertines should beware, however: the *yin mo*, the 'debauchery demon', is after them, and the skulls of his victims hang from a belt round his hips to prove it.

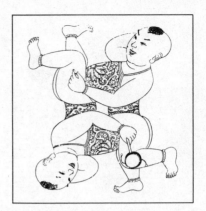

Four-fold happiness

Four
si

As a → *yin* number, four can stand for the West and also for the → earth, which was originally thought to be four-cornered, and which was itself subdivided into rectangles (→ *fang*). The → Middle Kingdom was imagined as lying in the middle of the Four Seas, surrounded by the four barbarian peoples. 'The "Four Mountains" was the title given to the leaders who entrusted the feudal lord with the maintenance of the peace in the "Four Directions", a charge which he accepted by opening the "Four Portals" of his residence' (Marcel Granet on ancient legends

in connection with the Emperor's tours of inspection).

As arithmetical shorthand for the geometrical properties of a square, or indeed any rectangle, four can obviously generate an extensive symbolic field, but it is in point of fact less used in a symbolic sense than five, which has the advantage of being able to include the (to the Chinese) all-important middle as a fifth direction.

As a corollary to the yearly process of the four → seasons, we have the 'four sections (periods)' (*jue*), each of 15 days, which initiate these seasons – the periods of the summer and winter solstices and of the spring and autumn equinoxes. The first day of each of these periods was known as the 'four separations', and on these days sexual intercourse was forbidden.

The 'four gates' (*si men*) is a reference to the four journeys undertaken by the young Siddharta Gautama, journeys which convinced him that he must give up his way of life as a prince and become → Buddha. The

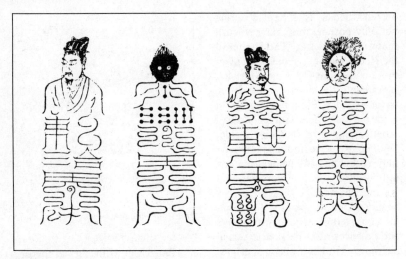

The Masters of the Four Directions: an amulet for repelling evil spells

'four great kings' (*si da wang*) are Ma, Zhao, Wen and Li; it is they who protect the jade-ruler in the four regions of the world.

The 'four arts' of the → scholar (who himself belongs to one of the four → callings) are symbolised by the → lute, the → chess-board, the → book and the painting. Each is also symbolised by a celebrated man who excelled in it: thus, Yu Bo-ya (*c.* 500 BC) in music, Zhao Yen (3rd century AD) in chess, Wang Xi-zhi (later than 3rd century AD) in calligraphy, and Wang Wei (Tang Dynasty) in painting.

The 'four treasures of the scholar's study' are ink, paper, → brush and ink-slab (Indian ink is bought as a solid in cylindrical form, and has to be rubbed down on a moistened stone before it can be used). The 'four-coloured play-stones' (*si se pai*) are playing cards of the old type, narrow and rectangular (→ games). Their use was forbidden in Taiwan.

The 'Four Books' (*si shu*) are the Analects of Confucius (*Lun-yu*), the 'Book of Mencius', 'The Great Learning' (*Da Xue*) and the 'Doctrine of the Mean' (*Zhong Yong*): since the establishment of Neo-Confucianism as the state religion in the Song Dynasty, these four books have enjoyed almost more popularity than the ancient 'Five Classics'. Confucian influence is also unmistakable in the doctrine of the 'four bonds' (*si wei*), i.e. the four cardinal virtues: propriety, integrity, righteousness and modesty.

Chinese Communism saw the ideology of the feudal period in terms of the 'four old things' – old culture, old customs, old habits and old ways of thinking – and proceeded to attack on each of these fronts.

For many Chinese, the word *si* = four is taboo, as it is phonetically close to *si* = death.

Fox
hu-li

狐狸

In China, as in Europe, the fox is known for its cunning; and being cunning it can live to a great age. Furthermore, it can turn itself into a woman when it reaches fifty years of age, into a girl when it is a hundred, and after a thousand years it can become a celestial fox – but few foxes achieve this!

The thousand-year-old fox has nine tails and is noted for its extreme sensuality. It was a thousand-year-old fox which assumed the form of the beguiling Dan-ji and led the last Emperor of the Shang Dynasty into such evil ways that he finally lost both his empire and his life. This tale is related in the famous Ming novel 'The Metamorphoses of the Gods' (*Feng-shen yan-yi*).

Texts dating from the dawn of our era identify the fox as a demonic creature upon whose back spirits ride. Then again it is described as a harbinger of good luck. In the main, however, it has always been an erotic symbol, and for about two thousand years it has been associated with venereal diseases. Hundreds of stories tell how a ravishingly beautiful girl appears one night to a young → scholar while he is studying, and how he makes love to her. She disappears in the early morning but comes back each evening. The scholar gets weaker and weaker – until a Taoist informs him that the girl is really a fox which is sucking him dry in order to imbibe the essence of immortality. Stories like this are confined to North

The nine-tailed vixen and the Japanese ape Songoku (woodcut by Hokusai)

China, to such Palaeo-Asiatic tribes as the Orok and the Gilyak, and to Korea and Japan. They are not found south of the Yangtse. In any case, the fox of Korean and Japanese folk-tales differs markedly from its Chinese counterpart. Fox-women often claim that their surname is *hu*, which is phonetically identical with the Chinese word for 'fox'.

In old Peking there were many houses in which foxes lived (they were, of course, invisible). These foxes were under the jurisdiction of a fox-official who lived in a tower at the eastern side-gate of the city. The families who shared these houses with the foxes put out food for them, and did nothing to stop them when they made a noise at night. Otherwise, the foxes would retaliate by putting filth in the family's food supply. Fox-women can be distinguished from ordinary women by the fact that they never change their clothes, which, however, never look soiled. In this connection, it is worth noting that 'fox-smell' is a term for 'under-arm sweat'.

Magpies, bamboos and plum-blossom: signs of friendship and harbingers of happiness

Friends, The Three
san you 三友

Pictures showing → pines, → bamboos and → plum trees, or bamboos, → a stone and plum-trees, are different versions of the 'three friends in winter' motif. They do not die: they remain constant and blossom before the spring comes. The motif can be used as a greeting to people who are poor or lonely.

In the Analects Confucius refers to 'three friends':

There are three friendships which are advantageous, and three which are injurious. Friendship with the upright; friendship with the sincere; and friendship with the man of much observation – these are advantageous. Friendship with the man of specious airs; friendship with the insinuatingly soft; and friendship with the glib-tongued – these are injurious. (Book XVI, ch. IV) (tr. Legge)

There is a clear reference to this passage in a poem by Su Dong-po

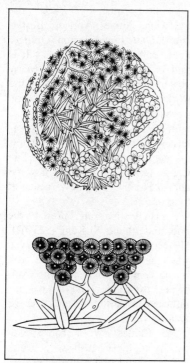

Above: Bamboos, pine-trees and plum-trees
Below: Pine-trees and bamboos

this is really a taboo-word for *tian-ji* meaning 'celestial cock', as it was believed that the frog's seed fell together with the → dew from → heaven. In various provinces there was at one time a cult of the frog, which led in turn to its being banned as an article of food. In other regions, however, frogs were bred for sale. Until well into the Middle Ages, it was widely believed that the frog could turn into a → quail.

Like the → toad, the frog is of course a → moon creature, but in folklore there is a lot more to it than that. In Taiwan, the word for 'green frog' is taboo among young girls because the creature is supposed to resemble the body of a girl. Instead, they refer to it as the 'water-chicken'. In Korea, a dream about a frog is supposed to foretell the birth of a son. An ancient text assures us that one of a human being's two → souls, – the *hun* – looks exactly like

(1036–1101) in which he speaks of the pine and the bamboo as the three (*sic*) friends who are advantageous: probably 'the three friends' were so well-known in the eleventh century that the third could be readily omitted for metrical reasons.

Frog
wa 蛙

Among the peasants, the frog is often called 'partridge' (*tian ji*); but

A summons: 'Protect all living things'

a frog. Finally, 'frog-mouth' means the glans penis. But many references to the frog are obscure and difficult to interpret. Rulers, high officials and poets often found the croaking of frogs disturbing: so, it is said, they told them to be quiet – and the frogs obeyed!

Front/Back
qian-hou

前後

In Chinese, 'front' is associated with the South and with the element → fire, and it is imbued with → *yang*, the male principle. Accordingly, the → Emperor sat facing south when his court was in session, and the imperial palace was always orientated on the South, as was, indeed, by the rules of geomancy, any suitable site for a burial place.

'Back' was associated with the North, with → water and with the female principle → *yin*. Subjects approached the Emperor from the South. 'Left/right' corresponded mainly to 'East/West'. On old Chinese maps, North is at the bottom of the sheet, South at the top.

symbolical imagery. (See the following: Apple, Apricot, Bottlegourd, Date, Finger-lemon, Orange, Pear, Pomegranate, etc., etc.) It is said in the 'Book of Rites': 'Many flowers and few fruits: that is the working of → heaven; but many words and few deeds – that is the fault of men.' Some of the → Immortals can be recognised from the fruits associated with them: thus → Lan Cai-he (a basket of fruit or flowers) and → He Xian-gu (the → peach of long life).

A man bearing fruit represents the poet and scholar Xi Kang (223–62). He was so fond of fruit that even when he is portrayed without fruit in the company of a girl who leans against the window, no one has any difficulty in getting the message: 'Xi Kang loves fruit.'

No Chinese word corresponds exactly to the English word 'fruit'. A basic distinction is made between 'wet' and 'dry' fruits. Neither the → banana nor the → lichee counts as a 'wet' fruit (aqueous fruit), however, perhaps because in neither case can the skin be eaten.

Apples and oranges make very acceptable gifts when visiting the sick – not least because both are very expensive.

Fruit
guoz

果子

Like many → flowers, the Chinese fruits also provide a rich field of

Fu-xi

伏羲

Fu-xi is the first of China's three cultural heroes, the three demiurges who are supposed to have laid the

Fu-xi

foundations of Chinese culture. Scholars have calculated that he must have lived long before 3000 BC. For example, he is credited with having 'invented' the eight → trigrams of the *Yi-jing*, although the 'Book of Changes' itself has been ascribed to the much later Zhou-gong, the Duke of Zhou. Fu-xi is also supposed to have instituted marriage, as well as inventing fishing nets and the → fish-cage. Flying in the face of Chinese morality as it was later to develop, he married his sister → Nü-gua; and reliefs dating from Han times show the two in close embrace like intertwined snakes, with Fu-xi himself holding in one hand the protractor which is the symbol of building and architecture. The protractor also serves as the symbol of the magic and curative forces in nature.

Fu-xi is often shown with a calf's head and the scaly body of a → dragon.

G

Games
youxi

Many games that now enjoy world-wide popularity were invented in China: kite-flying is perhaps the most obvious example. Then there is the magic square, which it is said appeared to Emperor Yu one day when he was walking by the river Lo. And → chess itself, of which there are many varieties in China, is supposed to have been developed from a mysterious document known as the 'Plan of the Yellow River'.

The first known reference to playing cards also occurs in ancient Chinese literature. They appear to have developed from the ancient game of 'pot-throwing' (*tou hu*) during the Tang Dynasty (618–906), the apogee of Chinese culture. Since then, Chinese playing cards have

Playing cards and dice

been rectangular and very small: they are often compared to the leaves of plants. It is particularly at → New Year, when the children get lots of toys, that women play the 'leaf-game' (*ye-zi xi*).

The domino too is first mentioned in ancient Chinese documents, and here again fact and fancy are inextricably mixed up as in the case of other games.

Dui-z is a kind of party game, played by → scholars and literati. One player utters a sentence; the second player then utters a parallel sentence – i.e. each component of the second sentence must formally and positionally reflect the corresponding component in the first sentence: noun–noun, verb–verb, compound–compound. The sentences are often laced with quotations from classical texts and puns.

On open-air games, see Ball, Snow, Swing.

Garlic
suan

Garlic is a lucky plant; it is an antidote to poisons of all sorts. It plays considerable part in the festival of the 5th day of the 5th month. Garlic may also symbolise a rich progeny.

Gate
men

A gateway – particularly a palace gateway – was a symbol of the → Emperor; but it could also symbolise the family. Until modern times, city gates were closed in the evening, and not reopened until first cock-crow. At the summer solstice, they stayed closed all day, as this was held to be a peculiarly critical, indeed

The outer door of the Imperial Palace in Peking

dangerous period (→ feast-days). To keep demons away, a metal disc bearing a representation of a → lion's head was nailed to the top of the gate. The custom of painting portraits of two generals on the sides of the gate at → New Year continues to be observed today. These were generals in the service of one of the Tang Emperors, who murdered many people, including members of his own family. Haunted to distraction by their → spirits, he engaged the two generals to protect him; and today their portraits are enough to protect all the houses in the city. In South China it counts as very bad luck to leave either a gate or a door half-open.

'Gate-packet' (*men bao*) is a euphemism for 'bribery': one gives the bribe 'to the gatepost'. 'The one standing in the door' (*men-hu* or *meng-zhong ren*) is a prostitute, and, correspondingly, the 'man in the door' (*men ren*) is a male prostitute. The 'dark gateway' (*xuan-men*) is a metaphor for the vagina, but may also refer to a certain Taoist sect.

Gecko
bi-hu   壁 虎

The gecko is a small, lizard-like creature, which the Chinese like to have in their houses as it eats vermin. It climbs about on walls and ceilings, and is therefore known as 'Wall-tiger' (*bi-hu*). A magic poison (*gu*), used typically in South China, was prepared by putting a → centipede, a → snake, a scorpion, a → frog and a gecko in a pot and leaving them

The gecko as one of the five noxious creatures

for a year: the creatures gradually ate each other up, and the corpse that was found when the pot was opened was supposed to contain the → noxious poison of all five. The corpse was used for various magical practices, e.g. for bringing about the death of a hated rival. Another name for the gecko is *shou-gong*, i.e. the 'guardian of the palace'. Old texts tell us how a gecko was put into a pot on the 5th day of the 5th month and then fed for a year on → cinnabar powder. At the end of the year, it was pounded to pieces. The ointment thus obtained was rubbed on to the arm of a girl destined for the imperial court: the mark would vanish the first time the girl had sexual intercourse.

In one such story we are told that a girl who was supposed to be a prostitute was able to point to the mark on her arm, which, she said, had been put there when she was six years old – she was now fifteen.

Men who were going to be away on a long journey painted the mark on the lower part of their wives' bodies. According to one text, this ensured that the women would have no children; other texts say that the spot would disappear should sexual intercourse take place.

Geomancy
feng-shui

For two thousand years geomancy was the science of 'Wind and Water' (*feng-shui*). No one would build a house or select a burial spot without consulting the geomancer beforehand. In dire necessity, one could make do without advice from the → astrologer or from the adept at interpreting → oracles; but the *feng-shui* expert – who today might be described as an ecologist – could not be ignored.

'Ensure harmony in the → Middle', we are told in the 'Book of Rites' (*Li-ji*), 'and → heaven and → earth take their rightful places and all things flourish.' What mattered was so to channel and organise natural forces that these would exercise as favourable an influence as possible: so houses, bridges, walls, copses, etc., had to be planned and sited with extreme care. *Feng-shui* required knowledge of the earth's surface (*di-li*, which is the modern term for 'geography'), the study of → *yin* and → *yang* and mastery of a specific technology. For example, it was for the geomancer to align the angle of a door, which was often set askew to the house if the whole house could not be built at the angle recommended by geomancy. For

similar reasons, all the houses in a village street had to be the same height: those in front must not obscure those behind. 'Even outside the village no high building could be put up on the right-hand side (i.e. on the west side facing south), nor could a high tree remain. This was in accordance with the instructions of the white → tiger which lived at the right-hand side of every village. The green → dragon, however, which lived at the left-hand side of the village, did not object' (W. Oehler, *Popular Religion in China*).

It often took a geomancer weeks to locate a 'lucky' burial site. Ancestors had to be protected against the influence of evil → spirits, and here the expertise of the geomancer was needed. He would probably look for a south-facing hill-side, and arrange for protective walls on each side to keep off east and west winds. The underside of the grave could be protected by siting it over an underground water-course.

Geomantic instructions in a military manual of 1662

In sites where the *feng-shui* was 'weak', pagodas were often erected. If a large stream flowed by a town, there was always a danger that the current might carry the good influences and powers away with it. Where the stream ran towards a mountain, this might prevent dispersal of these influences; otherwise a pagoda was built, thus achieving by art what nature by herself had failed to do – ensure 'harmony in the Middle'. Even today pagodas are usually to be seen downstream from the town, opposite a bend in the river. The handbooks written on the technique of siting houses and graves can only be understood by those versed in astronomy and → astrology, and who can use the special compass necessary in geomancy.

Gestures
zhuang-tai 狀 態

In their everyday lives the Chinese make much use of symbolic gestures; but only one set of these has been studied in detail, – the sign-language used by traders to signal prices. For example, when the index finger of one hand is stretched out and the thumb is placed close to the other fingers which are clenched, this means → one. → Two is indicated by stretching out index and middle finger, while the thumb is placed against the fourth and little fingers. → Three is made by stretching out middle, fourth and little fingers, with the thumb and the index finger forming a ring. The other numbers

are formed as follows: → four: four fingers stretched out, the thumb kept down; → five: all five fingers stretched out; → six: thumb and little finger stretched out, the others closed; → seven: thumb, index and middle finger stretched out, the other two closed; → eight: thumb and index finger stretched out, in imitation of the Chinese written sign for eight; → nine: this too looks like the written sign – the index finger is curved, the thumb is placed close to the other fingers which are clenched; → ten: again, like the written sign: the index finger of the left hand is placed across the index finger of the right.

The hands can be used to express all sorts of actions, happenings, intentions, etc. Here we have room for only a few examples. Bringing the two fists together twice or thrice is a sign that you are about to attack someone: but this is only a sign for the benefit of third parties, not for the object of your anger. To him you signal your intention, as in the West, by rolling up your sleeves. If the stomach is stroked by the right hand held horizontally with the fingers stretched out and close together, this means, 'I've had enough to eat.' The right index finger poked into the lightly clenched left hand symbolises sexual intercourse. Rubbing the two open hands against each other means 'bankruptcy'. To signal that you cannot hear, you hold your two hands behind your ears with the flat of the hand turned sideways. To tell someone to 'get lost!' you hold the right hand with outstretched fingers across your body, the flat of the hand towards the body, and then jerk

Polite conversation: a scene from the popular novel 'The Robbers of Liangshan Moor'

hand and arm violently forwards. And if someone wants to tell you that you're talking rubbish, he moves his hand, the fingers stretched out and close together, once across his chest to right and left. Placing your hand on your chest means 'I'; if someone points thumb and index finger splayed towards you, and gestures with the arm, it is a sign that he thinks very little of you and is not going to be friendly.

So much for the hands. Other parts of the body are also used in gesture language. Bending the head a little, and shaking it slightly, means 'Shame on you'; stroking the cheek downwards with the index finger is another way of indicating this. Moving the hand to and fro in front of the slightly bent head which is

again gently shaken, means 'This has nothing to do with me.' To indicate that you cannot stand someone (who is not present) you stick your lower lip out, wrinkle your nose and frown (not too much). To express astonishment, you open your eyes and mouth wide. To express 'I'm not quite sure' you scratch your head gently (again, not too much, as that would suggest that your hair needs washing).

Putting the teeth on the lower lip indicates 'I'm going to hit you.' Drawing in the lower lip expresses annoyance or uncertainty: one often sees children do this to foreigners. Sticking the lower lip out, on the other hand, means that you don't believe what the other person has said.

Knitting one's brows and pursing the lips expresses annoyance, discontent or disgust. When a child sticks its tongue out, it is not simply being rude as in Western society, but is expressing fear. Children pout their lips to show that they don't want something, e.g. to eat. A bad smell is indicated by wrinkling the nose slightly, knitting the brows and moving the right hand to and fro before the nose.

The open hand held palm downwards while the fingers are moved up and down (the arm pointing downwards) means 'Come here.' It is a very frequent gesture, and one that is instantly understood by taxi-drivers. The same message can be expressed by holding the right hand palm upwards, putting the thumb to the middle finger and then beckoning with the index finger. This gesture, however, is not acceptable between persons of different sex.

In the sign language of the dumb, the thumb indicates → heaven; the index finger, the → earth; the middle finger, the → father; the fourth finger, the mother; and the little finger, one's own wife.

'Spitting' is also a gesture, equivalent to 'crossing oneself'. It is a safeguard in a thunderstorm, and spirits dislike being spat at (this is clear from the oldest → medicinal text yet found). If you meet a funeral procession in the street you should spit: as you should when you see a shooting star.

Ghost
gui 鬼

In general, the Chinese word *gui* denotes a demon of whom we have every reason to feel scared. It is often the spirit of a dead person: in this case, members of the family to which it belonged are not frightened of it: that is, it is not a *gui* – unless, of course, they have neglected it or insulted it, but a *shen*. The → souls of others, however (i.e. non-family), might well be intent on getting their own back for insult and injury suffered in life. Then again, they might be driven by need to take offensive action: this goes in particular for the souls of those who had died in remote parts, far from their families, and who receive no sacrifices (the so-called 'Hungry Spirits'). Popular etymology links the word *gui* = demon, ghost, with *gui* = return home.

Gui wear hemless garments. They themselves cast no shadow, and their

Zhong-kui exorcises the ghosts

voices sound strange to us. They are very short-sighted and see only a red glow; we see them as a sort of dark cloud. In parts of South China it was believed that *gui* could act as servants to living men. Today, in both China and Taiwan, the press campaigns against the belief in ghosts, but the press reports themselves make it clear that this belief is by no means a thing of the past.

'*Gui*-traffic' is an expression for sexual intercourse. A 'Ghost Carriage' (*gui-che*) is supposed to be a bird with nine heads; the South Chinese believe that it comes into houses and robs inmates of their souls. It is particularly important not to put children's clothes out to dry in the open air, as the blood of this bird or one of its feathers may fall on them, and the children will then be taken ill. The 'Ghost Barrier' (*gui men guan*) is in the underworld, at the entrance to the first hell. The spirit passes through this barrier in the first seven days after death. In South China, the 'Ghost Mother' is believed to give birth to ten ghosts at a time, all of which she devours the same evening. In some texts we read of 'Ghost Pregnancy' which is an imaginary pregnancy, conjured up by dreams. 'Foreign ghosts' (foreign devils) (*yang gui-zi*) was a less than complimentary expression for Europeans and Americans. It is not much used nowadays.

Ginger
jiang

薑
薑

Ginger is an important ingredient in many Chinese dishes. Confucius, we are told in the Analects, was 'never without ginger when he ate'. The elaborate system of correspondences which underlies so much Chinese thought required that sauces should be prepared according to season with ginger, vinegar, wine or salt. Only → honey was invariably included: 'since what is sweet corresponds to the earth which lies in the centre' (Marcel Granet).

As the ginger root often resembles a finger, women were told to keep off ginger during pregnancy, as the child might well be born with more than five fingers.

Ginseng
ren-shen

Nowadays, ginseng is in great demand as a tonic to which all sorts of curative and restorative properties are attributed. In ancient times, the plant was mainly produced in the mountainous regions of what is today the province of Shanxi, in North China; later, Shandang (also in Shanxi) became famous for its ginseng.

The roots of the ginseng plant are fairly long and often look like a small child. It is said that ginseng not only looks like a child but can also cry like one.

At the present time, it is mainly in Manchuria and Korea that ginseng is produced. According to an old legend, it was a beetle which brought a red child (i.e. ginseng) to Manchuria. There is a well-known folk-tale about a man who is offered ginseng to eat; he refuses to eat it, believing it to be a boiled child.

Ginseng plays an important part in modern folk-tales current in the province of Jilin. There is one about a Buddhist monk who mistreats his young pupil. Every time the monk goes out, a child with a red cummerbund comes to play with the pupil. When the monk learns about this, he tells his pupil to fasten a thread to the clothing of his visitor. This is done, and later the monk finds the thread on a ginseng plant; so he digs up the root and boils it. While the root is boiling, the monk has to go out for a moment; the pupil lifts the lid of the pot and eats the contents. He gives the soup to his dog. When the monk comes back, the dog eats him up.

In the many fanciful tales connected with ginseng, one of the main protagonists is always a child.

Girl in spring

Girl
nü hai　　女孩

The role allotted in traditional Chinese society to young girls – indeed, to women in general – emerges very clearly from the customs associated with → birth, → name-giving, and with the annual *qi-qiao* festival. Indeed, male and female → children were treated in very different fashion from birth onwards. The *qi-qiao* festival was held on the 7th day of the 7th month (the festival of the → Spinning Damsel): in the light of the full moon, girls had to try to thread their needles correctly, and if they succeeded this was a sign that they had pleased the goddess and would be skilful in all forms of handiwork.

Girls are often compared with → flowers: → pomegranates, → gourds, → orchids, → peonies, → peach-blossom, and → plum-blossom are favourite symbols.

The animal world is also drawn on: the → frog, the → parrot and the → horse are favourite symbols, while → red and → green may further symbolise a girl's developing → beauty.

Formerly, the heroic maiden → Mu-lan was held up to girls as a paragon of filial piety (→ *xiao*). As an exemplar of the heroic warrior-maiden, she has lasted into the era of the modern Peking Opera and appears in popular comics and in war films. (See also Swing.)

Glow-worm
ying-huo-chong

螢 火 虫

The glow-worm is a symbol of → beauty and of steadfastness: the latter quality, no doubt, because when the great → scholar Jiu Yin was a boy he was so poor that he had to study at night by the light of glow-worms. Nevertheless, he passed all his examinations with great distinction.

Glue
jiao

膠

The love between a young couple is often described as 'as firm as lacquer and as lasting as glue'. A special form of glue made, so it is said, from the sinews of the → phoenix, and used for sticking broken → bow-strings together, symbolises the reunion of a pair of lovers after a long separation.

Goldfish
jin yu

金 魚

The Chinese are very fond of goldfish and keep them in bowls in their homes or in ponds in the temple gardens. The Chinese words meaning 'goldfish' are phonetically identical with the two words meaning 'gold in abundance', so goldfish make a very acceptable wedding present. When represented together with a → lotus (*jin-yu tong he*) the goldfish indicates 'gold and jade (*jin yu*) joined together' (*tong he*, which is homonymic with *he* = lotus). A picture showing a pair of goldfish is a symbol of fertility: but the goldfish may also represent a widow's lover, or a man supported by a prostitute.

Good Luck, The Five Gods of
wu fu

五 福

The gods of good luck are usually represented as men clad in the red robes of → officials. They confer long life (often symbolised as a man with a → crane and → flowers); → riches; welfare (a man with a → vase); virtue; health.

The five gods of good luck with three wine-barrels

A → bat is often shown fluttering round each of these gods. Again, the three → constellations may be added.

Five bats on their own symbolise the five gods and their gifts.

Goose
e

Like the → mandarin duck or the → phoenix, the goose is in China a symbol of → married bliss. The goose takes one partner for life, as a woman should. So a goose makes a very suitable engagement present. This is a very old custom, varied on occasion by an exchange – the bridegroom's family sends a gander, the bride's family reciprocates by sending back a goose. Neither of these ever ends up on the table.

The 'little calendar of the Xia Dynasty' marks the first month as follows: 'The wild goose flies to northern regions', and in the 9th month 'the wild geese migrate'. Brass boxes sometimes have the following inscription on the lid: 'May the flying wild goose lengthen (your) years' – a reference to the way in which seasons are announced in popular calendars, and to the reliability of a bird which never fails to turn up on time. As a migratory

A wild goose as bearer of good news

'May the wild goose on the wing lengthen (your) days (years)'

bird, the wild goose, like the wild duck, can be a harbinger of separation; but then again they can both be regarded as messengers, bearers of glad tidings from a spouse far away in northern lands.

Wild geese are represented as flying in pairs, and so a picture of wild geese makes a good wedding present (→ marriage). A picture showing a man with two geese in front of him is a reference to the calligrapher Wang Xi-zhi (321–79) who, so the legend goes, was particularly fond of geese and fed them with Chinese ink.

Gourd (Melon)
gua

Several kinds of gourd and melon are native to China. The watermelon alone is an importation from Western Asia; for this reason it is called 'Western gourd' (*xi gua*).

It is said – and the saying may be as old as → Confucius – that one should not stoop or bend down while passing through a field of gourds, lest one be suspected of stealing. On the day of the Feast of Women (the 7th day of the 7th month) women in Central China make offerings of melons, and on the 15th day of the 8th month (i.e. the night of the full moon) they make melon cakes. In the autumn, young girls go into the fields and pick melons, in the belief that this will bless their marriage with sons.

There are some interesting beliefs in Chinese folklore in connection with the water-melon. The written character for *gua* (see above) can be divided down the middle, and if the top ends are brought together each half can be read as the character for 'eight'. 'Twice times eight' is a metaphor for a marriageable girl (by our reckoning she is only 15 years old). One can put this graphically by saying that the girl 'is as old as the divided gourd (*po gua*)'. The expression can also refer to her first menstruation or even to her deflor-

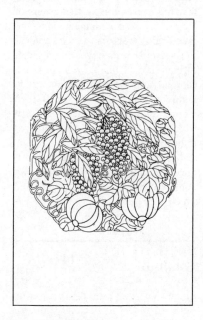

Ornamental fruits with two gourds

ation, if one thinks of the red-coloured inside of the water-melon. 'Melon-seed' is a poetic expression for a girl's teeth.

In the province of Canton, a melon must never be presented to anyone as a gift, as the word *xi* in *xi-gua* = water-melon is pronounced in Cantonese exactly like the word for 'death', 'dying' (*si* in *guo yu*). (See also bottle-gourd.)

Grave
fen-mu 墳墓

The grave was often looked upon in China as the dwelling-place of the deceased person. There are countless versions of the story in which a wayfarer comes by night to a fine house in which he is received and looked after by a young woman: when he wakes up in the morning he finds himself in a grave. Other legends tell how a pregnant woman dies and then comes every day from her grave as a living woman to feed the baby. The food she buys is paid for with 'death-money' (i.e. worthless paper money, not coins) as it later turns out. People look for the grave, and find in it a living child.

At burial, the dead were given everything they might need: household goods; in the case of rich people, even horses and a carriage. For this reason, the imperial tombs were guarded by 'grave-watchers', who ran their profession as a sort of enslavement or bondage, passed on from father to son. Some idea of the unimaginable wealth that went into the tomb along with an Emperor can be got from the partial excavation of the grave of Shi Huang-di, the first Emperor of China (3rd century BC).

Until quite recently, the dead were buried at 'favourable' spots specially recommended by an expert in → geomancy. If this were neglected, there was always the danger that one's ancestors would be unable to rest in peace and that their descendants would therefore be plagued by bad luck and all sorts of unpleasantness.

It was customary to plant trees round a grave: trees which in after years gave shade to wayfarers on the hot plains, timber for building to the peasants, and beneath the trees grass for the cows. Cremation – now officially favoured – was once practised only by Buddhist monks, or as a punishment for criminals. By the Middle Ages, however, funeral offerings were often burned. In later years and nowadays, these offerings are represented by paper models which are invariably ritually burned.

In olden days, people kept 'house urns'. This may be connected with the ceremony of the 'second burial' which is still fairly common in South China. A couple of years or so after initial burial the body is exhumed, the bones are cleaned and then placed in a clay urn about 50 cm deep. These vessels can be found for sale at markets in Taiwan. On the walls of the tombs of rich people, we often find paintings representing scenes from the life of the deceased, or scenes which are still well known in the theatre. (We know this because the scenes have titles which are today titles of plays.)

Green
lü   綠

Green is one of the colours that life takes on, and it is the emblem of the spring. Dreams in which green colours figure invariably end happily. A modern text has it that green indicates complete inner peace. Several of the gods and goddesses, e.g. the god of literature, go about in green robes. In the 8th century, → officials wore green.

Once upon a time, the fairy → He xian-gu (one of the eight → Immortals) felt tired, so she removed her shoes and stockings. When the other gods and goddesses looked askance at this indecorous conduct she ran away, but one stocking was caught on a → lichee twig and was left hanging there: this is the origin of the expression 'hanging up the green'. But green can also be a negative symbol. A man wearing a green turban (*dai lü mao*, or *lü jin*) is a cuckold, and the 'family of the green lamps' are prostitutes. The 'Green Youth' (*lü-lang*) is an evil spirit which attacks and kills girls at puberty.

The Chinese attach great importance to combinations of the two complementary colours, red and green.

Guan-di   關帝

Guan Yu was one of those who helped Liu Bei to become Emperor of West China and to found a short-

Guan-di (in foreground)

lived dynasty there in the 3rd century AD. Guan Yu was subsequently given the honorific name Guan-gong. He fell from power after the death of Liu Bei, but was gradually elevated to divine status in the centuries that followed. Until quite recently, temples to Guan-di (his name as a god) were to be found in almost all of China's larger towns. He was venerated as a god of war, and also as a god of justice and righteousness: parties to a dispute often took their case to his temple to be settled. In the Chinese theatre, he is a main protagonist in the many plays based on the 'Romance of the Three Kingdoms'. Here he is portrayed in the uniform of a general and on horseback. He is instantly recognisable by his red face.

Guan-yin 觀音

Guan-yin, the goddess of mercy, was originally the male Buddhist saint Avalokiteśvara (the patron saint of Tibetan Buddhism, who is incarnated in the person of the Dalai Lama). The name 'Avalokiteśvara' was translated into Chinese as 'he who listens to the sounds (of the world)' (*guan yin*). In Indian and Tibetan art, Avalokiteśvara was portrayed according to Indian concepts of beauty – i.e. with feminine softness of curve and well-developed breasts. It is probably for these reasons that people took Guan-yin for a goddess (as attested from the 9th century onwards). However, pictures of men with the upper part of the body uncovered usually show them with rather more in the way of bosom than females of the same social background have to offer.

Guan-yin is often shown in a Madonna-like posture, with a child in her arms. She is accompanied by a boy with a bottle, and a girl carrying a → willow-twig. On the South Chinese coast she is often identified with → Ma-zu, a goddess worshipped since the 11th century at least by boatmen and fishermen. The similarity in names has also led to her being regarded as the wife of Guan-gong (see previous entry). The legend of how she gets the better of → Lü Dong-bin after he has annoyed

Guan-yin, the Chinese 'Madonna'

her beyond endurance, is very popular.

Another legend tells how the willow-twig is put into the bottle, thereby becoming 'unworthy'. The willow-twig was thereupon transformed into a prostitute, which is why the brothel quarter has ever since been known as 'Flower streets and Willow lanes'.

Guang-han gong

廣 寒 宮

The 'Palace of the Wide Cold' is on the → moon; it is surrounded by beautiful gardens and seductive girls. The expression is used metaphorically to mean the process of falling in love with a girl whom one might well imagine to be as beautiful 'as the fairies in the moon'. Formerly, the palace with all its attractions often appeared in dreams, but, say the Taiwanese, since the Americans landed on the moon – not any more!

H

Hair
tou-fa 頭髮

All Chinese have black hair. Shining
black hair on a woman is called
'Cloud-hair' and is admired as
particularly → beautiful, especially
when the growth of hair is also
strong and luxuriant. Naturally wavy
hair is found only in South China
and in Taiwan, where it is not
uncommon. In any description of a
beautiful woman, her hair is usually
the first thing to be mentioned. In
medieval texts, we find references to
people in Northern Turkestan who
had 'yellow' i.e. fair hair, and to
slaves from the Burmese borderlands who had curly hair.

Body hair is scant and regarded
as undesirable. However, men are
proud to sport a good growth of →
beard, and in Chinese opera, high →
officials and military dignitaries are
always represented with exaggerated
beards.

*A lady with decorative head-dress on the
way to Xi-wang-mu*

Halberd
ji 戟

The halberd is an ancient Chinese
weapon which is often used as a

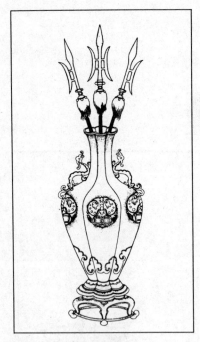

Three halberds in a vase

motif in ornamental and decorative art. It symbolises luck, happiness (*ji* homonym of *ji* = halberd); or it may be a way of wishing the recipient good luck in his examinations (*ji* = rank, grade).

A frequent grouping shows a → vase with three halberds in it and a → musical stone: → fish hang on the halberds and there is an → axe beside them.

Hall
tang　　　　堂

From the Chinese point of view, the main reception area in a house. The 'reception hall' was of cardinal

importance (→ apple, birthday, canopy). The word *tang*, however, can also refer to a business undertaking of any sort.

The word is also applied to the lachrymal sac under the eye: other metaphors for this are 'the recumbent silkworm' and 'the dragon palace'. Ideally this part of the eye was well developed and reddish in colour. A woman whose *tang* was dry and wrinkled or even liver-spotted would not have any children.

A *tang-ke* ('hall-guest') was a girl working the 'Flower-boats'. The *cai-tang* ('Vegetarian Hall') was the common denominator to which (according to Maximilian Kern) all Taoist sects were reduced in popular parlance.

Han Xiang-zi
韓 湘 子

Han Xiang-zi with his flute

Han is a historical figure – nephew of the celebrated scholar Han Yu (768–824). He lived in the early 9th century and renounced public life in order to study with the sage and holy man → Lü Dong-bin. It was said of Han that he could make flowers grow and blossom at will. He became one of the eight → Immortals. His symbol is the → flute.

Hare
tu-z
鬼 子

The hare is the fourth creature in the Chinese → zodiac. It is resident in the → moon, just as a → raven is in the sun, and it is there still for everyone to see. As much as two thousand years ago, it was already being represented along with pestle and mortar and a cassia-tree twig. It uses the mortar to pound → cinnamon twigs, and is a symbol of → longevity. Sometimes it is called 'jade-hare'. According to many texts, there are no male hares, and hares become pregnant by licking newly sprung plant shoots: to give birth, she spits the young from her mouth. A picture showing two men watching a third who is spitting three hares from his mouth, is a reference to Tang Mu, who was forced to eat his boiled son: when he vomited, it was three hares that came out.

There are also stories of how Emperor Wen-Wang of the Zhou Dynasty spat out three hares one after the other. They consisted of the flesh of his own son which had been made into meatballs and set before him (homonymic similarity between

The hare in the moon

tu = hare and *tu* = to spit out, may play a part in these fancies).

The belief that there are no male hares may be connected with the fact that the 'female' partner in homosexual intercourse was known as the 'hare'. 'Hunting a hare' meant going to a brothel to look for a young man; 'hare-pup' is a very strong expletive. 'Female hare' (*yin-tu*) is an expression for the vulva.

There are many references to 'white hares'. In one novel, the god of the planet Venus (the white planet) lets himself be shot at in the form of a white hare, so as to help the hero to find his mother. A hare-lipped child results if the mother eats hare flesh during pregnancy. In Taiwan, the hare-lip is said to result if, during the last month of pregnancy, the mother has cut up material or fabric in the room where the 'god of birth' happens to be dwelling.

The well-known trick – still performed by conjurers in the West – whereby a hare jumps out of a cloth which the conjurer has folded up and laid on the ground, is mentioned in a medieval text.

A picture showing six boys round a table on which stands a man with a hare's head, is a reference to the lunar festivities held on the 15th day of the 8th month. It expresses the wish that the children of the recipient will rise in the social scale and enjoy a peaceful life.

Hat
guan

The Chinese words for 'hat' and 'official' are homonyms (*guan*): so, the hat is a symbol of the → official.

Sometimes a picture shows father and son in ceremonial dress: the father with his cap of state on his head, holding a → sceptre in his hand, and the son with a head-dress which indicates that he has come first in his final examinations (*zhuang-yuan*). The message expressed by such a picture is 'May your son accompany you to court' or, 'May father and son both grace the highest office in the imperial service.'

Embroidered handbag: above, a boy wearing a hat riding a dragon. 'May you be rewarded with an official post!'

Heart
xin

As in the West, the heart plays a dual role as seat of life and seat of the emotions and affects. A medieval hero caught in a conflict of loyalties is said to have torn his heart out: but he went on living, so he asked a woman who was selling 'heartless vegetables' if a man could live without a heart. She said 'No' whereupon he fell dead. The author of the novel in which this episode occurs, is at pains to stress that she should have said 'Yes!' 'Heart and liver' (*xin-gan*) is a term of endearment used by women to their lovers.

Hearth
zao

Every Chinese house has a hearth. The kitchen, however, is not supposed to be in the house but rather in a small adjoining building. The hearth and the kitchen are the province of the wife, the lady of the house; the man has nothing to do with them. Over the hearth or close beside it is a statue or a picture of the hearth-god. Ensconced in his niche, he watches what goes on in the house and reports accordingly, once a year, to the supreme god. This takes place at → New Year; and before he goes aloft to report, many women smear his mouth with honey, so that he will have nothing but 'sweet' things to say. Colour-printed fabrics show the hearth-god surrounded by children, as he is also the protector of the family.

It is absolutely taboo to have sexual intercourse in the kitchen, in front of the hearth-god. His face is blackened by the smoke of many fires. All Chinese gods (except Buddhist ones) were originally living beings on earth, and these kitchen gods are supposed to have been soldiers unjustly put to death long ago by imperial command.

Square carpet (earth) with a round black field in the centre (heaven)

Heaven
tian   天

The sky is regarded as male, and it is paired with the → earth. 'Heaven is invisible and generates, earth is visible and forms,' we are told in the chapter entitled 'Reflections on the Beginnings' in the *Lü-shi chun-qiu* ('Spring and Autumn Annals of Lü Bu-wei'), the first Chinese encyclopaedia. This definition ties up with one of the oldest creation myths, in which heaven and earth are thought of as a conjugal pair engaged in never-ending intercourse. As more and more children were born from this union, they ran out of room so they had to lift heaven further up, thus forming a space between their parents on which they could live. In other legends, heaven is represented as a personal god who controls human life. 'Luck comes from heaven' ran an inscription which often used to be seen over house gateways, and Chinese is full of proverbial sayings and wise saws about the good and bad luck heaven sends us according to our deserts.

The word *tian* is also used in the sense of 'fate, fortune, lot'. A mother who loses a child says 'Heaven' meaning that it is heaven that has taken her child away. One of the terms that Christian missionaries settled on in their search for an apt translation of the Christian 'God' was *tian-zhu* = Lord of Heaven.

Other deities also live in heaven, and later mythology has arranged these in various 'ministries' on an analogy with the → Emperor and his administrative hierarchy on earth. Some gods live on the earth where their duties lie; a few days before → New Year they pay an official visit to the 'Emperor Above' (*shang-di*) – e.g. the → hearth-god – to report on how people have been behaving throughout the year. In one of the best-known novels, a rain-god dares to depart from a commandment given him by the supreme god and is therefore severely punished. One can get some idea of the deep veneration in which heaven was held in early times from a passage in the work of Qu-yuan (4th century BC): heaven is father and mother of mankind: therefore whoever is in tribulation and sore distressed should call on heaven, just as anyone who is sick or sorrowful should cling to his parents.

'What is below heaven' (*tian-xia*) is a long-established term meaning (a) the Chinese Empire, and (b) the civilised world.

boys with shoulder-length hair; one of them often holds a → lotus (*he*) while the other has a bowl from which rises a cloud of steam. In this cloud we can see five → bats, or, on occasion, a → horse and other prized objects. The He-he are a symbol of concord and harmony between married couples, and, as is obvious from their emblems, gods of → riches.

He-he 和合

The He-he are Heavenly Twins: their name means 'togetherness' or 'harmony, concord'. They may have originated in the shape of the poets Han-shan (the poet of the Cold Mountain) and his friend Shi-de (the foundling): the former was a hermit in the Tian-dai range of mountains, the latter was a foster child of the prior of the Guo-qing monastery where he was in charge of the kitchens. They are often represented in art.

On a non-historical plane, the Heavenly Twins are portrayed as

The two He-he

Hell
di yu 地獄

Chinese hells are really purgatories, as a limit is set to the amount of time a sinner spends in them. The literal translation of *di yu* is 'earth-prison': the sinner is sentenced by an infernal

The tortures of the damned in the sixth hell: blasphemers are clamped between boards and sawn into strips

accommodate new cases. Thus, in the 19th century a special sub-hell was instituted for men and women who indulged in dancing: the men had to stand on a glowing-hot dance-floor and embrace a woman who turned into a skeleton.

Each hell has its own judge and a staff of ruffians who are strictly organised in a bureaucratic hierarchy. Conditions in these hells are described by people who have visited them in a state of trance. Graphic pictures of scenes in hell are to be found on temple walls (at least in Taiwan).

Legend has it that even living → officials can be summoned to hell, to assist in adjudicating difficult cases. On their return home, they have reported on conditions in hell, where, they say, it is always dark, with no distinction between night and day. According to other sources, however, night and day do alternate.

These notions of hell and infernal punishment came, it is most likely, from India along with Buddhism. The Indians imagine an equal number of 'hot' and 'cold' hells, but the Chinese have only one hell in which sinners suffer cold as a punishment. Recent research suggests that even before the arrival of Buddhism in China, the Chinese had some idea of an underworld (as of a → heaven) but nothing is known of what form punishment took in it.

The judge in the eighth hell (Temple wall-painting in the Dong-yue Temple in Tainan, Taiwan)

judge. Chinese hells are ten in number: the first is the court-room where sentence is passed, the last is the place where, after punishment, sinners are reborn as human beings or as animals, according to their merits. Each hell has 16 sub-hells, which are variously equipped to inflict different punishments. Some texts mention 18 sub-hells: but sinners are inventive, we are told, and hell has to go on growing to

Hen
ji

Like the → cock, the hen, or even the picture of a hen, can drive away evil → spirits: they are afraid of it. In North China and Korea, the hen was the object of a special cult. It was taboo in these regions to eat poultry, and both cocks and hens were reared not for their eggs and meat but for their long tails and for their ability to crow well.

The Lolo, a Tibeto-Burman minority people in South China, have a legend according to which there existed, at the beginning of the world, two hens, one white, the other black: each laid nine eggs, out of which came good people and bad.

Hen with five chickens, symbolising good relations between parents and children

In South China and in Vietnam, eggs were used in consultation of the → oracle; the bones of a hen could also be used for this purpose. The blood of black hens was held to be particularly efficacious against spirits. In popular parlance, 'hen' or 'wild hen' is a metaphor for 'prostitute'.

Herb of Immortality
zhi

The 'wonder-working herb', the so-called 'drug of immortality' (*zhi* or *ling-zhi*), is often mentioned in classical Chinese literature, and popular prints still show it held in the mouth of a → deer, or in the beak of a → crane: a reduplicated symbol of → longevity.

Ling-zhi is represented in all sorts of forms. In Chinese it is sometimes described as a kind of *cao* = grass, plant. One ancient text says that it grows throughout the year on an island in the Eastern Sea: it looks like water-grass with long leaves, oval and pointed, and whoever takes it will live for ever and ever. Other texts describe it as a sort of morel, and in many illustrations it looks just like a → mushroom with stalk and cap. *Zhi* may also stand for rapid growth, i.e. a meteoric public career; it may also symbolise fertility especially when shown collectively.

As a hallucinogen of greater symbolic and alchemistic significance, *zhi* is something quite different from the powdered preparations known variously as *han-shi* ('cold minerals') and *wu-shi* ('five minerals'), which came into use towards the end of the Later Han Dynasty. The former was taken deliberately as a stimulant; and of the man who discovered its potency it is written (by Huang-fu Mi, 215–82) that he immediately gave himself up to → music and → sex. In contrast to the 'herb of immortality', the 'five minerals' powder had no religious or cosmological connotation: its spread was due entirely to its potency.

Hero
ying-xiong 英雄

Ying-xiong is the modern Chinese term meaning roughly the same as the word 'hero' does in European languages. There is an older word – *xia* – which still occurs in the compound *wu-xia* = 'warlike hero'. The *wu-xia* is the knight-errant, the star of popular novels (and films made from them) which enjoy such a vogue in present-day China.

In many ways, the ancient *xia* may be compared with the hero of medieval epics and romances. He comes from a middle-class family and is often poor. His appearance is rarely described; what matters is his character. He takes instant decisions, without pausing to consider the repercussions. When called upon to do so, he will devote all his strength to protecting the weak and downtrodden. He helps friends and strangers alike, in the course of his fight against injustice. If his friends have suffered he avenges them, and is then capable of

excesses of cruelty. He often tries to improve his friends morally.

In contrast with many a hero in European literature, he must be able to control his sexual appetites. Typically, he is cool, even lacking in interest, towards his wife. One very popular story tells how a hero exposes himself to extreme danger over a long period to rescue a girl who then falls in love with him. He takes her home to her parents, who naturally assume that intimacy has taken place during the long time they have spent alone together, and ask him to marry their daughter. He turns the request down with cold dignity: his mission was to rescue the girl, nothing more. He departs and the girl kills herself. Twenty years later, when he has become Emperor, the hero remembers her – only to learn that she has long since been dead.

Female heroes – heroines – do occur, but they are rare. It may happen – as in one well-known novel – that the heroine was a nun before launching forth into worldly adventures; but the religious element plays no determining part in this.

Heron
lu

The heron in its favourite habitat of lakes and rivers crops up over and over again in the work of the great Tang nature poets. Thus in Wang Wei:

Over the wide marshlands a heron
spreads its yellow wings

Heron and lotus

He Xian-gu with the magic lotus flower

And orioles are singing in the full summer trees.

Lu = heron is a homonym of *lu* = way, path. So, a picture showing a heron together with a lotus means 'May your path (*lu*) be always (*lian*, which is a homonym of *lian* = lotus) upward.'

rescued by Lü Dong-bin, another of the eight Immortals, who brought her into the group. The legend runs as follows: 'She had sworn never to marry, and her stepmother didn't know what to do with her. One day when she was cooking rice, grandfather Lü came and released her. As she rose up into the air, she was still holding the ladle in her hand' (Richard Wilhelm, from a verbal account).

He Xian-gu

何 仙 姑

He Xian-gu is one of the eight → Immortals, and the only woman among them. She is symbolised by the → lotus, and sometimes by the → peach. She is supposed to have been attacked by a demon and

Hibiscus
fu-rong   芙 蓉

This plant, popular also in the West, symbolises fame (*rong*) and riches (*fu*); or, by extension, fame and splendour. The scent of the hibiscus is compared with the attractive power of a → girl. As a poem puts it: 'When rain falls on the hibiscus, it opens in the fifth watch of the night (i.e. shortly before dawn).' This means that, if things go well, a lover will be joined with his beloved. The sentiment is spelled out more clearly in a poem which tells how the lover picks hibiscus blooms in a garden.

The term 'water hibiscus' refers to a young girl in her bath. A brothel can be described as a 'hibiscus curtain'. An unusually attractive woman is a 'hibiscus face'. Indeed, the comparison of the hibiscus with a beautiful young woman is a very obvious one.

Honey
mi   蜜

It was mainly in South China that the honey of wild → bees was collected. It was supposed to be lucky to dream of eating honey.

The word *mi* also means 'sweet', and the pleasures of sexual intercourse are described as *mi*.

Horse
ma   馬

The horse is the seventh creature in the Chinese → zodiac. In Old Chinese, there were many words denoting different sizes and colours of horse. The fact that these words have all died out is a pointer to the declining role of the horse in recent history.

Horses have always fetched a good price in China. The strongest came from Mongolia; smaller but very

sturdy and dependable horses came from Tibet. Of course, some of the best horses were imported from Western Asia, e.g. Arab horses which, it was said, 'sweated blood'. There was an ancient cult of an 'ancestral horse', a deity of some kind to whom sacrifices were made. In the *Yi-jing* the → dragon (male) and the horse (female) are the two creatures chosen to represent the two sexes; but in later mythology, the horse symbolises the → *yang* (male principle) while the female principle (→ *yin*) is symbolised by the cow.

A string of eight horses represents the famous horses of King Mu, who is supposed to have lived in the 10th century BC. In the great Ming novel 'Journey to the West' (*Xi-you ji*) we find the expression *yi-ma* = 'horse of the will', as a metaphor for wilfulness and inconstancy. A galloping steed is probably a reference to the mount of General Guan Yu (later → Guan-di), which was called 'Red-hare-horse'. The white horse which often appears in Buddhist texts stands for purity and loyalty.

A picture showing a man and a horse laden with precious things expresses a wish for an official post

A warrior draws an arrow from the breast of his lord's wounded horse

with the comfortable living that goes with it. A → monkey (*hou*) riding on a horse expresses the wish that the recipient of the picture may be rewarded with noble rank (*hou*) straight away (*ma shang* = literally, 'on horseback').

In modern Taiwan, 'horse' is a vulgar expression for 'girl-friend' – but the use of 'horse' as a coarse way of referring to a girl is very ancient. As far back as the 16th century we hear about a market in the town of Yang-zhou where 'skinny horses' (*ou-ma*) were sold. More than a hundred prostitutes were on offer, and clients could bargain with the girls directly without having to make use of a go-between.

The expression 'getting off the horse' refers to a shaman who is calling on the gods to visit him. In the language of prostitutes, 'riding the horse' means menstruating; and a 'horse-bucket' (*ma-tung*) is a toilet bucket, a symbol for babies in → marriage ritual. 'Horse-eye' is a metaphor for the orifice of the penis, and 'the horse shakes its hoof' is one of the 30 positions in sexual intercourse.

I

Ice
bing 冰

A picture showing a child sitting on ice on a winter's day is a reference to Wang Xiang, one of the 24 exemplars of filial piety (→ *xiao*). When his mother, who was ill, said she wanted to eat some carp in the winter, the boy went to the frozen river and sat on it long enough to thaw through the ice: immediately a big carp sprang out.

'Cracked ice' is an expression for marital pleasures in old age. An 'iceman' (*bing-ren*) is a marriage broker – usually a woman. The semantics of this are noteworthy: a man once dreamt that he saw someone standing on ice speaking to someone else under the ice. The dream was interpreted as follows: 'On the ice stands the male element (*yang*), under the ice is the female element (*yin*). You must mediate between them.' That is to say, man and woman are divided by ice, and this division can be set aside only by the 'icebreaker', the marriage broker, not by the couple themselves.

Immortals
xian 仙

Chinese 'saints' are men and women who have in their lifetime achieved or developed supernatural powers, and who have been elevated, after death, to the status of gods. There are hundreds and hundreds of them, and they are supposed to lead happy care-free lives for ever and ever in the Kunlun Mountains or on the → 'Islands of the Blessed' in the Eastern Sea. On earth, they are mainly revered as *genii loci*, i.e. their cult is linked to specific places. It is important to remember that the word *xian* can be applied to living people who have shown extraordinary talent and skill in some field. A man may be a *xian* because of his

The Feast of the Immortals

prowess as a poet, as a swordsman or even as a drinker; and *xian* often figures as part of the professional name of a prostitute.

The eight Immortals (*ba-xian*) form a special group of 'saints'. They are often depicted all together as a group, though sometimes we see them in groups of three. Membership of this select group has varied over the centuries; at present, the following belong to it: Zhang Guo-lao, Zhong-li Quan, Han Xiang-zi, He Xian-gu, Lan Cai-he, Li Tie-guai, Lü Dong-bin and Cao Guo-jiu. (See separate entries.)

In village temples the altar is covered with a length of fabric on which the Immortals are shown as a group. In pictures they often appear in their role of well-wishers; or they are shown crossing the sea to the feast given by the Queen Mother of the West (→ Xi-wang-mu), the feast of the gods and of → longevity. Then again they are shown standing on a terrace or in a small pavilion, greeting the god of longevity who is flying past on a → crane.

According to the texts, they can also come back to earth where they meet, for example, a poor man at a bridge, who holds out his hand for alms. One of the Immortals scrapes a little of the dirt off his skin, fashions it into a pill and offers it to the beggar – who refuses it in disgust! In another version of this tale, the beggar has the wit to try the pill first on dead fish: when they come to life, he too swallows the pill and becomes an Immortal.

The Taoist group of the eight Immortals is sometimes combined with the more Buddhist grouping of the eighteen → Luo-han.

Incense
xiang

The word *xiang* simply means 'fragrance'. The sandalwood which is the main source of incense comes from South-east Asia. In ancient China, incense was burned in special incense bowls. Nowadays incense sticks are used almost invariably, and these are placed in an altar vessel before the image of the god to whom the offering is being made. Often the ashes are gathered up and taken as a kind of medicine. Incense is mentioned in the very earliest Chinese texts on Buddhism; today it is used in all temples, and also in the small shrines which many of the faithful maintain in their own homes.

'Mosquito incense' (*wen-zi-xiang*) is usually green and takes the form of little coils which smoulder under the bed all night and keep the insects away.

Insignia, Imperial

Some authorities attribute → nine insignia to the Emperor, others credit him with → twelve. The list of nine runs as follows: → dragon, → mountains, → pheasant, pond-weed, grains of rice, the *Fu* pattern (symbolising right and wrong), the → axe, flames, sacrificial bowl. The addition of the Sun-raven, the Lunar Hare and of a constellation in the shape of a right angle gives a list of twelve, which then corresponds to the twelve months of the lunar year.

The series of twelve insignia is as follows: the → sun (red), the → moon (white), the Seven-star → Constellation (often shown as a triangle), → mountains, → dragon, → pheasant, the *Fu* pattern, the axe, two sacrificial vessels with representations of → monkeys and → tigers, water-plants (representing wood), → fire, → millet. In this chain, the 5th and 6th members are animals; the 7th symbolises the Emperor's power over life and death, and members 8 to 12 symbolise the five → elements.

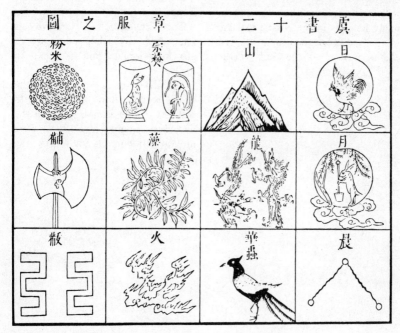

The twelve insignia

Iron
tie 鐵

We know that iron was being used in China as early as in the second millennium BC. However, it was not until about 400 BC that it came into general use for making plough-shares and weapons.

It symbolises strength and righteousness. The evil sea-dragons (*jiao*) fear iron, and for this reason iron figures were sunk in rivers and dams. In South China there is a so-called 'iron-tree' which blossoms only once in 60 years. Thus it stands for the cycle of → sixty, and symbolises long life, since this cycle represents the average life-span of a man.

'Iron shoes', well-known items in many legends in the Near East, are mentioned in the classical novel 'The Metamorphoses of the Gods' (*Feng-shen yan-yi*) (ch. 54).

Islands
dao

The Chinese 'Islands of the Blessed', the Chinese paradise, where the → Immortals dwell in eternal happiness, are usually portrayed as rocky islands off the South-east Coast. Legend has it that these are three islands off the East Coast of China, named → Fang-zhang, Peng-lai and Ying-zhou. Some scholars have tried to identify these as the Peng-hu Islands, which lie near Taiwan. There is, however, some evidence to suggest that the islands once lay immediately off-shore between Qingdao and Shanghai, and that they became subsequently joined to the coast as part of the province of Jiangsu.

The emblem of → longevity is intensified by the addition of growing → pines and → cranes in flight.

In earlier times, shrouds for the dead were often adorned with pictures of 'the islands', so that the deceased might feel they were already enjoying eternal felicity.

J

Jade
yu　　　　　玉

Jade, which occurs in several shades ranging from white to dark green, has always been the favourite gemstone in China. Not everything described as 'jade' is in fact jade; for example, nephrite is also called *yu*. In ancient times, jade was found in the border areas between the provinces of Henan and Shanxi; later, the best jade was held to be that found in Khotan (in Xinjiang) and in Burma.

It was an ancient custom to place a piece of jade in the mouth of a dead person in the belief that this prevented decomposition. It was used very widely for decorating belts; statues of considerable size were also made from jade. On their 70th birthday men were given a short rod of jade.

Genuine jade is always cool to the touch; for this reason the skin of a → beautiful woman is compared to it. It symbolises purity. 'Playing with jade' (*nong yu*) is a metaphor for sexual intercourse: 'handling jade' (*pin yu*) means cunnilingus. 'Jade-sap' (*yu-jiang*) is a woman's saliva, 'jade-fluid' is semen or vaginal secretions, the 'jade gate' or 'jade wall' is the vulva, the 'jade stem' is the penis. A young girl has a 'jade bearing' and 'jade legs', and her breasts are as firm as 'warm jade'. All of these are still in current use: they are always complimentary and usually have a sexual connotation.

The word *yao* refers to a type of jade which cannot be positively identified. A favourite motif in art is the 'jade pond' (*yao chi*) in the palace of → Xi-wang-mu, to whose feast (held on the day when the thousand-year → peaches ripen) the → Immortals come bringing their gifts. This is an auspicious event, and pictures representing it express the wish that the recipient may enjoy a long life and every happiness. It is therefore a very suitable gift for older men.

The 'Jade Emperor' (Yu-huang-di) is the supreme god in Chinese popular religion.

The Jade Emperor, or Great Ruler of Heaven, with his court in session

Jupiter
mu-xing   木星

Jupiter, the planet of the → East, goes round the sun in about → twelve years. So it is often called in Chinese *tai-sui* = Great Year, in contrast to the earthly year, which consists of only twelve months. There was in ancient times a belief that 'Great Year' could fall to earth in the shape of a large lump of flesh set all around with eyes. It had to be beaten to death or drowned, as otherwise all life in the neighbourhood would cease to exist.

In association with the 'Jupiter Year' (the planet is sometimes known as the 'Planet of the Year', *sui-xing*) there is also a Jupiter cycle of twelve symbols. These are notated by a series of two-character expressions whose exact meaning is no longer clear. The cycle was used sometimes in dynastic computation, and appears on ancient inscriptions. It is now virtually unknown.

K

King
wang 王

In the Zhou Dynasty, *wang* was the title of the supreme ruler; later it was adopted by the rulers of feudal states, and still later extended to princes in general. Nowadays, 'Great King' is an expression meaning 'tailor', and indeed, in general, the term can be used of anyone using a specialised skill. 'King Eight' is a strong expletive, comparable to 'cuckold'. There is a not very convincing explanation for this, to the effect that the character *wang* should be written as *wang* = to forget: then the expression would refer to a person who has 'forgotten' the eighth (virtue) – feeling of shame. Among the Hakka, a non-Han minority in South China, 'King' is a metaphor for → 'fish'.

Kingfisher
fei-cui 翡翠

The kingfisher looks like a → swallow, we are told in ancient texts, and is mainly found in South China and Vietnam. Because of its malachite-hued plumage it was highly prized, and came indeed to symbolise → beauty. The → eyebrows of a beautiful woman are described as 'kingfisher-eyebrows'. One of the 30 positions used in the Chinese art of love-making is known as the 'kingfisher-contact'. In general, the bird symbolises sexual enjoyment and conjugal happiness.

Kiss
qin-zui 親嘴

Among the Chinese and Japanese, kissing is not such a common practice as it is in the West. It is indeed mentioned in early texts, but always as *pars pro toto*, i.e. as symbolising sexual intercourse. It is in this sense too that it is understood throughout China: e.g. in the wedding ceremonies of the Tanka, held on the night of the full moon (→ toad). Kissing in public – in the West, a casual matter of no particular significance – was until very recently strictly taboo in China. Students caught in the act could even be sent down from the university.

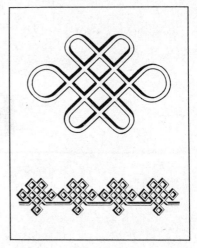

Knot, The Endless
pan-zhang 盤 長

The endless knot and 'lucky knot' ornament

The endless knot swallows its own tail, one might say: *pan-zhang* means 'long coil' or 'long twist'. It is one of the → eight Buddhist symbols and symbolises long life uninterrupted by setbacks. It is also called a 'lucky knot'.

In Hinduism, it is believed to be the mark on the breast of Vishnu.

Another tradition has it that the endless knot is a stylisation of the entrails of a defeated enemy. The phonetic similarity between *zhang* and *zang* = entrails no doubt plays a part here.

The endless knot is much used in China as an ornamental symbol and is worked into a literally endless variety of designs.

L

Lan Cai-he 藍 采 和

Lan Cai-he is one of the eight → Immortals: sometimes regarded as female, at other times as a hermaphrodite. His emblem is a basket of fruit or flowers, or, less frequently, a → flute or a bowl.

According to the *Tai-ping guang ji* (978), a collection of tales of the weird and wonderful, of gods and strange people, Lan Cai-he wore a ragged blue gown. He was often to be seen in market-places, sometimes wearing only one shoe. He is the patron saint of minstrels.

According to another tradition, Lan was a female singer, whose songs foretold the future.

Lan Cai-he with a basket of flowers

Landscape
shan-shui 山 水

Literally translated, the Chinese words for 'landscape' mean 'mountains and water'. Nothing could be more appropriate: in fact, the great majority of Chinese landscape pictures show exactly that – mountains and water.

However: 'It is not a mountain in itself and by itself that is understood here and represented. Rather, it is the mountain with everything around it, woods and waters, clouds and mists, and a thousand other details drawn together in one indissoluble unity. "Mountains without clouds are bald, and without water where is their charm?" (Guo Xi). And so the mountain is joined by the second of the primeval elements – water' (Otto Fischer, *Chinesische Landschaftsmalerei*).

The flat Chinese plain is hardly ever depicted: the plain was regarded as an object of more interest to the farmer than to the landscape painter. Here and there the mountains may indeed level out into flat areas, but these are not fields but 'gardens' and what grows in them is not corn or → rice, the staple foods, but fruit and flowers.

Human beings are often shown in Chinese landscapes. They are confined to the lower third of the picture and they are very small.

Here, nature seems to be tamed by the hand of the artist. We know that, like our ancestors in Europe, the ancient Chinese feared nature in the raw, the uncultivated → wilderness, and tried to avoid it as far as possible. Forests and wild mountains are the chosen haunt of meditating saints and bands of robbers. The Chinese were fond of laying out miniature landscapes in the grounds of their own houses, and these were often very charming. Every item in such a miniature landscape is very carefully chosen: stones representing the 'Mountain of → Longevity', and water representing the sea of happiness, are indispensable. These gardens form an earthly symbol of the Land of the Blessed.

The 'holy place of supreme joy' is a term for the vagina, a 'landscape' to be explored. Here, 'supreme joy' is a reference to paradise, which the devout Buddhist also hopes to reach.

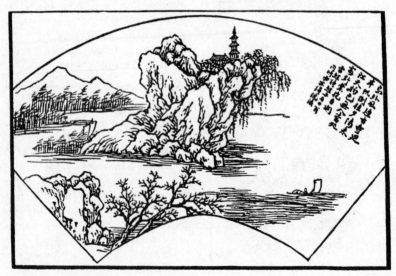

Mountains and water

Lantern
deng

Lanterns and lamps made from various materials are known to us from very early periods in Chinese culture. They occur in all sorts of shapes – cylindrical, cubic, spherical, etc. In one Vietnamese grave excavation a lamp in the shape of a kneeling man was found, and another shaped like a tree. Both were estimated to be around two thousand years old.

Nowadays, lamps are symbols of fertility. In the province of Yunnan, a lamp was placed under the bridal bed: this lamp was called the 'Children and Grandchildren Lamp'. Other lamps, called the 'All night long lamps', were placed beside the bed, one for the bridegroom and one for the bride. If these lamps went out at the same time, it was an auspicious sign for a long married life. In other areas, a lantern was hung under the bed of a pregnant woman. In Buddhism, light stands for illumination and knowledge.

Lanterns are signposts for guests and also for the → souls of the departed. They played a particularly big part in the so-called 'Feast of Lanterns' – the 15th day of the first Chinese month. This was at the same time the end of the New Year festivities, and the souls of the ancestors who had come to the celebrations had to be guided back to the world beyond: so lanterns made of paper and woven materials were hung up everywhere.

On the 7th day of the 7th month a second Feast of Lanterns was held in many regions, e.g. in Yunnan. Lotus-shaped lanterns were hung by the roadside, and little lamps were sent swimming along the rivers. The motivation here lay in the belief that

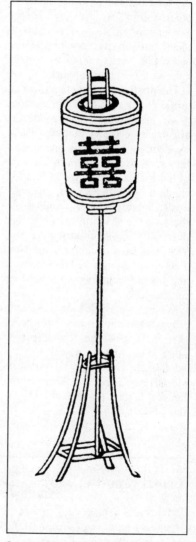

Lantern for a wedding feast

during the first 15 days of the 7th month the souls of people who had no relations, or who had died far from their families in remote places, could come back to earth. They were very hungry, having no relations to sacrifice to them; so they were on the look-out for offerings made to other spirits. Accordingly, special 'community' offerings were made to them, and on the day of the full moon they were guided by lantern light back to the underworld.

The first Feast of Lanterns was an occasion *par excellence* for families to vie with each other in producing artistically decorated lanterns. These were often so cleverly made that they spun round, driven by the heat of the wick, in the shape of dancing children or little horses. Scholars made 'lantern poems' and wrote them on the shade in the hope that passers-by would understand them. With this feast of lanterns the New Year festivities reached their climax, and thereafter life would resume its normal tenor.

Women were said to like walking along under lanterns, in the belief that they would be fertile (correlating *deng* = lantern with *ding* = adult male liable for military service). *Dian deng* = 'lighting the lantern' is then phonetically suggestive of *dian ding* = 'add a → son (to those one already has)'.

Lao-zi (Lao-tse) 老 子

Later tradition places the birth of the legendary founder of Taoism in 604 BC. This is generally discounted

today; indeed, many scholars doubt whether the book known as the *Dao de jing* ('The Book of the Dao and its Effectiveness') was written by Lao-zi at all. We do not know his real name; it was a later tradition that gave him the name Li Dan. 'Lao-zi' means nothing more than 'Old Master'. In the Middle Ages, the legend grew in China that towards

Lao-zi on his water buffalo

the end of his life he had left China and ridden westwards. From this, it was but a step to deducing that he had reached India where he was reborn as → Buddha: a typical piece of anti-Buddhist propaganda which was angrily denounced by the Buddhists.

Recent research has shown that the book he is supposed to have written, the *Dao de jing*, was certainly in existence as early as the 2nd century BC; and the text as reconstructed for that date is virtually identical with the text now extant. Nevertheless, we are still in no position to say exactly what these 81 short passages mean; they are written in a lapidary and elliptical manner, and the many 'translations' into Western languages must be regarded as no more than attempts to read into this arcane text whatever a given translator would like to find there. It has been suggested that the book is a kind of lecturer's note-book, containing key-words which the teacher would then amplify in class.

Anthropomorphic deities are

Lao-zi entrusting the Dao de Jing *to the border guard*

notably absent from the *Dao de jing*. The Dao begets the → One, whence arise the → Two: the Two generate the → Three, from which all things develop. (See Section 42.) Synchronically, the Dao orders and governs the world: diachronically, it makes the world develop the way it does. The Dao is like water; secret and deep it flows downward, offering no resistance and meeting no resistance.

For some two thousand years the ethos of the 'sage' has exercised a profound influence, on China, and later also on the West. 'Truthful words are not beautiful; beautiful words are not truthful . . . The sage does not hoard. Having bestowed all he has on others, he has yet more; having given all he has to others, he is richer still' (Section 81; tr. D. C. Lau).

In Chinese legend, Lao-zi is mistakenly associated with Huang-lao, 'The Old Yellow One', who is supposed to have been one of the five creators of the world. One of Lao-zi's avatars is particularly well-known: according to this tradition, his mother carried him for → 72 years in her womb, and then gave birth to him from her left armpit. He was born with white hair, and already an adept in many magic arts, by means of which he was able to prolong his life. He is supposed to have ridden to the West on a → water buffalo (or an → ox); when he came to the Han-gu Pass he instructed the border guard in the art of longevity and left with him a compendium of his teachings in five thousand words. The guard copied this out and then he himself became an → Immortal.

In art, Lao-zi is depicted as a bearded old man, epitomising → longevity. True to the legend, he is often seen riding on his water buffalo.

His Taoist 'followers' were priests and hermits who spent their lives in the study of the Dao, from which, according to popular belief, they derived supernatural powers. By means of → Immortality drugs they could prolong their lives, they rode on winds and clouds, and could be in more than one place at the same time. All of which had of course very little to do with Lao-zi and his teaching.

Left and Right
zuo-you 左 右

Like the distinction between → *yin* and → *yang*, the difference between left and right is relative rather than absolute. Like Western Europeans, the Chinese are mainly right-handed, but the left is not regarded as something 'sinister', as it often is in the West. This is bound up with Chinese cosmology and its system of directions. Traditionally, the → Emperor, as ruler of mankind, had his face turned towards the South when he received ambassadors and homage. The East where the sun rises, was then on his *left*, and the West where the sun sets, on his right. The left is the place of princes hence it is the more honoured side, as the East is the more auspicious direction. Among the minority peoples it is believed that the ruler's eye is turned towards the East to greet the

rising sun. This makes the South (on the right) the region of greater power, and the North (on the left) the region of weaker forces. → Geomancy plays a part here, and in the end it is often very difficult to arrive at any precise definition of 'left' and 'right'. Various pronouncements were made on the subject in the course of Chinese history. Thus, in ancient times, the Emperor's right-hand minister was superior in rank to the left-hand one; but from the 3rd century BC onwards, all → officials on the left-hand side were higher in rank than those on the right.

At home (→ hall) the householder sits on the eastern side, i.e. on the left, his wife on the western side (the right hand). At night, however, she takes the left-hand side of the bed and the husband the right: relative to sunrise she is still in the West, as her mat is immediately adjacent to the wall facing the rising sun. In the street, which is a *yin* object, i.e. it is subsumed by the female principle, the man walks on the right, the woman on the left. Group paintings of gods and goddesses have the former on the right-hand side of the picture, the latter on the left. In Tibetan art, it is exactly the other way round. Chinese Muslims regard the left hand as the unclean one.

Boys used to be taught to hide the right hand under the left (which corresponds to *yang*) when greeting someone, while girls were correspondingly instructed to conceal the left hand under the right. When shaking hands on a deal or making a formal gesture of agreement or friendship, the Chinese always offer the right hand. Little is known about left-handedness in China, but left-handed people seem to be regarded as deviants.

Lichee
li-zhi

The lichee is a South Chinese fruit with white flesh and a brown, rather large kernel. It is tinned and exported as a dessert fruit to Europe and America. In North China, dried longans and lichees are laid under the marriage bed in the hope that the union will be blessed with children. Water-chestnuts and lichees together express the idea of 'cunning' or 'smart' (*ling-li*).

Fruit in a bowl: lichees, lotus roots and water-nuts

Lily
bai-he

The day-lily (*Hemerocallis*) is supposed to be the plant that helps you to forget your troubles. It is also known as the 'Bringer of Sons', and is therefore often given to a young

The day-lily

woman on the occasion of her → marriage, or on her birthday.

There is a connection between this lily and the ancient custom of foot-binding. According to the legend, the last Emperor of the Qi Dynasty was so roused to ecstasy one day by the beauty of one of his concubines that he cried, 'Wherever she steps, a lily springs up.' Hence the appellation of 'Golden Lily' for artificially shrunken feet. The custom of foot-binding did not in fact become widespread until late in the Tang Dynasty (618–906).

Irises (*bai-he*; family *Iridaceae*) are effective in repelling evil → spirits, especially on the 5th day of the 5th month, when irises were hung up over doors. Eating irises is a way of prolonging your life.

Lion
shi-zi

獅子

The Chinese word for 'lion' is derived from Persian (šīr), and it was through embassies from Western Asia that the Chinese became acquainted with the animal. Among the gifts brought by ambassadors were lions which were kept in imperial zoos. Later, in Tang times (618–906), when Chinese armies penetrated deep into Central Asia, the Chinese may well have seen the animal in the wild for themselves.

The 'lion' which we see depicted in Chinese paintings and in sculpture bears very little resemblance to the real animal, which, however, plays a big part in Chinese folklore. In Song literature it is called the 'King of Beasts' (as it is in the West); a 17th-century novel describes it as a 'divine creature'. It is also the animal on which Mañjuśri (Wen-shu), the Boddhisattva of Wisdom, rides.

Lion with ball (stone rubbing)

Pairs of stone lions rival → dragons in popularity as guardians of official buildings and temples. The right lion is male, the left one female. Under the left paw of the male lion is an ornamental ball; under the right paw of the female is a cub. The number of bumps on the lions' heads depends on the rank of the official whose building they are guarding. The left lion could symbolise the office of *Tai Shi*

A lion and cub

(Grand Master), one of the highest in the Imperial State; the right hand lion symbolised the *Shao Bao*, the Junior Guardian of the Heir Apparent. Lion-guardians of this kind are known from the 3rd century AD onwards. According to one tradition, the lion cub is contained in the embroidered ball, as in an egg; but others say that this is not really a ball but a huge pearl which the lion is playing with in order to calm his nerves. The expression 'the lion throws the embroidered ball' is a metaphor for sexual intercourse.

One of the best-known dances is the 'Lion-dance' which is usually connected with the Feast of → Lanterns, held on the 15th day of the 1st lunar month. The dance seems to have reached China from Western Asia in the Tang Dynasty. At that time, acrobats wore wooden lion-masks and had tails made of threads. The eyes were gold, the teeth silver. The dance was accompanied by music. Nowadays, only one lion appears: as it dances along the street it threatens shops and stalls along the way, and can only be pacified by showering it with coins. 'Roaring of lions in He-dong' is an expression for a hen-pecked husband (He-dong is a place-name).

Pictures showing men riding on lions are almost invariably scenes from the classical novel *Feng-shen yan-yi* ('The Metamorphoses of the Gods').

Li Tie-guai 李 鐵 拐

'Li with the iron crutch' is one of the eight → Immortals. Once when he was asleep he let his → spirit go off wandering by itself, and when his disciples found him they thought he was dead and burned the body. When his spirit returned there was no body for it to enter: so Li looked around for a suitable body and chose that of a sick beggar. And that is how he came by his lame leg.

Another version of the story runs as follows. His sister-in-law wanted to see for herself whether Li had really acquired any magic powers during his stay in the mountains. He told her to say nothing about what she was going to see, then stretched a leg out under the hearth and lit a fire to cook rice. His sister-in-law, unable to hold her tongue, asked

Li Tie-guai with his bottle-gourd and bat

him about his leg – and ever since he has been lame.

Li's symbol is the calabash or the → bottle-gourd, from which a → bat is seen escaping. It was said that no less a divinity than → Xi-wang-mu herself had cured a boil on his leg and had initiated him into the art of acquiring immortality.

give them a coin and ten eggs. They proceeded to stand the eggs one upon the other on the coin, and when Liu Hai said that this was rather a risky thing to do, they answered that it was no riskier than the way he was earning his living in the service of princes. His eyes were opened, and he became a Taoist. Liu Hai is always regarded as a benevolent deity.

Liu Hai 劉 海

This god is usually depicted as a young man, standing on a three-legged → toad and swinging a string of coins (→ money) round him. There are all sorts of legends about him. Some say he was in the service of the Jin Dynasty, and became a minister at the age of fifty. Then he met two holy men who asked him to

Liu-lang 劉 郎

'He's a young Liu' they say of a young man who is keen to have his first encounter with the opposite sex. The reference is to an old story in which a man loses his way in the mountains and arrives at a magic → peach-blossom spring.

Liu Hai with his string of coins

Liver
gan 肝

The liver, so it was taught in ancient times, is one of the → five viscera (*zang*) which are correlated with the seven bodily orifices: 'The → eyes permit of weeping and they afford a clear view: as orifices they correspond to the liver, which is itself connected with → green as its symbolic colour' (Marcel Granet).

The liver was also held to be the seat of courage. This belief was so strong that men were known to try

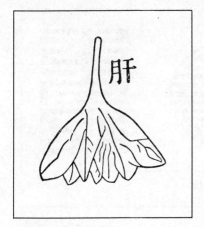

Representation of a liver

to eat the liver of an executed criminal in order to ingest something of his courage.

'Heart and liver' is a pet-name for one's sweetheart.

The god of longevity with attendant and the peach symbolising long life

Longevity, God of
Shou-xing

壽 星

The god of longevity appears on many greeting-cards as a fairly tall slim man with a long white beard, and an elongated skull, usually bald. In one hand he holds a → peach, the emblem of life, and in the other a stick of hard knotty wood. He is often accompanied by a boy-servant. Legend has it that he lives in a palace at the South Pole, surrounded by a large garden full of aromatic herbs, including the herb of → immortality. In this form he is frequently known as *nan-ji shou-xing* = the Immortal of the Southern Pole.

Shou-xing is a stellar god. His opposite counterpart is the Immortal of the North Pole, who is also known as the 'God of the Northern Dipper'. In Chinese cosmological symbolism the South is the region of life: the North is the region of death. Hence the saying that when 'the Old Man of the Southern Dipper' appeared, peace reigned in the Middle Kingdom. Sacrifice was offered to him to ensure a long life with health and happiness.

It is not by chance that the god of long life is represented as → bald in Chinese and Japanese art: his elongated skull resembles the penis, which is of course another symbol of life. Suitable attributes complete the picture of the 'old man': the → peach which he or his attendant holds, the → deer on which he rides, the →

Three ways of writing the character for 'longevity'

crane which bears him through auspicious → clouds.

Another symbol of longevity is → Peng-zu, the Chinese Methuselah.

In Taiwan, they call spinach the 'vegetable of long life', and eat it at → New Year festivities. The leaves are eaten before the stem. (See also Noodles.)

Loquat
pi-pa   枇杷

The loquat is the small yellow fruit of a tree which is also much used as a decorative shrub in America, though the fruit is rarely eaten. The fruit is called *pi-pa* as its shape resembles that of a Chinese musical instrument of the → mandoline family, which is also called *pi-pa*. It ripens early in spring, so counts as a lucky symbol.

'Loquat gateways and alleys' are brothels. Young → scholars were said to be 'running under the loquat blossom' when they visited celebrated prostitutes.

Lotus
lian-hua; he   蓮花

The lotus or sea-rose is of almost unique importance in Chinese folklore and symbolism, thanks largely, it would seem, to Buddhist influence: the lotus comes out of the mire but is not itself sullied; it is inwardly empty, outwardly upright; it has no branches but it smells sweet; it is the symbol of purity, and one of the → eight Buddhist precious things.

There are two Chinese words meaning 'lotus': *lian* and *he*. The former is phonetically identical with *lian* = to bind, connect (i.e. in marriage) and also = one after the other, uninterrupted; with *lian* = to love; and with *lian* = modesty. So the symbolic field covered by the lotus is limitless. For example: a boy holding a lotus in one hand and a → mouth organ (*sheng*) in the other: this means 'uninterrupted social advancement (*sheng*)'. A lotus bloom with a leaf and a bud indicates 'complete union'. A → magpie (*xi*) sitting on the stamens of a blown

A lotus in bloom

lotus, and picking seeds (*guo*) means 'May you have the joy (*xi*) of passing one exam (*guo*) after another (*lian*).' A boy with a carp (*yu*) beside a lotus (*lian*) means 'May you have abundance (*yu*) year in and year out (*lian*).' And so on and so forth. In Buddhism, the fruit, the flower and the stalk of the lotus symbolise past, present and future. The Buddha's foreskin (*bao pi*) is supposed to have been like a lotus flower. In one Chinese Buddhist text, it is said of the daughter of a holy man: 'Wherever she stepped, lotus flowers sprang up'; and about AD 500 a South Chinese Emperor staged the same sort of thing by having lotus flowers spread out so that his favourite wife could dance on them.

Another version of this tale makes the dancing floor out to have been a carpet with a lotus design. According to tradition, it was to enable them to dance neatly on the small blossoms that Chinese women had their feet bound. Men were supposed to find bound feet sexually stimulating. The custom is attested from about AD 900 onwards, and was not abolished until the end of the 19th century. Nowadays one may still find a few old women in villages with bound feet. The poetic name for the mutilation was 'the bent lotus'.

He in Chinese also means 'concord', 'unison', so a picture of two lotus blooms (or a leaf and a blossom) on one stem expresses the wish for 'heart and harmony shared'. The lotus seed-box with its many seeds symbolises fertility.

Love is symbolised by juxtaposing a lotus (representing the girl) and a → fish (symbolising the young man). The red lotus blossom symbolises the female genitalia, the lotus stem the male.

In Tibetan Tantrism, the thunderbolt (*vajra*) becomes a male symbol when it is associated with a lotus. Courtesans were often called 'red lotus'. When a man says that he has had the luck 'to come upon a lotus blossom with a double style' he means that he has met up with an old flame.

A blue lotus blossom (*qing*) stands for cleanliness (*qing*) and modesty. The lotus is also a symbol of the Immortal → He Xian-gu; and a picture of a man in a boat surrounded by lotus blossoms is a representation of the writer and philosopher Zhou Dun-yi (1017–73), who was particularly fond of the flower.

The presence of the word for 'lotus' in a man's name indicates that the bearer of the name is a Buddhist or is in some way connected with Buddhism; in women's names, it expresses the wish that the woman will be pure and respected.

A he-bao, a 'lotus package', is a silk purse which has the property of warding off spirits; a 'little purse', however, is a metaphor for the vagina. Purse and goldfish together symbolise the wish 'May you have gold (the goldfish) in abundance (yu = (a) fish, (b) abundance) in a purse.'

It was said in Peking that the lotus bloomed on the 8th day of the 4th month, i.e. on the birthday of the → Buddha. The 8th day of the 1st month is the 'day of the lotus'. If a woman sews on this day, she will have → menstruation trouble.

Lü Dong-bin

呂 洞 賓

Lü is one of the eight → Immortals: his symbol is the → sword with which he slays demons. He takes pride of place among the eight, and a wealth of legend has gathered round him. He is said to have lived in the Tang period: but other tales place him as late as the Song Dynasty. Two popular romances tell how he had to prove his power in ten ordeals. The best-known of these relates how one day he was drinking in a wine-shop and showed no signs of paying. Finally, instead of paying, he painted two dancing → cranes on the wall of the inn. These became so famous that mine host attracted far more customers and cashed in. When the debt was paid, however, the cranes detached themselves from the wall and flew away.

A similar story tells how he turned an ordinary well into one that produced wine for a certain time. On another occasion while the innkeeper is warming the wine, Lü causes the friend he is drinking with to live through his entire life in a dream ('The Yellow Millet Dream').

He flirts with → He Xian-gu, who thereupon becomes one of the Immortals. He is seduced by the whore 'Divine White Peony', that is

Lotus with magic bowl and the herb of immortality: 'Concord as your heart desires'

Lü Dong-bin with the sword

to say, he 'overcomes' her in a long love contest. In one of the clashes between the Song Emperor and the foreign Liao Dynasty which ruled over certain regions in North China, Lü took the part of the Liao, while → Li Tie-guai, another of the eight Immortals, was on the side of the Chinese. Finally, Lü is regarded as the patron saint of barbers.

Lunar Stations
su

The word *su* really means 'to lodge for the night' (corresponding to our expression 'to sleep together'). In the main, however, it refers to the 28 lunar stations – the 28 sections of the Chinese zodiac which the moon passes through in the course of its 28-day orbit round the earth. These constellations were known by the 5th century BC. Later tradition made them out to be the → souls of generals slain by the first Emperor of the Later Han Dynasty (1st century AD). Each of these stations is associated with an animal, as in the case of the 12 signs of the Chinese → zodiac. The lunar stations are shown on most compasses as used by → geomancers, and they play a cardinal role in ancient → astrology. Each sign (or a group of signs) corresponded to an ancient Chinese feudal state, and any unusual phenomenon in a sign was regarded as auguring something out of the ordinary in the corresponding province.

Luo-han 羅漢

In some ways, the 18 Luo-han (Arhats) of Buddhism correspond to the 8 → Immortals of Taoism. Theoretically, no less than 500 disciples of → the Buddha may, in the fullness of time, become Buddhas themselves, and statues of all these 500 can be found in certain temples. As a rule, however, the Luo-han are said to be 18 in number: 16 being of Indian origin, 2 of Chinese. According to the legend they cross the seas; and as in the case of the 8 Immortals, each of them is associated with a particular attribute. Thus, the first, Pin-tu-lo, has a book on his knees; the last, Po-lo-to-she, is riding on a tiger.

The 13th Luo-han, Ba-na-ta-ka

Among the non-Han Yao in South China, the word *Luo-han* means nothing more than 'young man'.

Lute (Guitar)
qin

琴

In ancient texts the Chinese lute is described as a 'cosmological instrument'. It was to be made from the → Wu-tong tree of South China, and was to measure 3 feet 6.6 inches (Chinese measures) long, so as to correspond to the year, 1.8 inches thick (= 3 × 6) and six-tenths broad: these two measurements corresponding to the six scales or keys. The upper surface was to be round and domed like the → heavens; the bottom was to be flat and four-cornered like the → earth. The top was to be broad to symbolise the scholars and men of culture; the bottom was to be narrow, symbolising the common people. To begin with, the *qin* had → five strings, but later this was increased to seven or nine (it is noteworthy that all of these numbers are 'male'). The lutes made by the Lei (= 'thunder') family were supposed to be the best. The 'Jew's harp' is a sort of → mouth organ.

'Lute strings' is a metaphor for the labia majora.

Qin *with a crane: 'May you be a good official'*

M

Magnolia
mu-lan 木蘭

From time immemorial, the Chinese have been growing magnolias in many varieties, both tree and shrub. In ancient times only the Emperor was entitled to own this flower: from time to time he would bestow a magnolia root on someone who had earned the imperial favour.

Formerly, the buds, the fruit and the woody parts were used as curatives, e.g. for anaemia. One kind of magnolia, known as *hou-po* and found in Sichuan, yields a Chinese medicine with remarkable restorative powers. Most of the medicinally valuable material is found in the bark, which is exported all over the world.

The magnolia blossom symbolises a → beautiful woman, though sometimes it is replaced here by the → peony. The popular name for the magnolia is *ye-he hua* = 'the flower of nocturnal togetherness'. *Mu-lan* is also the name of a celebrated

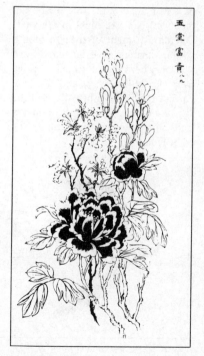

Magnolia, peony and wild apple

warrior-maiden who joined the army for the sake of her father and went on to make a successful military career for herself (→ Mu-lan).

Magpie
qiao

In popular parlance, the magpie has always been called *xi-qiao*, i.e. 'joy-bringing magpie'. Its call heralds good news or the arrival of a guest. The joy it brings is often → married bliss; this is because of one of the best-loved Chinese legends, the tale of the cowherd and the spinning damsel. Thanks to the forgetfulness of the magpie the two lovers can meet only on one night in the year. On the 7th night of the 7th month all the magpies leave earth and fly to heaven where they form a → bridge over the Milky Way, and thus the cowherd can rejoin his wife. On the 7th day of the 7th month it usually rains so that we on earth cannot see what is happening in the heavens.

In the *Shen yi jing*, the 'Book of the Gods and other Strange Things' (dating from the 4th or 5th century AD), we learn of a 'magpie-mirror'. The story runs as follows. Formerly, when man and wife had to separate they broke a → mirror and each of them took one half. If the woman succumbed in the interim to other men, her half of the mirror turned into a magpie and flew back to her husband. This is the origin of the practice of decorating the backs of mirrors with figures of magpies.

As the bird of good omen, the magpie is contrasted with the → raven, the bird of ill omen. The magpie is a → *yang* creature, partaking in male vigour. When the founding father of the Manchu Dynasty was fleeing from his enemies, a magpie perched on his head. The pursuit was called off, and thereafter the magpie was regarded as a sacred bird by the Manchus. They also believed that it dropped a fruit by means of which a heavenly maiden became pregnant.

The magpie makes its nest out of things it picks up on the ground. If

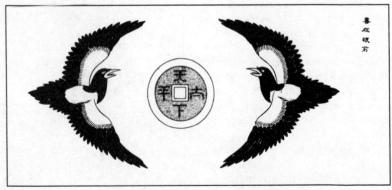

Two magpies, a coin with centre-hole and the inscription 'Great Peace over the whole world'

Two magpies: conjugal bliss

a magpie's nest is burned on the 5th day of the 5th month and its eggs given to a sick man, he will recover.

A picture showing 12 magpies expresses 12 good wishes. A picture showing an → official on horseback in the middle, surrounded by magpies, means 'May redoubled joy be yours (i.e. may you make a good marriage and have many children).' Here, the horse symbolises the high rank awaiting the offspring. A picture showing magpies (*xi*), bamboos (*zhu*) and plums (*mei*) means 'May man and wife (bamboo and plum) delight each other (two magpies).' Two magpies symbolise the wish 'May you meet each other in joy': this can refer either to a marriage or to conjugal sexual intercourse.

Ma-gu   麻 姑

Ma-gu is a fairy: she carries a bamboo staff with a basket hanging from it, and she is accompanied by a boy carrying a → peach. She is often depicted with unusually long nails, which she uses for scratching her back; her hair may be in a bun, or it may be down to her waist. She is also represented as the companion of → Xi-wang-mu. Many tales are told about her. She is supposed to have lived at the time of the Emperor Xiao (AD 147–68). During a banquet, her host became obsessed with the idea of how nice it would be to be scratched by her long nails, when his back got itchy. For these unseemly thoughts he was thrashed by an invisible whip, but the expression caught on and entered the language: 'as delightful as being scratched by Ma-gu'. Even the great Tang poet Li Tai-bo made poetic use of the reference.

There were temples to Ma-gu in many parts of China, and caves and mountains were named after her.

Ma-gu with the peach

Wherever she goes she is welcome as an auspicious goddess. Pictures of her along with the 'peach of immortality' or a basket filled with flowers or miraculous mushrooms, were brought as birthday presents.

It seems that her long nails gave rise to the idea of the → back-scratcher which is still in use today. It is usually made of wood.

Man
nan   男

Many Chinese paintings show a man or men: and we can only understand the symbolical content when we know who is being represented. A young man dancing, waving a string of coins, with a → toad in front of him, is → Liu Hai. If the man carries a sword, looks very fierce, and is surrounded by demons and wild beasts, he must be → Zhong-kui. If he is standing on a fiery wheel and despatching his enemies, he is → Nuo-zha.

Two old men who must be monks, to judge from their bald pates, are Han-shan and Shi-de (→ He-he, → broom).

A lengthy message of good wishes is conveyed by a picture of an old man carrying a child on his back: the child has a → musical stone, the old man has a staff with two → oranges and a → fan made from banana leaves hanging from it: nearby there is a second child, and a → bat flies round the whole group. We may spell the message out in telegraphese: good wishes – fate – good – lots of luck. It is a picture that is particularly suitable as a birthday gift for an older man.

Man is naturally identified with → yang, the male element, just as woman is identified with → yin. 'Male' and 'female' form a contrastive pair which takes many forms: straight and angular contrasted with round and curved, → heaven with → earth, out with in, lofty with low-lying. As depicted in Chinese literature, man reduces to two main types: the military man, rough, courageous and coarse, and the civil service official, who is mild and inoffensive. The latter does not make things happen, things happen to him. He lives modestly, is attentive to his parents and is generally passive. Hence he is readily seduced or led astray, with dire results for himself.

In the popular romance *Ping yao zhuan* ('The Defeat of the Demons'), a remarkable document of the 17th century (perhaps earlier: the date is not quite certain), we are told that the sexual drive is of equal intensity in men and women. So, if a man is permitted to take more than one woman, why should a woman be taken to task if she does the same thing? In keeping with his *yang* nature, man does 'outward' things: he works 'outside' the house, and the woman depends on him to provide for both of them. It is for this reason that she is supposed to be obedient to laws drawn up by men: for this reason she is to stick to one man and never be unfaithful. Gifted women, however, who surpass men in many ways, do not adhere to such rules, and they cannot be made to do so.

If you want to be rude about a man, you can call him a *nan-nü* = man-woman. And a well-known proverb puts a specifically male point of view: 'Ten men are easier to control than one woman: and ten women are easier to control than one child.'

A particularly derogatory expression common in novels for a woman of easy virtue is 'Dog-man-woman'.

'Men's Houses' or 'Youth Houses' in which unmarried men lived in group fashion were found among the minority peoples in South Chinese regions. The same sort of thing was known among the Cantonese Chinese, on the Ryukyu Islands and in Korea, and, no doubt, in ancient China, up to about two thousand years ago. Young men were at liberty to sow their wild oats, and gain → sexual experience. In South China there were until quite recently similar houses for unmarried girls who enjoyed sexual liberty. Certain men, as well as saints, are often depicted without shirts. They are always bustier than the women depicted in paintings.

Mandarin ducks with lotus

Mandarin Duck 鴛 鴦
yuan-yang

The mandarin duck, a familiar sight in parks in Europe, is native to East Asia. The birds live in pairs, and mate for life. So it is a natural symbol for marital happiness; and when two mandarin ducks are depicted, one with a lotus blossom in its beak, the other with a lotus fruit, this expresses the additional wish that the marriage will be blessed with sons.

'Mandarin duck curtains' and 'Mandarin duck coverlets' are used to decorate marriage beds. 'Mandarin duck pillows' often figure as wedding gifts: they are made of china and are painted with ducks.

'Mandarin ducks in the dew' is an expression for unmarried lovers. 'Mandarin duck union' is one of the thirty positions in sexual intercourse.

Mandarin Orange (Tangerine) 柑
gan

Like the other citrus fruits, the mandarin orange is native to China and South-East Asia. In Taiwan it is customary for the bride, on entering her future husband's house, to receive two mandarin oranges which she peels in the evening. This is supposed to augur well for a long happy life together. A *tian-gan* = 'celestial tangerine' is a ball with nails sticking out of it which is used for self-mortification by shamans in their religious ceremonies.

Mandoline
pi-pa

琵琶

The lute or mandoline seems to have originated in Iran. It is quite often used by shamans in their spells and incantations. Probably because of a similarity in shape the yellow → loquat is also called *pi-pa* in Chinese:

Princess Zhao-jun with her mandoline wrapped up

the fruit is a sign of good luck, and also seems to symbolise love.

A picture showing a woman in winter clothing, riding a grey horse and carrying a large mandoline, is a reference to Zhao-jun, who was one of the many concubines of a certain Han → Emperor. By the terms of a peace treaty with the Xiung-nu who lived in North China, the Emperor had to hand over a princess to them: so he got his court painter Mao to paint portraits of all his wives and concubines. Whereupon the ladies of the harem bribed Mao to depict them as raving beauties. Only the modest Zhao-jun failed to do this, so her picture showed her as very ill-favoured. Feeling that he could spare this one, the Emperor sent her off to the Xiung-nu; she became one of the ruler's wives. Later, the Emperor realised his mistake, and had Mao executed.

The expression 'Taking the mandoline under your arm' refers to a woman who remarries after the death of her husband.

Mandrake
ya-bu-lu

Some time before the 13th century at the latest, the Chinese were introduced to the mandrake by Muslims in Central or Western Asia. The Chinese name *ya-bu-lu* is derived from the Arabic *yabrūḥ*.

The traditional method of using the mandrake is as follows. A shaft is dug into the earth until the root of the plant is reached, and dogs are then used to bring it to the surface.

The dogs are poisoned by the aroma of the plant and die. It should then be concealed in the ground for a year, after which it is taken out and dried. A very small dose will rob a man of all feeling for three days, during which time he will seem to be dead.

Maple
feng

The Chinese word for 'maple' (*feng*) is phonetically identical with the word for 'designation' or 'appointment' (i.e. to a fief). In many pictures, a → monkey is shown

Monkey in a maple tree, reaching for the seal of office: 'May the seal you carry be that of a count (earl)'

perched in a maple. Below the monkey there is a bees' nest (also *feng*). The monkey is trying to catch hold of a packet wrapped in cloth which is hanging in the branches. The packet contains a seal of office symbolising the preferment which, it is hoped, awaits the recipient of the picture.

Marriage
jie-hun

By night – so the story goes – the mysterious old man in the → moon ties a magical and invisible red thread round the legs of new-born boys and girls. When they grow up, they are drawn together by a powerful bond of which they are completely unaware. Should their paths cross, a wedding is the inevitable outcome.

In pre-1949 China, marriage was not something that young people entered upon of their own free will. Rather, it was a 'political' act of union between two families, and therefore hardly something that could be left to the whims of the inexperienced. 'Love marriages' were until recently customary among the minority peoples in South China, a practice that was strenuously opposed by the Han majority.

As in the case of business agreements, the initial steps between the two contracting families were taken, not by the parties themselves, but by an intermediate third party, a so-called marriage broker (usually a woman, but sometimes a man). A

Marriage horoscope drawn up in accordance with astrological data

family with a marriageable child would get in touch with the broker and give him or her a more or less detailed brief. The broker then visited the other family, which could not, even if favourably disposed, agree without further ado: honour demanded some sort of prevarication, and negotiations could run on for a long time. When agreement was finally reached, the next step was for the broker to bring the 'eight signs' – year, day and hour of birth – for comparison with those of the proposed partner. This was necessary because everyone had to be satisfied that there was no → astrological impediment to the desired union. Even at this late stage, the whole thing could be called off; or, if the parties still felt that a marriage should take place in spite of unfavourable signs, certain modifications could be introduced. Gifts were then exchanged; a dowry was agreed, and gold, silver and jewellery were handed over, never land.

On the wedding day, the bridegroom arrives along with his friends at the bride's house, where entry is ceremoniously denied him until he

A nervous daughter-in-law meets her husband's parents

has given money to the guards. Then comes the feast. The bride does not take part in this: she sits all day on the bed in her bridal gown, and is not allowed to leave the room. When night falls, the bridegroom – often in his cups – enters the bedroom and lifts his bride's veil: this is when she sees her husband for the first time. The two are now left alone, though others often get a lot of fun out of boring holes in the paper window panes with their fingers to see what is going on. Until quite recently, it was the custom in some regions of China to exhibit the bridal sheet next morning (as used to be common in certain parts of Europe). A bride who turned out not to be a virgin could be packed off home straight away.

When choosing a bride certain things had to be borne in mind. For

The two He-he, the gods of marriage

example, marriage between families with the same surname was not allowed. In very exceptional cases, the Emperor could sanction such a marriage, but only if the families could prove that their forebears came from widely separated parts of China.

A man could marry only one wife, and she enjoyed certain specific rights. He could, of course, take one or more concubines, who were inferior in status to his wife, who could expel them from the house without consulting her husband. The concubines were at her beck and call for housework and so on. These concubines came usually from the lower classes, and their status was not covered by any sort of safeguard: a concubine was highly vulnerable – unless she could produce a son for a husband whose lawful wife could only manage to produce daughters.

Each wife had her own dwelling (usually a small house separated from the main house), in which she received her husband. Every man was expected to marry and beget children; homosexuality, practised by older men and by monks, did not constitute grounds for refusing marriage. Since 1928 monogamy alone is recognised by law; polygamy is forbidden, but has been slow to die out.

Attitudes to marriage have changed radically in present-day China. The main differences are that the part-time marriage broker has vanished, her place being taken by an amateur mediator, or a party member who also deals with the quality and quantity of the marriage gifts. This is mainly in country districts; in the towns, people are now largely free to choose their own spouses. In the universities, in factories and offices, this can be done much more easily than in the villages, though advice from parents and friends continues to be listened to with respect.

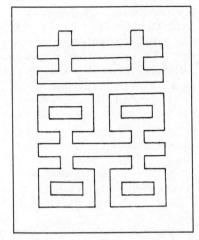

The joys of conjugal life

Married Bliss
hunpei 婚配

The oldest oracle bones extant are concerned with political problems and the happiness to be found in human togetherness. The relationship between man and wife is one of the → five ways which are accessible to all (*Li-ji*, 'Book of Rites').

Chinese thought and Chinese society have always conferred upon marriage and the family (including, in the case of the middle and upper classes, concubines) a status unparalleled in any other advanced culture. A syllogistic chain leads from order and harmony in the family to order and peace in the state; and the clan system constructed on the basis of Confucian family ethics has given China the biggest population in the world.

Both Buddhist and Confucian ideas on present suffering and the happiness that can be attained went into the making of Kang You-wei's vision of a new ordering of society. In his 'Book of the Great Equality' (*Da tong shu*, 1902) he specifies five barriers which must be torn down if this great equality is to be realised. The fourth chapter is entitled 'How to eliminate barriers between the sexes and give women equality'; the fifth deals with 'How to get rid of the Confines of the Family, and turn Humanity into "People of Heaven" '. Kang's book had some influence both on moderate reformers and on later cultural-revolutionary ideas.

Folk art, old and new, is rich in symbols depicting conjugal bliss. For some of these see the following: Goose, Kingfisher, Lotus, Magpie, Mandarin Duck, Narcissus, Orchid, Phoenix.

See also Fate, Feelings, Flying, He-he, Ice, Marriage, Rain, *Ren*, Red, Spring, Wood Oil Tree.

Ma-zu 媽祖

Ma-zu is a goddess who is worshipped especially on the coast of South China. She is accompanied by 'Thousand-mile Eyes' (Qian-li yan) and 'Favourable-wind Ear' (Shun-

Ma-zu in the temple of Chang-hua (Taiwan)

feng er), both of whom she captured on Peach-blossom Mountain, and who help her to rescue → fishermen in peril on the deep. On 14 April 1960 her 1,001th birthday was celebrated in her temple in Peikang (Taiwan) (traditionally she was born on 19 April 901). Her cult has spread along the coastal regions and up the big rivers of China, and has even reached Brazil and California. In her role as goddess, Ma-zu is given the title of 'Queen Empress of Heaven' (*tian-hou*).

Meander
hui-wen

This type of strip ornamentation, which is still used a great deal on carpets and similar articles with decorated borders, makes its appearance as far back as the Neolithic age, when it was used on pottery. The motif occurs in many forms. Often it consists of → squares within squares in endless series. As this pattern bears a strong resemblance to the Chinese written character meaning 'to return' (*hui*) the meander pattern symbolises 'rebirth'. A similar figure is the *hui-hui-jin*, the basic element in which is formed by two squares fitting into each other (*jin* means 'brocade' or simply 'patterned weave'). The meander design is related to the → swastika motif.

Meander patterns

Medicine
yao-xue

The oldest book on Chinese medicine is supposed to be the 'Book of the Yellow Emperor' (*Huang-di nei-jing*), compiled, we are told, by the mythical Emperor Huang-di, to whom is also attributed the oldest book on sexual practices (*Huang-di su-wen*). In their present form, both of these works seem to have been put together around the turn of the millennium. Medical texts which have been recently excavated in burial sites, introduce us to the medical knowledge available in the China of before 200 BC; they are certainly older than the classical

命醫去毒

Hua-to operates on Goan-di

works ascribed to Huang-di, and more closely related to the *Ben-cao* (see below). In these newly discovered texts, the two main components of Chinese medicine are already clearly recognisable: on the one hand, remedies based largely on herbal materials which must be prepared in certain prescribed ways; and on the other, instructions for the use of these materials some of which we would regard as magic spells or incantations. Both of these components have held their ground and are practised even today, except where Western medicine has managed to break through. 'Magic' medicine of this sort is not practised by anyone the Chinese would call a 'doctor', but by a shaman who usually performs movements and actions in a state of trance, in which either he goes to the spirits and gods

or they come to him. The shaman prescribes no medicine, except perhaps ashes from the → incense burned during the ceremony. Any effect that this treatment may have upon the invalid is purely psychological.

Doctors in ancient China who prescribed medicines made from herbal matter or from parts of animals, were divided into three categories: at the top were the state doctors, upper-class men who, in addition to their training in traditional medicine, had studied the medical texts available and had passed a state examination. They were called 'Great Doctors', held state posts and were summoned to court if the Emperor or one of his high officials were ill. The second group also belonged to the upper class: they were state officials who had studied medicine as a sideline in their free time. Should a friend or a relation fall ill they would do what they could to help. They never asked for payment but expected gifts on suitable occasions such as major feast-days and holidays.

The third category was drawn from the lower classes of society. Its members were often the sons or grandsons of doctors. Practitioners belonging to this category often had their own private books of remedies and treatments, which were carefully guarded from rival eyes. They worked in small shops or on the streets, and they took payment for their advice. These practitioners are still active, and the present regime has been trying to lay its hands on their secret texts, partly in order to make use of information possibly contained therein, and partly to curtail the influence of its owners. 'Barefoot doctors' have attended basic courses in first aid, hygiene, the use of ordinary medicines and of drugs available only on prescription. Apart from this they also roll up their trouser legs, take off their shoes and work in the fields – hence their name.

The standard work on all diseases and remedies is the *Ben-cao gang-mu* (the 'Encyclopaedia of Plants and Roots') the core material of which was written down about two thousand years ago. Over the centuries it was extended and amended until a definitive edition was produced under the Ming Dynasty (1368–1644). The work contains a full description of all plants, their properties and their use in medicine, and Western researchers – botanists, doctors and pharmaceutical firms – have also turned to it for information. It is noteworthy that, when the basic material was being collected, paediatricians, specialists in women's diseases, and even horse doctors, were already active in China.

Characteristic of Chinese medicine is the absence of surgery. The traditional view was that the human body as provided by one's parents should not be mutilated in any way. Men who were castrated to become eunuchs, kept the parts removed and had them buried with them at death. Nor was circumcision known in China till about fifty years ago, again because of a strong belief in the inviolability of the body as given.

More than two thousand years ago, attempts were made to provide Chinese medicine with a theoretical basis, by correlating it with the system of the five → elements or 'states of being' (*wu xing*). Illness ensued when the balance of forces in the body was not in equilibrium with those in the environment. Correct use of the adequate medicine could restore the lost harmony, and the patient got better. To take a simple example: a cold could be cured by taking a medicine that contained warmth. Due balance between warmth and cold, between dryness and moistness, is of universal significance over the whole corpus of Chinese medicine. Certain groups in South China like to eat dog-meat. But, since the dog is correlated with 'hot', it cannot be eaten in summer. As soon as the cold weather returns, dogs vanish from the streets to reappear on menus in restaurants.

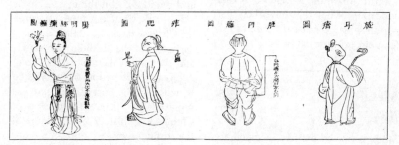

Representations of external complaints

Menstruation
yue-jing

月 經

During menstruation, a Chinese woman is not allowed to go to a temple, take part in a pilgrimage or have sexual intercourse. By Chinese reckoning, menstruation begins at 14 years of age (corresponding to 13 by Western reckoning). The term *yue-jing* = 'month-period' is often replaced by such metaphors as 'little red sister has come', 'the red news', 'the monthly news', 'the first tide', 'the red general grasps the door', 'riding a horse'. 'The dirty cloth', 'the monthly cloth' – the cloths used in menstruation – can be used along with the blood of a black dog, the penis of a white horse plus a lot of dirty water, to ward off black magic. The menstrual blood of virgins is supposed to be of medicinal use in sexual troubles.

If a cloth used in menstruation is buried under the threshold, the woman will always remain in the house and never run away. Another way of insuring this is to burn the cloth on the 7th day of the 7th Chinese month and sprinkle the ashes on the door frame.

Little attention is paid to sexual education. When they have their first period, girls do not even dare to ask for help or information.

Metal
jin

Metal is one of the five → elements or 'permutations of being'. The word *jin* is often used as equivalent to 'gold': its symbolic correlatives are the West and the colour white.

According to the ancient teaching contained in the *Hong-fan* ('Great Plan') metal also has correlatives in the five viscera (the lungs), in the five bodily functions (hearing and understanding) and the five heavenly signs or symbols of the seasons (cold). In the *Huang-di nei-jing*, the breviary of ancient Chinese medicine, 'metal' is further correlated with one of the bodily orifices (the nose) and with one of the affects (grief). The basic concept is that of relationship with the West and with autumn as the season in which vegetation dies: the time of death and, in ancient Chinese society, the time for executions to be carried out. Metal (→ sword) is hence significant as the instrument of execution.

Middle
zhong

The written sign for 'middle' represents an arrow striking the centre of a target: the same sign can be used as a verb meaning 'to strike in the middle', 'hit the mark'.

From very ancient times onwards the Chinese have called their country *zhong guo*, the 'Middle Kingdom', and they still call themselves *zhong guo ren* = 'the people of the Middle Kingdom'. The term *zhong guo* was replaced at different times over China's long history by the name of the ruling dynasty; and our word 'China' comes presumably from the name of the Qin Dynasty (*c.* 250–206 BC). The Russian word *Kitai* derives from the name of the Kitan Dynasty which ruled North China sporadically (AD 1125–1234) (cf. English 'Cathay'). The ancient capital, Lo-yang, was shown by Chinese astronomers to be very close to the centre point of the earth. Indeed, theoretically, the seat of the → Emperor was to be 'in the middle', although, in point of fact, most Chinese capitals have been situated in the West or the North of the country. The Emperor faced the South, so that he could follow the progress of the sun from dawn through midday to evening. His subjects had to approach him from the South; and Chinese maps on which the Emperor could survey his realm, had the South at the top of the sheet, the North at the bottom.

The term 'Middle Kingdom' was understood not only in a geographic sense, but in a moral sense as well. In the Taoist book *Lie-zi* we already find it described as a land of diametrical opposites which counterbalance each other and replace each other: 'Within the Four Seas lies the Middle Kingdom: it lies to the north and the south of the Yellow River, and to east and west of the Great Mountain (*tai shan*) in an area of over a thousand miles (→ square). Cloudy and clear are clearly distinguished, and so warm and cold succeed each other. Dark and bright are clearly divided, so day and night follow each other. Among the people are the clever and the stupid. Nature thrives luxuriantly, arts and crafts are richly developed, ruler and people occupy their proper places, and morality and justice support each other.'

As 'Middle Kingdom', China saw herself in the centre of 'all below heaven' (*tian xia*), as the quintessence of civilisation. Beyond her borders, 'outside', lived only barbarians.

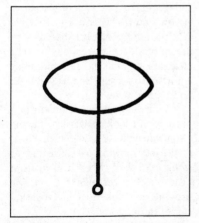

The old form of the written sign for 'middle'

Milk
nai

It is only in recent years that the Chinese have started to drink milk, although it has been used in cooking for much longer. Yoghurt made from sheep's milk was eaten at various periods of the Middle Ages. 'Mother's milk' is supposed to give you physical strength and sexual stamina, and to prolong your life. One may say disparagingly of a little boy 'Mother's milk is still wet on his lips.'

The Milky Way is known in China as the 'heavenly river Han'. (See also Dryness, *Su*.)

Millet
su

粟

Millet is widely cultivated, especially in North China. The 'Yellow Millet Dream' – an allegory of the illusory nature, the vanity of worldly preferment and honours – is very well known. A poor man bemoans his lot in a wayside inn. The sage Lü who is in an adjoining room hears his complaint and gives him a pillow on which the man falls asleep; meanwhile the innkeeper is making some millet gruel on the fire. In his dream, the poor man lives through all the pleasures of a good marriage, an illustrious career and the acquisition of many honours till he dies at the age of 80 – the very moment when he wakes up, to find that the yellow millet gruel is not even ready. Thus does the sage instruct him that life is nothing but an illusion, a short dream. Like a similar tale, the 'Dream of the Southern Branch' (*Nan-ke meng*), the 'Millet Dream' has often been used as a theme for operas.

Mirror
jing

Bronze mirrors were being used in China before the end of the second millennium BC. But the Chinese are still fond of telling the story of the peasant woman who wants her husband to bring her a comb from the town and, to help his memory, tells him it is something that looks like the new moon. But by the time the peasant remembers to buy the comb, it is full moon: he gets confused and buys a mirror. When his wife looks into it she flies into a rage: 'How dare you bring a concubine home – and such an ugly one into the bargain!'

It was popularly believed that mirrors made → spirits visible, and one still finds today so-called 'magic mirrors' on the back of which strange patterns appear when they are held in certain ways: in sunlight flowers, according to an ancient text, and in moonlight a → hare. The best magic mirrors were said to be those formerly produced at Yang-zhou in Central China – particularly, those made on the 5th day of the 5th month (→ feast-days). Buddhist priests used these mirrors to show believers the form in which they would be reborn. If a man looks into a magic mirror and cannot recognise his own face, this is a sign that his death is not far off. It is bad luck to dream of a dark mirror; but a bright mirror is a good sign. If a man finds a mirror, it is a sign that he will soon find a good wife.

A man who receives a mirror in a present can look forward to having a son who will rise to high civil office. A picture showing a bronze mirror (*tong jing*) with shoes (*xie*) in front of it, makes a very suitable wedding present: it betokens a life together (*tong*) in harmony (*xie*).

In a stock situation which occurs in many novels, a man who has to

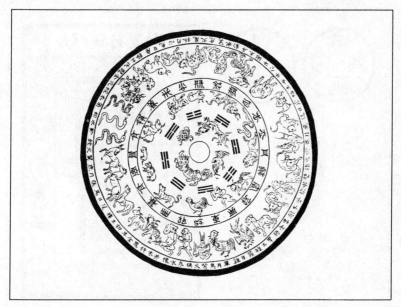

A mirror of the Tang Dynasty

leave his wife for a very long time breaks a mirror into two pieces; each partner keeps a piece. In this way they will know each other again, should the separation last so long that they cannot recognise each other. It was also believed that one piece of the mirror would turn into a → magpie and fly away if the partner holding the other piece were unfaithful. When the 'broken mirror is round again', the partners have been reunited.

Metal mirrors tended to become tarnished after some time, and a mirror polisher had to be brought in. But 'polishing the mirror' is a common term for fondling the female genitalia: it may also refer to lesbian love-making.

Money
qian

From the 7th century BC onwards, metal coins of various kinds were in use in China. The round copper coin seems to have developed gradually from the 'knife-money' used in East Shandong, where a small knife was once used as a token of payment; the round coin is a remnant of the knife handle along with the square hole used for hanging it up. Two or four inscribed characters were added, and the coin remained thus as the monetary unit used by the broad masses, until the early 20th century. The coins were threaded on a cord: a thousand of them formed the next unit in the monetary system. As motifs, coins are found in many

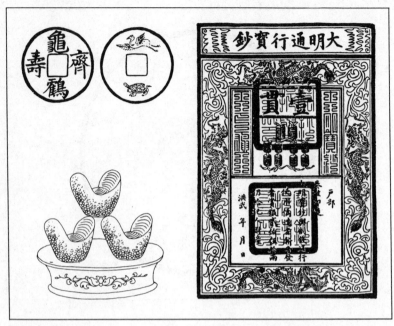

Top left: Coins as amulets. Bottom left: Three gold bars: 'May you pass the three state examinations'. Right: Paper money of the early Ming Dynasty

combinations. The word *qian* = money is phonetically identical with the word *qian* = before: hence, a → bat carrying money can be interpreted as 'May happiness be before your eyes' – and in this sentence, the word for 'eye' is the same as the word for the hole in the coin (*yan*). Two → magpies with a coin: this means 'May happiness be before your eyes.' A cord (*lian*) with nine coins symbolises 'uninterrupted happiness'. The coin is also one of the *ba-bao*, the eight symbols of riches (→ precious things).

Paper money has been in use from time to time since the 13th century, and plays an important part in the cult of the dead and in ancestor worship. Until recent years bundles of 10,000 Chinese dollar bills – issued by the 'Bank of the Underworld' – were burned to provide the spirits with whatever they need.

Coins were normally made from copper, though at a later date brass began to be used. In ancient China bar-silver was used as a currency, and was known as 'silver shoes'. The → shoe shape is used for the construction of ponds and flowerbeds in ornamental gardens.

From very early times, coins have been used as → amulets, as protective devices against disease-bearing demons, etc. In practice they were worn, either singly or in strings round the neck. The 'money that drives off evil influences' (*ya-sui-qian*) was a → New Year's Gift. In the Middle Ages it was the custom to pelt a young couple with money when they had sat down on their bed, and the bride tried to catch it in her apron. This was not ordinary money, however, but special coins bearing such inscriptions as 'Long life, riches and honour', 'Like Fish in Water' (which alludes to marital bliss), 'May you grow old in harmony', 'May you have five sons and one daughter.' Nowadays, the bride tries to blow the water out of a half-filled bowl so that she can pick up the coin lying on the bottom.

One of the most popular Chinese operas is called 'Shaking the Money Tree'. The money-tree, from which coins fall, is a frequent motif in pictures. This opera is usually performed by very young actors. It tells the story of a celestial lady's-maid who is bent on getting her share of worldly pleasures. So she goes down to earth where her behaviour is so appalling that the supreme god has to send down a couple of demiurges who take her prisoner and bring her back to heaven.

Today, the expression 'to shake the money-tree' often refers to a bawd who makes a lot of money out of prostitutes (→ Liu Hai).

Monk
he-shang 和尚

There are Buddhist monks and Taoist monks in China, and there are considerable differences between them. Buddhist monks (*seng*) are strict vegetarians and are forbidden to marry or to have sexual intercourse. They must not adorn themselves in any way, and their heads are shaven. They wear a uniform simple robe which nowadays is usually orange-coloured. After serving their apprenticeship they have to undergo an ordination ceremony, during which small cones

'Shaking the money-tree'

A Taoist monk mounted on a tiger

of incense are placed on their bare skulls, ignited and left to burn away, leaving deep scars.

Taoist monks also wear very simple clothing, usually grey, and eschew all adornment. However, they are not all celibate, nor are they all able to resist meat and alcohol.

Buddhist monks are often disparagingly referred to as 'bareheaded asses' (*tu lu*), a term with a double sexual innuendo, as the ass is regarded as a particularly randy animal.

Monkey upon monkey: 'May each generation be elevated to the rank of count'

Monkey
hou 猴

It is not only in Indian mythology that the monkey plays a leading part; it is also found in South Chinese and in Tibetan legend. Several varieties of monkey are native to South China; and according to one Tibetan myth, the Tibetan people are descended from a monkey. Tales of women who have been abducted and ravished by monkeys and who have then given birth to children, are common in South China, and several Chinese 'clans' attribute their origins to such a union.

Like the Indian monkey-god Hanuman, gods in Chinese legend sometimes appear in the guise of monkeys. The best-known of these is Sun Wu-kong, who accompanied the Buddhist pilgrim Xuan-Cang to India and came to his rescue in many a dangerous situation, though, on the other hand, Xuan-Cang had to put up with his tantrums and his penchant for practical jokes. Sun Wu-kong is one of the chief protagonists in the picaresque novel of the Song Dynasty, 'The Journey to the West' (also known as 'Monkey'). Some scenes from this novel have been turned into stage plays, and films, in which the monkey-god appears as a dancer with a whitened face, carrying a long pole. His dance always arouses general mirth.

Many temples were built to the monkey-god in South China. In these, he is revered and worshipped as Qi-tian da-sheng ('the great saint equal to heaven'). In the popular mind, however, he symbolises rather the adulterer. The monkey is the ninth creature in the Chinese zodiac, following the horse with which it is often represented. A picture showing a monkey mounted on a horse is called *ma-shang feng-hou*; and a homonymic reading of this title gives the meaning 'May you be straight away (*ma-shang*) elevated to the rank of count (*feng-hou*).' Such a picture was a very suitable gift for an → official, for example.

More frequently, we find a monkey shown holding a → peach (as in the classical novel *Feng-shen Yan-yi*, 'The Metamorphoses of the Gods'): the peach symbolises → longevity, and was stolen, according to one legend, from the peach-garden of → Xi-wang-mu.

Yet another motif in painting shows two monkeys on a → pine-tree. This can be interpreted as 'May you rank as count from generation to generation.' This is also the meaning inherent in a picture showing one monkey crouching on the back (*bei*) of another (*bei* = generation).

Moon
yue   月

The moon is associated with the female principle (→ *yin*), so the moon deity (→ Chang-e) is also female, and 'arises' in the West: that is to say, it is in the West that the new moon first becomes visible. Both the West and the autumn are female and the Chinese think that the moon is most beautiful in the autumn. Accordingly the Feast of the Moon was held on the 15th day of the 8th month (in the old Chinese → calendar, every month began on the day of the new moon, so full moon always falls on the 15th). However, autumn is also the time when executions are carried out, as all of nature is dying. For this reason, the moon was sometimes linked with the execution of criminals, while the → sun symbolised the virtuous. Finally, since the Emperor is associated with the sun, the moon symbolises the Empress.

The Chinese see a → toad or a → hare in the moon, but then again a man who is busy cutting down a → cinnamon tree, which promptly grows up again. Emperor Xuan-cong of the Tang Dynasty is supposed to have been taken up to the moon by a magician and shown the palaces and the beautiful → fairies who live there. From them, Xuan-cong is said to have learned an unearthly melody, an episode which in expanded form has provided the material for many stories and plays.

The Moon-palace is called → *Guang-han* ('Wide coldness'). The 'Moon-blossom' or 'Moon-pearl' falls from time to time on to the earth, and any woman who swallows it becomes pregnant. Women's feet mutilated by binding were much admired in ancient times, and compared with the beauty of the new moon – as were the eyebrows of beautiful women. The full moon, on the other hand, symbolised an attractive female posterior: though the phrase 'admiring the full moon' refers to a homosexual's bottom.

'The old man under the moon' has everybody's records in safe keeping, and from studying these he can tell which man will marry which woman: → marriage is determined by → fate, a theme which underlies many Chinese novels. Given the nature of the old lunar calendar, it was to be expected that certain numbers – seven, → twelve, → thirteen and twenty-eight – should acquire symbolical meaning (see also Number mysticism).

The extent to which the mid-autumn festival, the moon festival, has changed in character in recent times can be gauged from reports by two German eye-witnesses: First, Richard Wilhelm in 1926:

> The sacrifice to the moon takes place in the open air on the 15th day of the 8th month. All the fruits which are offered in sacrifice have symbolical meaning: the → gourds express the wish that the family may always remain united; the → pomegranates symbolise many children, the → apples augur peace. The cakes are round in shape like the full moon.

Secondly, Erwin Wickert in 1982:

'Moon-mood'

For dessert, our cook Lao Huo had provided small round cakes which were very sweet. The Chinese were moved to see these, because today being the 15th of the 8th month according to the old lunar calendar, was the day when the moon-feast used to be celebrated. This was one of the most popular of the Chinese festivals, when people went about in processions carrying Chinese lanterns. 'In our village,' said the Vice-President of the Academia Sinica, 'there was a moon-cake society. Every month, poor families paid ten pence into a fund kept by the baker. He could use the capital for his own purposes during the year, but on the day of the moon-feast he had to supply every member of the society with moon-cakes.' I asked him if this still went on nowadays. Our guest replied: 'No. But you can still get moon-cakes.'

Mountain
shan   山

In ancient China, mountains were special objects of veneration. Indeed, mountains played the same sort of role in Chinese cosmology as the Emperor did in society: they ensured cosmic order and permanence. The cult of the 'Five Mountains' (*wu yue*) has persisted into modern times. From time immemorial these five mountains have been places of sacrifice. They represent all five directions: Tai-shan is in Shandong in the East; Heng-shan is in

Hunan in the South; Song-shan is in Henan in the Centre; Hua-shan is in Shanxi in the West; and, finally, Heng-shan is in Shanxi in the North. (*Heng* in the latter word is written with a different character from that used for the Heng-shan in Hunan.) All five are wooded, which is a rarity in China, and numerous Taoist temples crown their summits. Along with these five mountains there are a few more which are sacred to Buddhists, especially O-mi in the western province of Sichuan.

In ancient times, the West was seen as the realm of the mountains. In the mysterious North-West towered the Kunlun, which we might well compare with the world-mountain Sumeru of Indian legend: each had nine terraces. In the fabled Kunlun were palaces, hanging gardens, springs from which the

water of life flowed. Whoever succeeded in climbing all the steps leading up to the Kunlun attained immortality. Indeed, the 'Supreme → One' (*tai yi*) dwelt in the Kunlun. The only divinity who received visitors in the Kunlun, however, was the Queen Mother of the West (→ Xiwang-mu). This is probably connected with an earlier belief according to which mountains – especially the Kunlun – were regarded as the place where 'the ten thousand things have their origins and where → yin and → yang alternate with each other for ever'.

The Chinese cosmogony differs from the Indian one in that the Kunlun is located not in the centre of the earth but in the West, at the source of the Yellow River. As Buddhism made inroads into China – i.e. since about the 1st century AD

Poet in the mountains

Expedition in the mountains

at the latest – Indian and Chinese cosmological concepts began to mingle with each other. Sumeru was now seen as the source of four great rivers which flowed north, south, east and west; and the Yellow River was, of course, the one flowing eastwards.

Virtually every mountain had its resident mountain god. The late classical belief that the spirits of the dead live in the mountains, persisted in North China, and sacrifices were accordingly made to mountains. In later times we find many reports of governmental attempts to ban the cult of mountain spirits, partly perhaps because of their erotic character: for example, young girls were 'married' to the mountain. The Wu-shan mountain in the western part of Central China is celebrated because a goddess once appeared there to a great prince with whom she performed the 'clouds and rain game'.

It was the mountains which generated → clouds and → rain, the Chinese believed. In pictures, cloud-capped mountains symbolise the earth, while waves symbolise the sea. The expression 'mountains and seas' (*shan hai*) refers to China as a whole; and this is also the title of the oldest geography book. A most solemn oath was to swear by 'mountain-oath and sea-oath' (*shan men hai shi*). The expression 'middle mountain' (*zhong yue*) may refer to the human → nose. A landslip in the mountains was taken as an unmistakable sign that the ruling dynasty's days were numbered: for mountain and → Emperor corresponded to and reflected each other.

The ancient tale of 'The Old Simpleton' (*Yu-gong*) acquired unexpected fame as a parable in the Mao era. This tells how the old man could no longer put up with having to go round a chain of mountains in order to get to the nearest village. Undeterred by the fact that he was already ninety years old, he made a start on digging a way through the hills. A scholar pointed out to him that he was really too old to take on such a task; whereupon the old man reminded him that his children were helping him and that his grand-children and great-grandchildren would certainly bring the work to a successful conclusion. It is obvious why Mao should have found this tale useful as an exercise in moral propaganda, but it is noteworthy that he invariably omitted to mention the end of the story as told in Lie-zi's original version: here, the gods of the mountains and the sea take pity on the old simpleton and report his case to the supreme god, Shang-di, who orders his demiurges to cut a way through the mountains forthwith.

On mountain spirits, see *Shan-xiao*.

Mountain Songs 山 歌
shan ge

These songs are in origin love-songs of the non-Chinese peoples who live in the mountains of South and West China. A young man on one mountain sings to a girl on another – she answers him, and love-songs of considerable length take shape. Dialogue songs of this kind are later found in purely Chinese settings. Love-songs sung by prostitutes on boats in the neighbourhood of Su zhou are also sometimes referred to as 'mountain songs'.

Mouth 口
kou

The old teaching on the → five viscera and the seven (or nine) bodily orifices was adduced as proof of the thesis that → man as microcosm was a replica of the cosmos itself. Within the human microcosm, the lungs were associated with the → eyes, the → liver with the ears: and in the same way, the mouth was associated with the spleen. The characteristic quality of the spleen

was trustworthiness, reliability – a rich speculative field for doctors and psychologists.

The written sign for *kou* represents an opening. Hence, the mouth can also symbolise the female genitalia, and one speaks of a woman's 'two mouths', the upper and the lower. The reduplicated sign (i.e. one 'mouth' above the other) is read as *lu*, and it denotes a note in the Chinese → musical scale.

Mouth Organ 笙
sheng

The Chinese mouth organ is a wind instrument consisting of several → bamboo pipes. It is mentioned in ancient texts. Nowadays, it is more typically found among the non-Han minority peoples of South China. The word *sheng* is phonetically identical with the word *sheng* meaning 'to rise in rank', so the

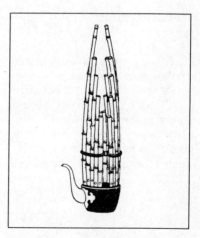

Mouth organ

mouth organ symbolises preferment. Another way of expressing this is to show a child holding a lotus seed capsule (*lian*). This symbolises the wish that one may 'rise further and further (*lian*) in rank'. Or, if the emphasis is on the child, 'May you continue (*lian*) to bring sons into the world (*sheng*) who will attain high rank.'

Moxa
aijiu

Moxa seems to have developed from cauterisation, and to be earlier than acupuncture. In the 3rd century AD moxa seems to have been used only on one or two places on the body of a patient. The erotic novel *Jin ping mei* mentions moxa as a sexual stimulant before intercourse (ch. 78).

Mucus (female)
yinshui

Erotic novels glorify women who secrete mucus in large amounts even before intercourse or without intercourse simply by observing another woman in love. The mucus is variously called 'Spring water', 'Jade juice', 'water of the waves', 'bubbling spring', or 'erotic ford' and is drunk by men as an aphrodisiac.

Mu-lan

Mu-lan, who is also known as Hua Mu-lan, is the best-known warrior maiden in Chinese mythology. Her father had been called up for military service, and, as he was past the age for this, he should have been able to send his son instead. As he had no son, his daughter put on man's clothing, mounted her horse and went off to represent him. She served twelve years in the army, with such distinction that she rose to high rank, without ever being recognised as a woman. When, after the wars, some of her comrades came to visit her, they were greatly astonished to find her unmistakably a woman and sitting on her weaving-stool.

She still ranks today as the paragon of a filial daughter (→ *xiao*).

Mushroom
gu

The true i.e. the edible mushroom (*jun* or *gu*) is often mentioned in Chinese literature. The question of drug-taking in the great cultures of the past has been investigated by, *inter alia*, R. Gordon Wasson (see his *Soma: Divine Mushroom of Immortality*), who claims that the Chinese knew and made use of hallucinogens such as the fly agaric. Crucial evidence here seems to be afforded by the *zhi*, also known as the 'miracle-working *zhi*', which can be rendered in English as 'mushroom of the spirits', 'miraculous

The warrior maiden Mu-lan (stone rubbing)

mushroom', 'auspicious mushroom' – all of these being with reference to the longevity the *zhi* is supposed to confer.

Cammann has objected that the *zhi* when depicted never looks like a fly agaric, but rather like a kind of morel. It is often shown together with other plants and objects, the group as a whole always symbolising longevity. In a more general sense, *zhi* is described as a herb of → immortality.

'Mushroom Palace' (*zhi-cheng gu*) is the palace made of gold and silver which is supposed to be located in the Peng-lai → Islands.

Music
yue

Five kinds of musical instrument were known in ancient China, each of which corresponded to a human property or relationship. They were: the → musical stone symbolising uprightness; stringed instruments standing for purity and faithfulness; leather instruments associated with leaders in war; the → lute symbolising the moon, and the lute or → mandoline symbolising conjugal harmony. → Confucius was deeply

Confucius playing on the cosmic guitar

versed in the music of his time, and it is said that wherever he travelled in feudal China he could assess the state of government in any place from the quality of the music he heard there. In this connection, 'immoral' (lewd, lascivious) (*yin*) music is mentioned – presumably a reference to erotically stimulating dance music, which was always enough to make Confucius take to his heels.

Good music expresses the harmony between heaven and earth. 'When the drums thunder, the cymbals and musical stones clash, when flutes and violins, dancing and singing fill the air with their noise, this is bound to jar the nerves, stimulate the senses and make life effervesce. But music made by such means does not induce pleasure. We may say: the noisier the music, the more depressed people become, the more the state is in jeopardy and

the more the prince declines. Thus is the very essence of music destroyed' (from the 'Spring and Autumn of Lü Bu-wei', tr. Richard Wilhelm).

From the 6th century AD onwards, classical Chinese music was gradually ousted by Central Asian music and musicians. (See also Mouth Organ, Drum, Flute, Number Mysticism.)

Musical Stone 殸
qing 石

The musical stone is one of the oldest Chinese and Vietnamese musical instruments. It seems to have developed from the xylophone. It is often represented in stylised form as a kind of set-square. Its phonetic identity with *qing* = blessings, good luck, has led to its being used to symbolise 'good luck'.

The musical stone

Muslims 回教徒
hui-jiao-tu

The Muslims who live mainly in Xinjiang, the westernmost province of China, in the heartland of Central

Asia, are the largest minority group in China. They speak Uigur or related Turkic languages, and differ also in physical type from the Chinese. Some of these Muslims came as traders to China as long ago as the 9th century. In South China, the Muslim population is physically indistinguishable from the Chinese, and its members speak only Chinese. In folklore they are connected with the motif of the 'treasure trove': a Chinese finds a curious object, which a Muslim sees and wants to buy at an unheard-of price. The Chinese decides that what he has found must be very valuable, so he refuses to sell it. He tries to make use of it himself, and destroys its magic properties in the process.

In folk-prints, Muslims are usually shown bearing treasure: they have a god of → riches, etc. A picture showing these themes is a suitable present for a merchant, to whom one is wishing good luck and good business.

Mussels
bang 蚌

How do → swallows get through the winter? According to ancient Chinese myths, they turn into mussels! In late autumn they set out for their hiding-place in the ocean where the change takes place. Peasant calendars tell us that mussels are only full when the moon is full: at new moon they are empty. As for → sparrows, they too have to hide somewhere during the cold season – so they turn into oysters.

A certain kind of oyster found in the province of Fukien is called *li*. Because of phonetic similarity, this suggests *ti* = male child (normally used as meaning 'younger brother').

In Japan and Korea, the female genitalia are called 'mussels'. In Taiwanese, the word *la* = mussel has the same connotation.

N

Nails
ding

Hammering nails into things is either a way of appropriating them, establishing a claim to them, or a way of protecting them against evil spirits. Formerly, one used to see nails with Medusa-like heads hammered into gateways of Chinese houses: these were supposed to ward off illnesses, or to promote the chances of having sons. Perhaps we have here transference of meaning suggested by the phonetic similarity between *ding* = man, male adult, and *ding* = nail. Long → fingernails play a certain part in mythology (→ Ma-gu).

Nakedness
luo

The Chinese have a predilection for covering things up, and it is not surprising to find that in general they dislike and disapprove of nakedness, which they regard as something suitable only for savages.

In very ancient times, ritual disrobing was associated with certain ceremonies – the rain-making ceremony, and the ceremony of 'surrendering oneself'. In general, however, people in China go to bed wearing clothes: even in the marriage bed, partners keep at least some of their clothes on. There is a well-known tale about a girl who lets her fan fall into the water: she takes her clothes off to retrieve it, and is observed by a man. She demands that he marry her at once, as only a married woman can be seen nude by a husband.

There is another tale about a town that was being besieged. The attackers were getting nowhere until they came up with the idea of sending a troop of women forward who were naked from the waist down. The defenders stopped shooting; but then they retaliated by making a troop of monks stand completely naked on the city wall – and then the attackers stopped shooting too! A rain-making ceremony consisted in getting two teams of naked men and women to strike each other.

In the Middle Ages, adulterous women were punished by being beaten on their bare posteriors; in particularly bad cases, the woman was stripped completely naked before being beaten. Until recently, nude female dancers in Taipeh were liable to be punished. At all times, of course, there have been eccentrics who ran about naked, but no one paid any attention to them.

Thus, nakedness may mean any of three different things: it may indicate nothing more than a primitive state of civilisation; it may be an indictable offence or part of the punishment for that offence; lastly it may serve a ritual purpose as in the rain-making ceremony (it may also be part of a trick).

Name-giving
mingming

Chinese names have two components. Every Chinese has a surname or family name (*xing*), which is written first: that is, it precedes the given name. The *xing* consists almost invariably of a single character, and is therefore monosyllabic. Altogether, there are hardly more than 400 different family names, with the result that millions of Chinese are called Wang or Li. Until the Revolution of 1911, persons with the same family name could not marry, apart from exceptional cases – for example, if it could be proved that they had had no common ancestor for at least two thousand years. Families kept genealogical records which in many cases extended back into prehistoric times, and which are in general reliable from about AD 1200 onwards.

Before the Revolution, when a woman married she did not lose her family name altogether, but often retained it along with her new family name, i.e. that of her husband. (This is still customary in Taiwan.) When a child is born it first of all receives a pet-name such as 'little lion' or 'little fatty'. A little later, it gets its personal name, its *ming*, which usually consists of two characters. The *ming* is chosen according to certain rules which are often set out in verse form. All the children, or at least all the sons belonging to the same generation, get the same character as first (or, more rarely, second) component of the *ming*. As we saw, many millions of Chinese have identical family names, and two persons with the same family name *may* be related. It is here that the code poem plays a part. For example, suppose that a visitor turns up who has the same family name and who also knows the code poem in which his *ming* appears. From this, host and visitor can at once establish whether or not they belong to the same generation of one family. This in turn will affect the manner in which the visitor is received, and the way in which he is addressed. Thus, it is almost impossible for an impostor to pass himself off as a relative.

At the age of ten, or shortly there-after, the child is given a second name. This is a monosyllable or disyllable which is chosen by the father as particularly suited to the child in question with an eye to its future success and happiness. This second name – the *zi* – is therefore symbolic. It is used by friends and strangers alike. Adults may add further names to those they already possess.

Within the family, brothers and sisters are referred to in terms of relationship only: 'older brother number two', 'younger sister number three', where 'older' and 'younger' are with relation to the age of the speaker. Again, within the family, such forms of address as 'old two', 'maternal aunt two' and so on may be used.

Artists sign pictures with one or another of their names, depending on the identity of the person for whom the picture is intended. Special reference works list the various names used by artists. In general, it may be said that Chinese names tell us more about the character and personality of their bearers than ours do; they are not standardised.

Narcissus
shui-xian 水 仙

The literal meaning of the Chinese words *shui-xian* is 'water-immortal'. As the plant blooms round about the → New Year, it makes a suitable symbol of luck in the coming year. It is supposed to have been introduced

Narcissus and peony

into the southern Chinese province of Fujian by Arab traders, about AD 1000. It is in the folklore of this province that the narcissus plays a significant part, and flower growers there try to breed varieties that look like tigers or fairies.

A picture showing a narcissus (*xian*), → stones and → bamboos (*zhu*) can be interpreted as 'The immortals (*xian*) wish (*zhu*) (you) long life (bamboos).' Like the → orchid the narcissus symbolises a married couple.

Navel
ji 臍

The umbilical cord should not be cut with a knife; it is much better if the mother bites it off. In Central China, however, it is burned off, sometimes with hot tongs. A nice navel should look like a → bean. If a woman has a large, deep navel, it is a sign of her strength and beauty. A protruding navel is regarded as ugly and probably indicative of illness.

In one ancient text, the province of Shandong is described as 'the navel of the world'.

Needle
zhen

Needlework was taboo at certain times of the year: thus, from → New Year's Day to the 5th of the 1st month, a needle could not be used in case it should enter the eye of the Buddha. A woman who does needlework on the 3rd day of a lunar month will soon be a widow; if she uses her needle on the 9th her parents will die an untimely death, if on the 10th she may give birth to a girl, but never a → son. The eye of the needle is female, the point is male.

Nephrite
yu

The usual translation of the Chinese word *yu* is 'jade'. However, many pieces of 'jade' are not true jade at all but nephrite. This is particularly the case in Taiwan, where pure jade is not found at all. Nephrite is less transparent than jade and it is a darker green; like jade, however, it is polished and used for making jewellery and weapons.

Its firmness and elasticity probably explain the very frequent use in novels of the term 'nephrite stem', meaning the penis.

New Year
xin-nian

The Chinese New Year lasts not for a day but for two weeks. It is a family feast: sons come home from far-off places, and newly married daughters visit their parents.

It is the time of year when people are in contact with the world of the spirits via the → hearth-god, who goes aloft on the 24th day of the 12th month to report on what he has witnessed during the past twelve months.

The story goes that a certain hearth-god, thoroughly disgusted and fed-up with his year, begged the Jade Emperor in heaven to annihilate the human race. Before anything could be done, however, the other gods came to intercede for mankind; whereupon the Jade Emperor told them to go to earth and see for themselves what went on there. In the meantime, on earth, people had stopped working, tidied everything up and laid on the festivities – and this was the beginning of the New Year Feast.

Before the feast begins, → father and eldest → son go to the family graves and invite the ancestral spirits to their home: pictures of them are hung up, candles and incense are lit. 'The doors are protected by the two genii of the door and by lucky symbols in red against evil → spirits;

New Year picture designed to ward off evil spirits

and when the doors are closed people settle down to wait for midnight, taking great care not to pronounce any word that might have inauspicious connotations' (Richard Wilhelm).

In preparation for the feast, the streets are also decorated with → lanterns of every shape and colour, paper dragons and shadow-pictures. 'On the walls brightly coloured pictures are hung up for sale; most of these depict chubby, well-nourished → children, or the friendly domestic spirits: → Guan-di, the tutelary god with his red face; → Guan-yin, the goddess of mercy with her falcon, which brings her the chain of prayers from earth-dwellers, and with her → vase of twigs that shower blessings . . . and of course the god of → riches: he is never

Modern New Year pictures

absent from any country store' (Richard Wilhelm).

The conclusion of the Feast of Lanterns on the first full moon after New Year also marks the end of the whole festival.

Nine
jiu
九

The square of → three is a very potent male number, which plays an important part in the *Yi-jing* (the 'Book of Changes'). Thus, regarding the first hexagram: 'When only nines appear, this means: a troop of headless → dragons appear . . . the whole sign *qian* (= the creative) is set in motion and turns into the sign *kun* (= the receptive)' (tr. Richard Wilhelm).

The ancient 'Book of Rites' (*Li-ji*) enumerates nine rites: 'Initiation ceremony of a male child, marriage,

Nine sheep (or goats) under the sign of the triple yang

audience, embassies, burial, sacrifice, hospitality, ceremonial drinking, military traditions. In addition, we are told that these nine symbolise the five permutations of matter (→ elements).

Expounding the principles of things, the earliest Chinese encyclopaedia, the 'Spring and Autumn of Lü Bu-wei', says: '→ Heaven has nine fields, → earth has nine regions, the country has nine → mountains, the mountains have nine passes, in the sea there are nine islands.' The mythical → Emperor Yu is said to have subdued the nine big rivers in the form of the nine-headed → dragon: he travelled over the nine provinces and measured them, i.e. he divided the earth into nine → square fields each of which he then further subdivided into nine smaller fields.

On the lines of the nine provinces, there arose in Han times the concept of the 'Nine Wells' (*jiu quan*) as a term denoting the realm of the dead (→ hell). On the 9th day of the 9th month the feast of the 'double *yang*' was observed: men went up into the mountains and drank wine from → chrysanthemum flowers. Old Peking, which was built in keeping with astrological advice, has a holy of holies in the centre, and eight access avenues – i.e. nine parts.

Noodles
mian-tiao

We know from grave excavations that noodles were in general use in the Tang Dynasty (618–907). They used to be made from pure wheat or rice, but nowadays a mixture of maize, peas and beans is more commonly used. In South China, they are eaten particularly at → New Year, as they symbolise → longevity. 'Packet of noodles' is a term for the *Mons veneris*.

North/South
nan-bei

The people of North China are said to be quiet and level-headed, unlike the Cantonese in the South, who are turbulent, revolutionary and less reliable. But no one seems to have come up with a plausible reason why this should be so.

The Old Man of the North Pole with snake and tortoise

Ancient Chinese cosmology recognised two antipodes – the 'God of the Northern Dipper' and the 'God of the Southern Dipper' (→ longevity).

'South Wind' (*nan feng*) is a term for 'homosexuality', since it is phonetically identical with *nan-feng* = 'male custom' (i.e. sodomy).

Nose
bi-z

According to the ancient Chinese doctrine of correspondences, the nose is the bodily orifice corresponding to the lungs: and as it sticks up out of the face, it is also compared with the penis. 'The human middle' (*ren zhong*) is the line joining the nose to the mouth: the expression graphically symbolises the pleasures of sex.

As regards men, a large nose is considered preferable to a long one. Most of the girls in brothels had short noses, which was supposed to indicate a high degree of sexual awareness. As in Turkey, biting the nose off is a sign of extreme jealousy.

Noxious Creatures, The Five
wu-du 五 毒

The → centipede, the → snake, the scorpion, the → gecko and the → toad: these are regarded as the five noxious creatures, which people in North China try to expel on the 5th

The five noxious creatures

Nü-gua 女媧

Nü-gua seems to have been the sister of → Fu-xi, who was also her husband. Like him, she has a → snake's body or a fish's tail. She could transform 70 different things per day. Together, she and Fu-xi 'invented' marriage. But her main claim to fame is that she could smelt and fuse things. One day when the gods were engaged in combat, one of the four pillars holding up the earth got broken: whereupon Nü-gua used her skill to smelt stones and mend it. However, she didn't get the height quite right, with the result that the firmament sags a little at the south-eastern corner – and this is why all the rivers in China run towards the South-east.

day of the 5th Chinese month. This particular day is close to the summer solstice – a critical moment of transition, when mankind is particularly exposed to danger. In South China, the Dragon Boat festivities are held on the same day (→ dragon). Painters were fond of representing the heroic → Zhong-kui, surrounded by the creatures: the grim-visaged hero is busy slaying them, thus freeing the world from the evils they betoken.

Each period in Chinese history has its own way of denoting and interpreting the 'five evils'. In the People's Republic, *wu-du* means 'bribery and corruption, tax evasion, misappropriation of state property, slapdash work due to using inferior materials, theft of state economic information'. (This definition is from the Chinese–German Dictionary published in Peking in 1964.)

She is also regarded as the inventor of the → mouth organ, and she codified the (religious) music of China. According to other traditions she invented the → flute, and created human beings from figures of clay which she baked in an oven: some got overdone, which accounts for the black races; others were taken out too soon and these are the white races. Yet another tradition tells us that once upon a time a brother and sister lived in the Kun-lun: their names were Fu-xi and Nü-gua, and no one else existed. They did not wish to contract an incestuous marriage, so they sought the advice of the oracle by letting two clouds of smoke ascend upwards: these united in the sky, a sign that it was their duty to marry. When intercourse took place, Fu-xi thought it

Fu-xi and Nü-gua

proper to cover his bride's face – which is what many women still do, according to an old text.

It is said of Nü-gua that on many occasions she has come to the help of hard-pressed heroes. On the other hand, she was instrumental in bringing about the death of Emperor Zhou-xin, the last Emperor of the Shang Dynasty, because he had made up a suggestive poem about her.

In stone relief work, Fu-xi and Nü-gua are shown with the lower halves of their bodies intertwined. Nü-gua is on the right, with a pair of compasses in her right hand; Fu-xi has a square-measure in his left hand. These insignia convey an impression of 'sound customs'.

Number Mysticism
mishu

祕 數

The cardinal importance accruing to number symbolism in ancient China may be gauged from the fact that every dynasty selected a number as a kind of modulus for its reign. The chosen number might be one of the numbered tones in the old pentatonic music, which automatically linked it to one of the → five colours. It followed from this that when a change of dynasty took place, the colour of court dress had to be altered, and a new scale was chosen for the court music, as European countries change their national anthem after a revolution. There is a story that one of the old philosophers was once upon a time called upon to bring about a change in a valley where it was always cold: all he had to do was to play the 'right' music – and the valley warmed up!

Any one numerical symbol refers to a whole complex of facts and pseudo-facts – which is not to say that other numerical symbols cannot be brought into correlation with this same complex. In fact, number in China is as readily capable of 'change' as are many other things: the category of 'change' is basic to Chinese thought.

The lunar year on which the Chinese → calendar was based (the

Cycle of → Twelve) generates a number system which can be used in reckoning all other astronomical and chronological data. Chinese → astrology uses a system of → 'Ten Heavenly Stems' and → 'Twelve Earthly Branches' (→ lunar stations).

Such doctrines as that of the two natural principles → *yin* and → *yang*, of the heaven-earth-man trinity, of the → square as the ruling figure, of the five → elements or 'permutations', and of the eight → trigrams, give rise, as might be expected, to endless numerological speculation. → Geomancy also derives ultimately from a form of number mysticism.

Along with their many practical uses, the natural numbers gave the Chinese for thousands of years an insight 'into the way things are held together and into the alternating cultural systems in which we may discern the rhythms of cosmic life' (Marcel Granet).

See separate entries on the cardinals, numbers One to Ten, Twelve, Thirteen: also, Twenty-four, Thirty-six, Seventy-two and Ten Thousand.

Nuns
ni-gu　　尼 姑

Nunneries were instituted against the will of → Buddha, mainly at the behest of Ananda, Buddha's favourite disciple. From the historical sources it seems that the first convent was set up in China round about AD 350.

A woman who did not wish to marry could expect to meet with little understanding and no sympathy. It is related of one provincial governor that he had all the nuns in his province rounded up and weighed. They were then forcibly married off to available bachelors at the best going rate – for pork!

There were times when women flocked to convents in considerable numbers. A Chinese proverb ran: 'If a woman refuses to serve a husband and bring up children, let her enter a nunnery!' The first nunneries exclusively for women date from AD 972: from then onwards, nuns could no longer be initiated along with monks.

It is considered bad luck to see a nun on the street between New Year's Day and the 3rd day of the feast.

Nuo-zha　　哪 吒

This is a youthful god: he stands on a fiery wheel, in combat with his enemies. According to one tale, he is the son of the Heavenly Ruler of the North, at fault in that he revered only → Buddha and not his parents. Then again, he is the son of Li Jing: he was born after a three-year pregnancy as a lump of flesh which his father dashed to pieces. His deeds are related in the novels *Feng-shen yan-yi* ('The Metamorphoses of the Gods') and *Xi you ji* ('Journey to the West').

O

Occultism
midao　秘道

From the days of → Lao-zi and →
Confucius onwards, the educated
upper classes in China have been on
the whole enlightened, rational and
concerned with life here and now
rather than with a shadowy beyond.
Pari passu with this rationalist
approach, however, there persisted
a cult of ancestor worship, laced with
all sorts of → astrological practices,
→ geomancy, → medicine, augury
and → oracles, and → number
mysticism. The task that both Confucians and Taoists set themselves was
to arrive at a complete understanding of the self, as part of an all-
embracing ontological ethics. 'Union
in the spirit' guided both schools
even when such mythological and
alchemistic factions as that of the
Taoist Huai-nan-zi (179–122 BC)
arose, when Taoist secret societies

sprang up all over China and when
Confucianism for its part hardened
into an increasingly doctrinaire
system.

'→ Heaven and → hell are in
men's minds': this is the key-note of
the Chinese attitude to the world
beyond, which we find cropping up
again and again throughout Chinese
history. In later stages of Confucianism, funeral procedures and
ancestor worship were developed to
a degree where genuine auto-sugges-
tion followed as a matter of course.
'Through fasting and meditating on
the life of the deceased, obsessive
concentration on his appearance, the
sound of his voice, his habits, the
filial mourner is brought to such a
state of mental receptiveness that
often he almost sees his dead father
and hears his voice' (Richard
Wilhelm). In any case, it is not easy
to distinguish, where the Chinese are
concerned, between ceremonial
behaviour, on the one hand, and
genuine feeling expressed as feeling,
on the other.

Members of an occult sect performing their rites

The uncertainty which Confucius connected with the concept of life after death – a concept which made ancestor worship a duty, an uncertainty which adumbrated free thinking (Richard Wilhelm) – left the broad masses untouched. Many Chinese, not content with simply venerating → spirits and deities, sought closer contact with them. A rich field of activity opened up before the various sects and occult movements. Times of political upheaval, e.g. the Boxer Rebellion, brought these movements floods of converts: e.g. the → Fox Movement, which involved the worship of 'the third father Hu', as Hu the Fox was manifestly able to heal the sick and offer help in other crises of everyday life. Then there was the Swastika

Society, which devoted itself to charitable ends, and which still has today its adherents in South-east Asia.

Until the thirties of this century, China swarmed with sects such as these and with occult groups. Some were highly ritualistic, like the 'Dragon-flower sect' (*long-hua*), whose antecedents can be traced back to the → 'White Lotus Society' of the Ming Dynasty: ritualistic penitence, sexual practices and the mass burning of incense were popular means of inducing access to the subconscious. Other secret societies discarded ritual and devoted themselves to more practical affairs of everyday life – e.g. the Xian-tian ('Earlier than Heaven') sect and the Wu Wei ('Do without Ado') sect.

Spiritualistic practices are still found today – e.g. in a temple, a square board is strewn with sand or

The 'White Lotus' sect

ashes, over which two men hold a rod: during the seance, the rod 'moves by itself' and makes characters or signs on the board. A specialist is then brought in to decipher and interpret these 'messages from the world beyond'.

See also Amulet, Soul.

Odour
qi-wei

It is true that the classical literature distinguishes → five odours. These are: goatish (associated with the East and with wood); the smell of burning (associated with the South and with fire); fragrant (associated with the earth and the middle); rancid (associated with the West and with metal) and putrid (associated with the North and with water). But, as far as ordinary people are concerned, only two come into question: nice smells and nasty ones. 'Fragrance' (*xiang* or *fang*) is a stock encomium for everything concerning a woman – her bedroom, her clothes, her hair, skin, body and genitalia. A brothel is described as 'the hell of fragrance and powder'. The tongue of the beloved is a 'soft fragrance'. Virgins have a 'scent of purity'. 'Curious scents' can have a stimulating effect, e.g. a woman's sweat. But the smell of a woman's bound feet (common in old China) was also a 'curious scent'.

An expression frequently used to describe the feelings of young men is 'sympathy with the scent and caring about the → jade'. Many men dream of 'sweet perfume'. A very curious expression is 'listening to the scent'. 'Adding scent' is a custom observed on the eve of a wedding: relations of the bride come and throw → money into a chest in which there is → incense. 'Scent' in this expression is equivalent to 'incense', which is still burned today in temples as part of the act of worship. There are 'incense clocks' which consist of a coin fastened to an incense stick. When the stick burns down, the coin falls into a bowl with a tinkling sound. Short periods of time can be measured in this way, e.g. the time it takes a story-teller to relate something, etc.

'Incense-head' is an expression denoting a shaman; 'scented flesh' is a taboo expression for dog-meat.

Stench (*chou*) is not often mentioned. A particularly awful stench is → 'fox-smell' which is typical of foreigners (i.e. Europeans) and which, according to a modern novel, is simply unendurable. The smell of armpits also comes into this category.

Official
guan

Both in the theory of the state and in the social hierarchy of ancient China, the official's role was of cardinal importance. Education, the organisation of public works, military affairs and jurisdiction were all in the hands of powerful officials. Their activities even had a cosmological dimension: for some of them were astronomers who looked after the → calendar and, at the same

An official in court dress with a bat: 'May the divine official bring good luck!'

the value of an astute choice of personnel and of a highly organised administration. Duty trips – i.e. postings to more or less remote parts of the Empire – were an integral part of the theory of the state (→ tally).

Officials shown in Chinese → New Year pictures are very often gods dressed in court clothes with cap (→ hat), chest and body sashes, and wearing ceremonial → shoes. The official holds in both hands a scroll bearing the words *tian-guan ci fu,* i.e. 'May the heavenly official bring (you) happiness.' Before a performance in the popular theatre an actor in similar dress comes on and greets the audience with these words.

time, recorded and interpreted the astrological signs (→ astrology).

The Taoist concept of *wu wei* ('activity in non-activity') was interpreted by later philosophers as meaning that the official had to be active and efficient, while the monarch did nothing. It was enough for the ruler to choose the right sort of officials who would then discharge all his duties, leaving him to enjoy his supreme rank in majestic peace. As Han Fei-zi puts it: 'His doing is non-doing, and nothing is left undone.'

So much for the theory; in practice, matters were at all times rather different, though the ancient → Emperors were not slow to recognise

A child dressed up as an official offers wine to a high official

The heavenly official is the first member of a Taoist trinity, which also includes the earth official and the water official. All three appear on the 15th day of the 1st month, the beginning of the ternary period of *shang yuan*, which runs to the 14th day of the 7th month. (The other two periods are *zhong-yuan*, from the 15th of the 7th to the end of the 11th month; and *xia-yuan*, from the 1st of the 12th to the 14th of the 1st month. These periods have to do with the cult of the spirits of the dead.)

A career as an official offered many advantages and privileges, and could only be attained via success in the very difficult and exacting state examinations. Thus good wishes for success (often depending on a pun) can be read into certain symbols: cf. the following entries: Aubergine, Bean, Boat, Chrysanthemum, Maple, Monkey. Scholars, who were almost always also officials, also came to occupy a very high place in the hierarchy of officials.

Originally, *tai bao* = 'great protector' was the title given to one of the Emperor's highest officials. Later it came to refer to a gang-leader's sidekick. Today it is used to mean a juvenile offender.

Olive
gan-lan

橄 欖

For climatic reasons, the olive tree grows better in South China than in the North. The tree seems to have been introduced to China from Persia, where – as in South-western Asia in general – it had been cultivated since the 3rd millennium BC. Being → green, the olive symbolises life; and from it is brewed a sort of → wine or → tea which used to be drunk at → New Year.

One
yi

—

One Chinese dictionary gives 67 meanings of the character *yi*, giving a total of 3,417 compounds. Another takes 923 folio pages to deal with this single character: confronted with this, the publishers gave up the idea of producing a complete dictionary of numbers.

According to ancient Chinese philosophy, there was in the beginning the 'Greatest and Highest' (→ *tai ji*) whence issued the 'Great Monad' (*tai yi*); this in turn divided into the → two principles, → *yin* and → *yang*, which generated the five → elements or 'states of being' (wood, fire, earth, metal, water); from these five elements the → 'ten thousand things' (*wan wu*) arise.

Confucian thinkers and → Lao-zi alike stressed in their own ways that the 'One' is the Undivided, the Perfect Entity. 'Great is the original power of the Creative One, to whom all beings owe their existence. And this power flows through the whole of Heaven' (Elucidation to the first hexagram of the *Yi-jing*: 'the Creative One').

And in Lao-zi:

There is a thing confusedly formed,

Born before heaven and earth.
Silent and void
It stands alone and does not
  change,
Goes round and does not weary.
It is capable of being the mother
  of the world.
I know not its name
So I style it 'the way'.
(Tr. D. C. Lau, Penguin Books,
  1963, p. 82)

Onion
cong

The onion often serves as a symbol for 'clever' (*cong*). There is one particular kind of onion known as 'stag-onion' which a pregnant woman should wear at her waist if she wants a son. Chinese vegetarians do not eat onions. If onions are put under the bridal bed, the husband is unable to deflower his bride. The fingers of a woman are compared to green onions. Women who go to the onion field on the 15th day of the 1st month and dig out onions, will get good husbands.

Open, To
kai

'Opening' and 'concealing' are related concepts in Chinese. Anything that runs counter to good moral custom should be 'concealed'. One of the key concepts of Confucian ethics is *chi* = shame (the basic meaning of the character is 'to stare hard or fixedly at something').

→ Sexual matters are neither openly displayed nor described in plain language: they are *nei-bu* = 'belonging to the interior'. Pictures and metaphors may, however, reveal what language prefers to veil. Thus 'breaking the seal' refers to defloration; going with a prostitute is 'opening the heart'; an orgasm is described as 'opening of joy'. If you make love twice in the same evening 'the plum blossom is opening for the second time'. 'Opening thrice' refers to three very specialised ways of making love.

Oracle
shenyu

In prehistoric and early historical China, prognostication was practised by means of oracle bones and tortoise shells. Holes were bored in the shells or in the shoulder bones of cattle, into which hot rods were inserted: cracks then appeared on the obverse side, from which answers of the 'yes–no' type were derived. Similarly, something that had just happened or was about to happen could be identified as 'auspicious' or 'inauspicious'. The method could be varied. For example, glowing metal could be held close to the bore-holes in the shell which then cracked in various ways, or bones could be prepared and thrown into the fire. The text of the question was always scratched onto shell or bone, so that these oracle bones provide us with what amounts to historical documentation – in fact, the most important source,

The sign of change in the Yi-jing

so far discovered, for the history of the Shang period (*c.* 1500–1050 BC). Similar oracle bones, sometimes furnished with authenticating dates, were used until recently by various ethnic minorities.

In early Chinese culture, oracles of this kind provided important guide-lines which ordered and channelled the stream of events and possible reactions. 'The oracle priests functioned as indispensable coordinators in a world which was split between the wilderness and the town, between this life and that beyond, and where the dividing partitions were thin enough to allow continual traffic and exchange between them' (Wolfgang Bauer).

In the later practice of prognostication by means of the yarrow plant 50 sections of yarrow stem were laid out: certain divisions and subtractions were then performed which were construed as 'correspondences' to → heaven, → earth, → man, → the seasons. Odd and even residues of whole or broken yarrow stems were then formed into → trigrams which were subsequently expanded into hexagrams. This is the principle underlying the celebrated *Yi-jing*, the 3,000-year-old 'Book of Changes'. This consists of a logically expanding system of 64 hexagrams, whose accompanying explanations ('The Verdict', 'The Picture') are supposed to enlighten the enquirer with regard to his own situation. This is not a simple binary prognostication of the 'good/bad' type: rather it identifies, with the help of tossed coins or staves, the contingent situation of an individual and the possible or likely developments therefrom. 'As long as things are still happening, they can be directed' (*Yi-jing*, tr. Richard Wilhelm).

If the *Yi-jing* has become something of a fashionable craze in the West (via translation into Western languages) this is not the case in the East, where the book is now used by scholars only, as it is no easy matter to interpret commentaries and explanations whose authenticity is itself far from certain. Nowadays in most East Asian temples – and especially in South-east Asia – there are bamboo canes containing 12, 24, 28, 49, 64, 100 or 120 short rods. The enquirer chooses one of these and shakes the container till a rod falls out. He looks at the number written on it and then chooses the correspondingly numbered slip from an adjacent board: on this he will find the answer to his questions concerning his → fate. Attendants are employed to read the slips of paper to the illiterate, and to explain their content to anyone who cannot understand it. These answers are obviously simplifications and vulgarisations of the text of the original *Yi-jing*.

In addition there are books that interpret dreams; and some people try to foretell the future from strange noises in the ears or twitching of the eye (*yan-tiao*).

Orange
ju-z

橘子

Oranges grow in South China. They were regarded as very suitable presents for children. The story was told of Lu Ji, who was given two

Two oranges and two fishes in a basket: '(May) every year (be) happy!'

oranges for himself but who ate neither and presented them both to his mother; he was thus known as an example of → *xiao*, the attention to filial duty which the Chinese prize so highly. *Ju* = orange is phonetically very close to *zhu* = 'to wish or pray for good fortune' (*zhu fu*); and accordingly, the orange is regarded as a harbinger of good luck and is often eaten on the second day of the → New Year Feast. On this day in ancient times the Emperor had oranges distributed to his officials.

A related fruit is the bitter orange (*yuan*), which symbolises the phonetically equivalent → fate, destiny (*yuan*).

Orchid
lan

蘭

The word *lan* can also mean → lily or iris. The symbolical significance of the orchid has to do mainly with its scent. An 'orchid-room' is the dwelling-place of a young girl or the bedroom of a married couple. A beautiful woman's breath is like the perfume of an orchid. The word *lan* = orchid occurs in women's names only.

Old texts mention bathing in orchid blossom. But this may be a euphemism for bathing in filth which was supposed to be a cure for possession by → spirits. In general, the flower stands for love and beauty. 'Golden-orchid Bond' (*jin lan qi*) is a close friendship between two men or women, which is not necessarily sexual. A man can say to his wife: 'Above (on earth) we have the (bond of the) golden orchid, below (the earth) we have the same grave.' The relationship between two homosexuals can also be described as a 'Golden-orchid Bond'.

The 'Golden Orchid Club' was limited to the Shun-de area in the province of Guangdong. This was a 'young-girl-house' where girls went to live at puberty and where they led a fairly free existence: there were also similar houses for young men. One governor of the province found the freedoms enjoyed by these girls so offensive that he had the eyes of their fathers and brothers painted red in token of the scandal they had brought upon family life. Once the parents had chosen a suitable bridegroom, a girl would then be extracted forcibly from the 'Golden Orchid Club' and married off. However, some girls refused to stay with their husbands and went back to the Club to live – whereupon the husbands proceeded at once to take other wives. This custom probably arose among the Zhuang, one of the largest non-Han minorities in South China.

Orchids in a → vase may mean 'concord', after the passage in the *Yi-jing* which says: 'When two people are in concord, their sharpness (→ metal) is broken. Words of concord are fragrant as orchids.'

Oriole
ying

Because of its beautiful song, the oriole is the bird of joy and of music. In paintings representing the → five human relationships, the oriole symbolises friendship.

'The swallow harmonises with the oriole' is a form of love-play, for which another metaphor is 'The oriole is randy and the butterfly plucks.' A 'floating oriole' (the Chinese word *liu-ying* suggests rather 'wandering oriole') is a prostitute: prostitutes were often singing-girls into the bargain. A 'wild oriole' is a free-lance prostitute, i.e. non-registered. An 'oriole-swallow' is a bar-maid, and 'oriole-flower-halls' are top-rank brothels.

An orchid

Oriole on cherry twig

Otter
shui-ta 水獺

Literary evidence goes to show that even in the Middle Ages otters were being trained to catch fish. The otter is the symbol of sexual activity, indeed hyper-activity: according to popular belief its sexual appetite is so insatiable that when it cannot find a female partner it embraces a tree and dies in the process. That is to say, its penis remains fixed in the tree, and can then provide a very trustworthy aphrodisiac.

There are many tales of otters in female guise seducing men.

Owl
xiao 鴞

For the ancient Egyptians the owl was the bird of the dead, as it was in ancient India; for the Greeks it was a symbol of wisdom, while the Romans eyed it askance as a bird of ill-omen. The Chinese agree with the Romans; the appearance of an owl heralds disaster, and in this the bird is the opposite of the → phoenix, the harbinger of happiness and fortune.

Its bad name appears to rest mainly on the belief that young owls could not learn to fly until they had picked out the eyes of their mother – not something likely to appeal to people who value filial piety as highly as the Chinese do!

Many authorities identify the owl with the 'demon chariot', a being which originally had ten heads, till a dog bit off one of them. The monster

Embroidered handbag with owl (upper right)

has been bleeding ever since, and children's clothes should not be left out in the sun to dry, as it may cast an evil spell on them.

Big staring eyes are typical of demons, and the owl is certainly gifted in this respect. But in ancient China, the owl cannot have been viewed with dislike alone, as many bronze vessels are extant which are owl-shaped, and roof-finials often took the form of sculptured owls which were supposed to shelter the inmates from 'thunder and fire'.

Ox (Cow)
niu   牛

The ox (cow) is the second animal in the Chinese zodiac, where it follows the → rat. The word *niu* is used in Chinese as a generic term, covering the animals which are distinguished in English as ox, cow, bull, etc. To Chinese, the *niu* is the animal that draws the plough and acts as beast of burden. Even today, many Chinese will not eat beef,

believing it to be immoral to kill and eat the creature which helps them with the harvest, and which therefore deserves their thanks. It is likely that this taboo came into China with Buddhism, as it suggests a connection with the Buddhist ban on meat, especially beef.

More than one medieval Emperor issued edicts prohibiting the slaughter and the consumption of oxen. Similar edicts of a more rigorous nature were issued in Japan. In South China, again, there was a popular cult of the ox (or the → water buffalo) which had nothing at all to do with Buddhism. The ox symbolises the spring, as work on the land began in spring with the ceremonial ploughing, in which at one time the → Emperor took an active part. There existed 'ox-temples' for the 'yellow ox' (*Bovina communis*). Oxen of other colours were not rare; and one old story tells

Boy with kite on an ox

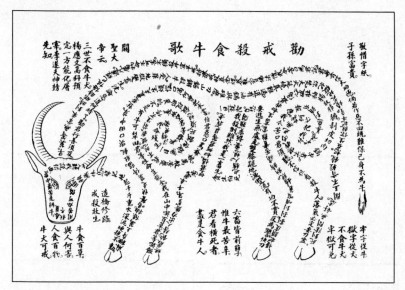

An ox delineated in Chinese characters

how two black and two blue oxen came out of the → river in the neighbourhood of the city of Lo-yang, and fought with each other. The connection between the ox and → water is of very long standing: and at one time, stone or bronze figures of oxen used to be thrown into rivers if the dykes were threatening to give way. Several legends tell how an ox came out of a tree, ran into the river and was then revered as a god. Common to all of these legends is a popular belief in the strength of the animal.

Bull-fighting was known among some of the aboriginal minority groups in South China, and the sport was taken over by the Chinese. Two bulls were matched with each other: the loser was slaughtered and eaten by both parties to the contest. Often, these 'bulls' were in fact water buffalo. Some authorities say that these contests are ritual re-enact-ments of a fight with a river god in the shape of an ox which took place in West China. Clearly, however, we have here a fertility cult, as during the fight the aboriginal women danced and beat drums with an abandon reserved otherwise for their → 'Drum-dance Feast'. This feast took place at the end of the harvest: in Korea on the 5th day of the 5th month.

Oyster
li

In many dialects the word for oyster (*li*) is identical with the word for 'younger brother' (*di in guoyu*). Oysters presented to a woman who has just given birth express the wish that the new baby may soon have a younger brother.

P

Panther
bao

豹

The word *bao* means 'leopard' or
'panther'. Neither animal is common
in Chinese painting. In the older
literature, there is, at most, rather
frequent mention of the panther's
tail (*bao-wei*), which was a mark of
distinction, used to adorn war chariots. The panther itself is regarded
as a savage and cruel animal, and it
was probably for this reason that the
word *bao* = panther was taboo in
West China (*bao* = cruel, savage).
In actual fact, the animal symbolises
'taming savagery' (*fu-meng*); a
young woman who was beautiful,
but also headstrong and violent, was
dubbed a 'flowery panther' (*hua bao-
z*).

   In association with one or more →
magpies (*xi*), however, representation of a panther takes on quite a
different meaning. *Xi* can also mean
'joy, pleasure', and *bao* can mean 'to

*Panther and magpie as harbingers of joys
to come*

announce, herald'. So, such a picture can be interpreted as meaning 'May this picture herald joy for you' and it makes a very suitable family present.

Parrot
ying-wu; ying-ge 鸚鵡

The parrot is native to South China, but has been known all over the country for more than two thousand years: an ancient text mentions talking parrots. The bird is often depicted holding a pearl in its beak, accompanying the goddess → Guanyin.

By itself, the word for parrot can simply mean 'a young girl'. The expression 'the parrot invites (us) to tea' refers to a bar-maid or a girl in a brothel.

Parrots

Partridge
zhe-gu 鷓鴣

The partridge is regarded as a bird of the South. It symbolises elective affinity, as is already clear from the wise saws of a seasonal nature found in the ancient 'Book of Songs' (*Shijing*). The cooing hen partridge calling seductively to the cock at the time of the spring floods becomes a symbol for 'disorderly relations'. Hardly concealed here is a reference to Princess Yi-jiang, who outraged custom by marrying first the father, then the son (Duke Xuan of Wei, 718–699 BC). 'Construed as an allegorical aphorism, each and every traditional metaphor or simile reveals something of the way in which nature is ordered' (Marcel Granet).

Partridges

Parts of the Body 肢體
zhiti

In old Chinese thought, the parallelism existing between macrocosm and microcosm extended to the human body. The lower part of the body, the part which is nearer to the → earth, is ruled by → *yin*: it was associated with the West, and hence with the right side. Eyes and ears, however, are in the upper part of the body, associated with → heaven, with → *yang*, and with the left hand facing east. For these reasons, the status of 'left' was superior to that of 'right'. 'It is for these reasons that the left ear of a defeated enemy was cut off and his left eye put out. It was strictly logical then that one should use the right hand to consume the things of the earth: the right hand is the hand one uses, and the hand with which one kills, so it should be hidden' (Marcel Granet). Only very rarely does one see a person who uses the left hand to write with; and left-handed eaters are a great rarity who suffer at mealtimes.

Later, a comparison was made between the parts of the body and the institutions of the Chinese state. The diaphragm is the palace, the arms are the suburbs, the legs the boundaries, etc., etc. Again, the body is the ruler and the arms are his ministers; they must obey the body.

A modern fable tells how the different parts of the body strove together, each asserting its role over those of the others, until the whole organism perished.

Pass 關
guan

Fortified customs posts were built at border passes in the mountains, and in Chinese novels these posts are often the scene of violent combat. A children's game in Taiwan is called 'passing through the five passes'. Also in Taiwan we find the belief that when a child has reached the age of twelve, it has to pass through several passes, in each of which a 'god-general' shoots arrows at it. So, from their seventh or eighth year onwards, children have to be instructed in Buddhism so that they may stand some chance of getting through all the passes. The way before them will then be marked by stones bearing inscriptions, and when the demiurge fires his arrows they will be harmlessly deflected by the stones.

A popular motif in painting shows → Lao-zi at the Han-gu Pass, where he expounded the *Dao De Jing* to the border guard. This story provides the central theme of Bertolt Brecht's book *The Legend of Lao-zi's Going into Exile, and the Making of the Dao De Jing* (1939).

Pavilion 亭
ting

A frequent motif in Chinese painting is a small pavilion which is sometimes round, sometimes many-cornered. If this airy edifice stands on a steep rock jutting up out of

Pavilion on the island of paradise

Peach
tao

Hardly any other tree or fruit in China is so heavily overlaid with symbolism as the peach. Its wood and its colour kept demons at bay, its petals could cast spells on men, and the peaches of → immortality ripened only once in a thousand years (a figure stepped up in some accounts to three or even nine thousand years). Legend has it that this miraculous tree stood in the gardens of → Xi-wang-mu, deep in the fabled Kun-lun Mountains. On that rare day, when the tree bore fruit, the

the sea, surrounded by clouds, with cranes flying towards it, we know we are looking at the → Islands of the → Immortals, in the eastern sea – a kind of paradise in which the blessed spirits live.

Again, the pavilion may be built on the thick vapours issuing from the muzzle of a monster; in this case, the reference is to a Fata Morgana over the Eastern Ocean, which is also known as 'Sea-monster Market' (*shen-shi*). However, this may be a symbol for 'success' as *shen-shi* is phonetically reminiscent of *sheng-shi* = success.

Pavilions outside villages and towns protect travellers against rain; they are not infrequently the scene of chance or romantic meetings (between persons of different sex).

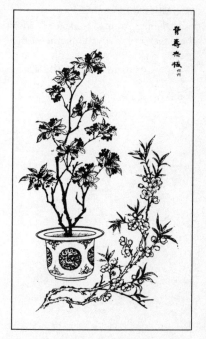

Peach-blossom and Osmanthus

goddess invited all the → Immortals to her palace and laid on a feast. But once, as we read in 'Journey to the West', the great Ming novel of the 16th century (*Xi-you ji*), the monkey Sun broke into the palace garden just before the wonderful fruit ripened, and, to the horror of the assembled guests, plucked and ate the lot. Not surprisingly, Sun became an Immortal.

The peach is the most usual symbol of → longevity. Until very recently, peach boughs were placed before the gates of houses at New Year, in order to drive away evil spirits; and bows were made from peach-wood so that demons could be shot down. Tutelary gods guarding the doors were carved from peach-wood. Later, paper models were used instead.

The immortality associated with the peach is a favourite theme of the great lyric poets of the Tang Dynasty. Thus in Li Bo (701–62):

Peach petals float their streams away in secret

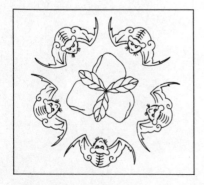

Three peaches, five bats

To other skies and earths than those of mortals.
(Tr. Arthur Cooper, Penguin Books, 1973)

This is a reference to the celebrated short story by Tao Qian (365–428) entitled 'The Story of the Peach-blossom Spring'. A simple fisherman follows a stream to a spring issuing forth from a cave, through which he passes to find another world where people lead a happy existence. This cave was often sought in the western regions of Hunan, and has been identified as a holy place of the Zhuang, a non-Han minority in South China. According to the Yao, another minority people in the same area, there are twelve peach-blossom caves, and they are stations on the way from this world to another life after death.

In popular parlance, however, 'peach-blossom spring' is used in more down-to-earth fashion as a metaphor for the vagina.

Peach-blossom is compared to the fine colouring of a young girl, but the term may also refer to a woman who is somewhat easy-going and only too ready to be seduced. 'Green peach-blossom' is a metaphor for a secret meeting-place of lovers. 'Peach-blossom eyes' are the moist, appealing eyes of actors playing female parts. In folk-poetry, the words 'A drop of peach-blossom stains the azure coat' refers to loss of virginity. 'To be peach-blossom mad' means 'to be confused with the pressures of puberty'. A 'Peach-blossom Cave' may simply be a coffin. From the great novel 'The Romance of the Three Kingdoms', the 'Peach Garden' in which the three heroes, Liu Bei, Zhang Fei and Guan Yu swear brotherhood, has become famous.

In the series of plants which symbolise the months, the peach stands for the 3rd Chinese month.

Peacock
kong-que

孔 雀

The peacock symbolises dignity and → beauty. It drives evil away; and it

Peacocks in flight

dances when it sees a beautiful woman. In Chinese legend it lacks the status it has in India, where the god of war is said to ride on a peacock, as does Sarasvati, the goddess of the poetic arts; and Indra himself is depicted sitting on a peacock throne.

Under the Manchus, peacock feathers were used as insignia denoting rank. In painting, they indicate an → official. A → vase with peacock feathers and coral can be interpreted as meaning 'May the brilliance of the feathers and the button be yours' – a reference to the practice of making the distinctive buttons for first- and second-rank officials from coral.

Pear
li

Pear-trees can live for a very long time, so it is not surprising to find them used as a symbol for → longevity. In one Chinese opera, a fruit merchant claims that his pears will make a marriage happy. But lovers should never cut up or divide pears since the word for 'pear' (*li*) is phonetically identical with the word for 'separation' (*li*). For the same reasons, relatives or friends should avoid dividing pears among each other.

Above all, no one should be given pears on the 15th day of the 7th month, for this is the day which the spirits of the dead spend on earth, and pears would bring their loss home even more forcefully to bereaved families.

Zheng-zi, Confucius's favourite disciple, who was celebrated for his piety, repudiated his wife because she did not cook pears long enough for the family meal. 'Pear blossom with rain drops' rates as a sight of very special beauty, and the phrase is used to describe beautiful women.

Pearl
zhu 珠

The pearl is one of the → eight jewels: it stands for purity and preciousness. The Chinese knew how to cultivate pearls before the beginning of our era, and long before the Japanese entered the field. Tears may be called 'little pearls'. In ancient times, a pearl was laid in the mouth of a dead person, perhaps because the → 'mussel becomes "pregnant" by reason of thunder, and the pearl grows by moonlight'.

The Chinese say that Tibetan monks have a 'seduction pearl' which gives them magic properties for sixty years. Any woman caught in its rays becomes desperate for love.

Peng-zu 彭祖

Peng-zu is the Chinese Methuselah. He is said to have attained the age of 800 years; at 70 he still looked like a baby. In an ancient collection of biographies of Immortals we read: 'Peng-zu said: Even if a man has no knowledge of magic, he can reach an

Peng-zu

age of 120 years if he relies on and looks after his own vital forces: but if he wilfully neglects to do so in some respect, he may not reach this age. Even the slightest acquaintance with the "Way" (*dao*) will enable him to reach 240 years: 480 years, if he has somewhat deeper knowledge. If he can make full use of his spiritual powers he does not need to die at all – but this in itself does not make him an "Immortal". The Way to cultivate → longevity consists simply in this: never offend against life. In winter one feels warm, in summer cool, and the harmony that imbues the four → seasons never fails; one adjusts one's body to the environment. In the dark room one enjoys women, without letting a covetous thought cross one's mind: thus is vitality given its head.'

Peng-zu is usually depicted as burning → incense and praying for a long life. Often he is surrounded by children. Such a picture wishes the recipient a long life.

Peony
mu-dan 牡 丹

The peony is the 'Queen of Flowers', the emblem of wealth and distinction. Its present name in Chinese, *mu-dan*, hardly appears before the 5th century AD; previously the flower was called *shuo-yao*. In the 'Book of Odes' amorous youths and maidens give each other *shuo-yao*. The *mu-dan* is presumably the 8th-century refinement of the old native peony. It occurs in various colours, but the red peony was, and still is, the most admired and valued. White peonies, which are a later development, symbolise young → girls who are distinguished by their wit as much as by their beauty. Legend has a woman called 'White Peony' (Bai mu-dan) who challenged the Immortal → Lü Dong-bin to a contest in amorous sports: the duel went on all night long, but she won in the end – by tickling him! The historian Ou-yang Xiu (1007–72) wrote a book on the white peony, and poets of the Tang Dynasty (618–907) sang its praises in their own inimitable manner.

Embroidered handbag: in the centre a peony surrounded by bats

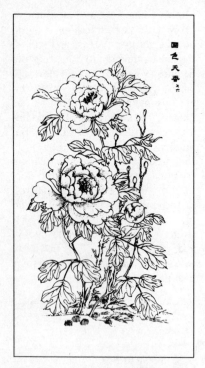

The peony, symbol of maidenhood

girl); 'When the peony begins to bloom, it is picked by the young man.' More specifically, the peony symbolises the female genitalia: 'When the dew (= semen) drops, the peony opens.'

In pictures, we find the peony along with the → lotus, the → plum-tree, and the → chrysanthemum: together, they represent the four → seasons, the peony being the flower of → spring. Together with the → hibiscus (*fu-rong*) it means 'flourishing (*rong*) in riches and reputation'. Other groupings are: with the wild apple (*hai-tang*) 'May your house (*tang*) stand in riches and credit'; together with the peach 'Long life, riches and reputation'; together with → pine-tree and → stone 'Riches, reputation and long life'.

At times, the peony became almost synonymous with 'flower' in general. A play dating from the Ming Dynasty tells how the Empress Wu was arrogant enough to order all flowers to bloom forthwith: only the peony disobeyed her. This episode is expanded in Chapters 3–4 of the later novel *Jing-hua yuan*. In popular parlance a 'peony' is a ravishingly attractive young woman. As folk-songs put it: 'I'm waiting for the peony to bloom in the garden.' 'When the peony blooms, its perfume spreads for 1,000 miles and attracts flowers and butterflies' (here 'flowers and butterflies' symbolise the young man, the peony is the

Persimmon
shi   柿

By itself, the persimmon (also called the date-palm or the Chinese fig)

Persimmon ornamentation

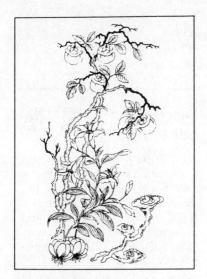

Persimmon, lily and miraculous mushroom: 'May everything proceed as you wish!'

symbolises 'affairs', 'matters' in general (*shi* = affairs, business). Together with a tangerine (mandarin orange) it symbolises the wish 'May you have good fortune in all your undertakings.' This is because the Chinese word for tangerine, *ju*, is phonetically close to *ji* = luck, fortune. A cake made from persimmons may be depicted together with a branch of a → pine-tree (*bo*) and an → orange (*ju* here taken as phonetically suggestive of *ji*): this grouping expresses the wish 'Good luck (*ji*) in a hundred (*bai*) undertakings (*shi*).' Coupled with the → lichee fruit, the persimmon means 'profit (gain) (*li*) on the market (*shi*)' – in other words, a favourable business deal.

As a → tree, the persimmon has four virtues: it has a long life, it gives shade, birds nest in it, and it

harbours no vermin. It is probably for these reasons that it used to be frequently planted in temple gardens.

Pheasant
ye-ji   野雞

The pheasant plays a rather prominent part in early Chinese literature. It was believed to turn into an oyster (or a → snake, according to some texts) in the first winter month.

The pheasant is one of the figures in an ancient board-game, where it is opposed by the → owl. In general, the bird was regarded as one of ill-omen. If pheasants did not cry at the beginning of the 12th month, a great flood was imminent. If they had still not started to cry by the middle of the same month, women became lascivious and seduced men. The pheasant was also supposed to cry at the first → thunder of spring, and again when the celestial → dog appeared or a comet was seen in the sky. One of the popular romances tells how a pheasant disguised itself as a beautiful woman and seduced a sweets-seller; however, celestial help arrives, and the pheasant is slain. In a 19th-century text, a pheasant leads a lover to his sweetheart – but she turns out to be a spirit.

The pheasant also figures in a series of twelve → insignia: here, it represents the Empress. In North-west China there was a celebrated place of worship – the so-called 'Storehouse of Chen' (*Chen-cang*) – which plays a very prominent role in

A pheasant

'golden pheasant' with long tail-feathers, was the symbol of an official in the civil service.

Phoenix
feng-huang

The Chinese *feng-huang* has nothing to do with the phoenix of Egyptian and classical antiquity, apart from the fact that it too is mythological. It is mentioned in texts dating from as far back as the end of the second millennium BC; and in a commentary to the 'Spring and Autumn Annals' (4th century BC), we are told that the male phoenix (along with the female → unicorn, and the five magic beings – the white tiger, the tortoise, the green dragon, the red bird and the dark warrior) is a

Chinese belief. The story goes that a boy was once chasing a pair of pheasants there. The cock pheasant took refuge in Chen-cang and turned into a stone, while the hen settled somewhere else a long way off. What actually happened is not very clear from the ancient texts, but today the expression 'to cross the storehouse of Chen' (it was built over water) means 'to indulge in secret extra-marital sexual intercourse'.

The South Gate of the Palace was known as the 'Pheasant Gate'. A

Male and female phoenix

sign that the land is being ruled by a just king. Confucius is referring to the lack of such signs from heaven (*fu-rui*) when he complains that the phoenix appears no more: presumably because the government is bad, and there is no prospect of improvement.

The *feng-huang* is the second of the four miraculous creatures, and the ruler of those which are feathered. Depicted together with a → dragon, it symbolises the Empress (the Emperor being represented by the dragon). Its use as a female symbol is of later date.

Chinese scholars consider it likely that the *feng-huang* was originally a god of the → winds, as the written character (see above) is derived from the character for 'wind' (*feng*). Some think that the *feng* in the creature's name refers to the male, the *huang* to the female phoenix: and that together the two words symbolise sexual union. Others take the bird to be a → *yang* creature (i.e. representing the male principle) and associated with the South. Its body, it is said, symbolises the → five human qualities: its head, virtue (*de*); the wings, duty; the back, ritually correct

Phoenix with nine young ones

behaviour; the breast, humanity; the stomach, reliability. Its feathers are, correspondingly, of five colours.

Some texts speak of a cinnabar red phoenix which is supposed to have been born in a cinnabar-cave at the South Pole; and the creature is then known as the 'Phoenix of the Cinna-bar-mountain'. Cinnabar is red – the colour of the South – and is the basic substance in Taoist alchemy. In Chinese philosophy, it is normal for alchemistic practices to have a sexual connotation, and this is reflected in the terminology; so the 'Phoenix of the Cinnabar-mountain' may also denote the female genitalia.

The expression 'the two phoenixes pierce the blossom' denotes connubial intercourse; 'false male and empty female phoenix' refers to homosexuality. In North-west China, the phoenix now represents the lover, while the → peony symbolises the beloved. This can be depicted as three phoenixes on whose backs children are riding: the children carry vases with peonies and other flowers. A picture with a dragon on the left and a phoenix on the right symbolises man and wife. A phoenix depicted on a woman's wedding dress indicates that she is 'Empress for a day'. A woman with particularly attractive eyes has 'phoenix eyes'. 'The phoenixes are dancing in pairs' is one of the thirty positions in sexual intercourse.

There is a description of the realm of Uttarakuru, the paradise behind Mount Meru, where, we are told, Feng and the 'white *luan*' are entertaining the Immortals with song and dance. This *luan* is supposed to be the female phoenix but it is always

described in the same way as the male – apart from one detail: a '*luan-man*' (*luan-sheng*) is a person who uses a planchette to ask the spirits questions. Answers, when they come, are usually in the form of poems. It is on record that a *luan-sheng* in a Taiwan village put 1,717 questions in three months: most of these questions being of a practical nature – what day is most suitable for a particular job, what medicine should one take, what sort of → amulet should one wear, etc. Here we see the creatures of mythology joining forces with → occultism.

Pig
zhu 豬

The pig is the last of the twelve creatures in the Chinese → zodiac: it symbolises virility. The Chinese pig can be → black or → white. The founding father of the Kitan, a non-Chinese people who came from Manchuria to rule large areas of North China between 916 and 1122, is supposed to have had a pig's head; and for this reason the Kitan would not, it seems, eat pork. Nor do Chinese → Muslims eat it, in keeping with universal Islamic precept. Since the god Xuan-tan is a Muslim, no pork should be offered to him in sacrifice either. → Girls should not eat knuckle of pork, as this suggests pregnancy; pregnant women are given this dish, however, as it is supposed to be very nourishing both for mother and

The pig betokens good luck in an examination

unborn child. 'Eating roast pork' is a metaphor for sexual intercourse.

The 'river-pig' (*he zhu*) is a kind of abalone or sea-mussel, which can be very poisonous indeed, but which is much eaten by the Chinese.

Pine
song 松

The pine is the favourite tree of Chinese painters: no other tree has been depicted so often in Chinese art. Since it can stand up to the cold and does not lose its needles, the pine symbolises → longevity and steadfastness. Pine-trees and cedars rank above all other trees, and epitomise self-discipline. Pines, → bamboos and → plum-trees are the → 'three friends in winter', although

the plum-tree does not really bloom till the early spring. Pines and → cranes symbolise the last years of a long life. The ancient custom of planting a pine-tree on a grave probably plays a part here.

The pine-tree is a key motif in Chinese poetry. Compounds like *song-lai* = 'the music of the pine-needles', and *song-tao* = 'the rustling of the pines', are poetic commonplaces. In the Analects (*Lun yu*) of → Confucius, there are several references to the pine: 'by being immobile it prolongs its life'. And again: the Master said: 'When the year becomes cold, then we know how the pine and the cypress are the last to lose their leaves' (Book IX, Ch. XXVII, tr. Legge). The theme is taken up again by the nature poets of the Tang Dynasty – for example, in the poem 'Pines in the Courtyard' by Bo Ju-yi (772–846): 'What good have they done me since I shared their lives? Little, if at all, have they eased the

Pine-tree with rocks and narcissi

The pine-tree: the tree that epitomises all trees

bonds of my heart. But they are "useful friends" to me, and they fulfil my wish for "conversations with wise men".'

Old pine-trees are much admired and venerated. One ancient tree that stood at the foot of → Tai-shan Mountain was made a mandarin of the fifth class by the First → Emperor. As pine needles grow in pairs, the tree is also a symbol of → married bliss.

and is the colour of → fornication. In one Chinese province, all the prostitutes had to have pink identity → tallies. *Hong-niang* (= 'red girls') was a general name for girls in brothels. It is also the stock name of a lady's-maid in many Chinese plays. The 'red girl' arranges assignations between her mistress and a lover, and in general does what she can to make the course of true love run smooth.

Pink
fen-hong

The literal meaning of the two Chinese characters above is 'powder-red', i.e. 'make-up red'; and characters meaning 'peach-red' are also sometimes used for 'pink'. The colour symbolises female flightiness,

Planets
xing

In contrast to the → constellations, the planets play no great part in Chinese mythology. Five planets were known to the ancient Chinese astronomers, which meant that they could be readily fitted into the extensive series of correspondences based on → five. Thus, a planet was associated with each of the five directions and with the attendant colour. In only two cases is choice of colour apt: Mars is red and Venus white. Since white is the colour of death, of the West and of autumn – i.e. of that season in which nature begins to decay – Venus is the star of the West, where of course the planet is seèn at its most impressive as evening star. Venus is known as the 'Big White One' (*tai bai*) and is associated with the male principle. Mars is associated with → fire and the South. It is also known as 'Fire-star' and as 'Punishment of heaven'. Its appearance in the sky heralds wars. → Jupiter is associated with the East and with the → element wood. Mercury belongs to the North and → water, and its symbolic colour is → black. Mercury is a symbol of the Empress. Lastly, Saturn is in the → middle, and its colour is that of the → earth, i.e. → yellow.

The plum-blossom loop

Plum
mei; li

Even before it has leaves, the plum-tree begins to blossom, the first tree in the spring to do so. Admittedly, in the cold of North China, this is only possible if the tree is kept under glass as a pot plant – which is what the Chinese do if they want the blossom to appear in the 'spring month' of the old calendar (corresponding to our January/February). The plum is described as 'ice-skinned and jade-boned' and is compared to a burgeoning but as yet innocent girl. It represents winter and virginity.

'In the corner of the wall, some twigs of plum blossom. Braving the frost, they bloom quietly for themselves. Even from a distance, you can see that it is not snow. And from somewhere a sweet perfume is wafted' (Wang An-shi, 11th century, tr. Lessing).

The five petals symbolise the five gods of good luck. 'Plum-blossom' (*mei-hua*) is a common term for the lady's-maids and serving girls of former times: the term has a connotation of sexual pleasure, as can be seen from its use to denote the cover on the bridal bed – 'Plum-blossom Cover'. But in a completely different context, 'plum-blossom' also refers to a way of foretelling human → fate, which is said to have been developed by the philosopher Shao

Plum-blossom

Yung (1011–77). A picture showing a scholar at his table laden with books, to whom a boy is bringing two sprays of plum-blossom, is a reference to the poet Lin Bu (967–1028), who was famous for his poems on this theme (e.g. 'The little Plum-tree in my Mountain Garden', *Shan-yuan xiao-mei*).

Plum-tree, → pine-tree and → bamboo are the three → friends of the cold season. A picture showing bamboo, plum-tree, children at play, an old man with two women and a lady's-maid, symbolises the following saying: 'The plum-tree puts forth many kernels (= children), the green bamboo (*xun*) brings many grandchildren' (*sun*, phonetically close to *xun*).

'Blue plum and bamboo-horse' is a term denoting a young couple who were attached to each other in early youth, before they could marry. 'Peach and plum' (*tao-li*) denotes students. Plums may also symbolise → eyebrows, as the Chinese words are similar.

'The plum-trees are in bloom for the second time' may mean a second marriage (possibly with a concubine) or a second round of sexual intercourse in the same night.

'Willow-plum-sickness' (*yang-mei bing*) is the Chinese word for 'syphilis', apparently because the lesions are supposed to look like plum-blossom.

Pomegranate 石榴
shi-liu

The Chinese characters mean 'stone willow'; and Chinese sources tell us that the tree was brought to China from the Near East in the 2nd century BC. As in the Near East, so too in China the pomegranate symbolises fertility as it is full of seeds (*zi*), by the rules of homonymic transfer, therefore, full of children (*zi*). It is one of the 'three fortunate fruits' – along with the → peach and the → finger-lemon. These fruits symbolise abundance and plenty. A picture of a ripe pomegranate, half-open, is a very popular wedding present. The inscription here will be: '*liu kai bai-zi*' = 'the pomegranate opens: hundred seeds, hundred sons' (in Chinese, the word *zi* can mean both 'seed' and 'son'). A pomegranate 'opens its mouth in laughter' (*shi-liu kai xiao-kou*). Girls like to put

A pomegranate full of seeds

pomegranate blossoms in their hair. If a girl is told that she is 'apple (*ping-guo*) and peach (*tao*)' what is meant is that she is 16 years old (*shi-liu* = 16, i.e. homonymic with *shi-liu* = pomegranate). When performing a sacrifice, pomegranates should not be used as the fruit is said to be too seductive. The pomegranate blossoms in the 5th Chinese month, in the summer, that is. It joins the → orchid, the iris and the wild apple as one of the 'blossoms of the four → seasons'.

Pomegranate, cap of office and sash do not express the wish (as one might expect) that a certain → official should be 'fertile', but that the title and rank he holds should continue in the family from generation to generation: for *shi* = pomegranate is a homonym of *shi* = generation.

Powder
fen

In ancient times, face powder was made from rice-starch, and it was

not until about two thousand years ago that mineral-based cosmetics began to be used. It seems that women have always powdered their faces in the interests of → beauty; and, as in Europe, prostitutes tended to lay it on very thickly. This is why prostitutes were disparagingly referred to as 'powder-heads' (*fen-tou*).

Precious Things, The Eight
ba-bao

八 寶

The → eight symbols of Buddhism and the eight emblems of the → scholar are also known as jewels or precious things. The Buddhist precious things appear mostly as decorative elements in embroidery (on altar curtains and altar cloths). Those of the scholar in general reduce to those specific to Confucianism in particular and consist of things which a scholar would value and use for writing purposes. The inventory may be extended to include the following fourteen objects: wishing pearls, → musical stone, clouds predicting good luck, → rhombus, → rhinoceros (horn) cup, books, pictures, → maple, → yarrow, → banana leaf, → tripod, herb of → immortality, → money, silver shoe.

A 'bowl of precious things' (*ju bao pen*) is often represented: in the background there may be a rich man sitting in state in his reception hall, and two or three children may play around him, symbolising → longevity, riches and sons. This is meant to express the wish that the recipient of the picture should be blessed with this world's goods: but the man in the background doesn't really fit in, as he is Shi Chong, a medieval ruler, who amassed enormous riches and yet died in poverty, as he himself had feared.

A lucky bowl occurs in the legend of Chen Wan-san, who lived *c.* AD 1400: he was an animal-lover and was always letting fish off the hook. He was therefore given a bowl which was instantly filled to the brim with money whenever he threw a single coin into it. This Aladdin's Lamp has a counterpart in the shape of the 'Money-shedding Tree' (*yao qian shu*).

The fourteen precious things

Pubic Hair
yinmao

Chinese has several periphrastic terms for pubic hair: 'black rose', 'fragrant grass', 'sacred hair' or, simply, 'moss'. It is often compared to a → beard. A woman with hairy legs is supposed to have a lot of pubic hair. The more luxuriant the growth, the more sensual and, hence, the more lecherous the woman is supposed to be. Clever women are said to have long, fine pubic hair; stupid women haven't got any, and are therefore called 'white tigers'. It is a sign of beauty if the hair forms an equilateral triangle and grows upwards.

Purple
zi

Purple is frequently associated with both → heaven and the → Emperor.

The Imperial Palace was known as the 'Purple Region'. On stage, heroes with purple faces can be recognised – like those with red faces – as loyal, imperturbable → officials. Nowadays, purple expresses grief and self-pity. The placenta is known as the 'carriage of the purple river'.

Q

Quail
an; chun 鶉

The quail is a symbol of courage, because in rural China quail-fights – like cock-fights – were a popular form of amusement. It used to be believed that the quail sang all summer, turned into a big field-mouse at the onset of winter, and reappeared as a quail in the spring (→ swallow). 'The quails go in pairs, the magpies fly two by two' says a famous couplet in the *Shi-jing* (the 'Book of Odes'), which was often used to make deeper political points.

'Nine quails together' means 'May nine generations live together in peace (*an*)'. In this sentence, the verb 'live' (*ju*) is symbolised by *ju* = chrysanthemum. In the nature of things, it is not a sentence that is very often appropriate.

Nine quails with a chrysanthemum

Prostitutes are sometimes called 'quails who sell their feathers (i.e. their skin)'.

R

Rain
yu

雨

Scratched on one of the oldest oracle bones (13th–12th centuries BC) that have come down to us, is the question: When is it going to rain? We can feel the urgency in these primitive characters – rain was vital to the agrarian economy of old China. Indeed, sacrifices to the rain-gods in time of drought were performed well into modern times.

'Wind and rain blow through the cosmos' (*Huai-nan-zi* of Liu An, died 121 BC). To command wind and rain was the privilege of spirits powerful in magic (*ling*).

Rain comes about when the female principle (→ *yin*) unites with the male principle (→ *yang*). 'Rain and Dew' represent contrasting poetical motifs which serve as emblems for certain seasons of the year. 'With rain is associated the representation of female properties,

雨
師

Rain-god on clouds

with dew the representation of princely munificence' (Marcel Granet).

The rainbow is seen as a resplendent symbol of the union of *yang* and *yin*: it serves therefore as an emblem of marriage. You should never point your finger at a rainbow.

But the rainbow can have another meaning, in that it may appear when either husband or wife is more handsome and attractive than the other, and therefore enters upon an adulterous relationship. The rainbow is then an emblem of → fornication or sexual abuse, and forebodes ill.

'Rainbow bridges' are 'flying' bridges made of tree-trunks unsupported by pillars. 'Rainbow skirts' have strips decorated in many colours round the bottom hem.

In early reliefs, the rainbow is shown as a → snake or as a → dragon with two heads. In West China they give it the head of a → donkey, and it rates as a lucky symbol.

Rang

Rang is a specifically Chinese concept, which can hardly be translated by any one word into a European language. It is perhaps best paraphrased as 'giving in in order to get something when there is no other way of achieving it'. At a very basic level, it may mean no more than stepping aside to let someone else pass on the street. More significantly, I may *rang yu*: i.e. cede rights or privileges which are indisputably mine, thus indirectly forcing someone else to make an equivalent concession. An → Emperor when forced to abdicate performed *rang wang*: that is to say, he surrendered the throne to which he had a traditional entitlement, in favour of

a usurper. The latter could not have the deposed Emperor put to death immediately, much as he would have liked to, in order to eliminate a possible source of political opposition; he usually did so some time later.

In everyday life it happens quite often that someone turns down a small gift, aware that if he accepted it he would be under moral pressure to repay it with a larger and more expensive gift.

Rat
da shu

The rat is the first creature in the old Chinese → zodiac. The story goes that the → ox was at the head of the string of animals which wanted to be included in the zodiac. But no one had noticed that a rat had got on to the ox's back, and when the creatures lined up to be appointed, the rat jumped down and was taken first.

The rat is associated with → money; when you hear a rat scrabbling around for food at night, it is said to be 'counting money'. 'Money-rat' is a disparaging way of referring to a miser.

Rats used to be left undisturbed on certain days in the year so that

1936
1948

1960
1972

Rat years

they could get married in peace! The days thus observed varied from one region of China to another – thus, the 3rd day of the 12th month, the 7th of the 12th or the 19th of the 1st. In a South Chinese legend, it is the rat which brings → rice to mankind. Rats can turn into demons – male demons usually, in contrast with the fox which turns into a female demon. When rats appear in a house, → cats soon follow, because they know that the family will soon be in poverty.

There is frequent mention in early texts of a rat-dance in which the rats stand up on their hind legs, place their front paws on their heads and sing.

Unlike the rat, the mouse plays little part in Chinese symbolism, perhaps because it does not do so much harm; perhaps also because both creatures have the same name in Chinese (*shu*). When a distinction must be made, the rat is called 'old mouse' (*lao shu*), or 'big mouse' (*da shu*).

Performing mice used to be shown in Peking markets at → New Year.

Rattle
jing-zhang

A rod or staff fitted with a ring at the upper end, from which further rings hang. It is an Indian symbol, and appears only in Buddhist contexts. The rattle symbolises the mendicant monk who warns small creatures on the ground to get out of his way lest he inadvertently step on them.

Raven
wu ya 烏鴉

On the oldest stone reliefs that have come down to us the raven is already depicted as the creature of the → sun, together with its counterpart, the moon hare. As the sun is associated with → fire and the moon with → water, we should expect to find a fire-bird in the sun, but this cannot be substantiated from the texts.

Legend has it that there were once ten sun-ravens which generated so much heat that mankind was likely to perish – but then the archer Hou Yi shot nine of the searing suns down. So now there is only one

The archer Hou Yi, shooting down the nine suns. These are symbolised by the ravens lying on the ground

raven in the sun – but it has three legs.

A red raven was the symbolic creature of the Zhou Dynasty (c. 1050–256 BC), because the Zhou identified themselves with the sun. A three-legged raven was the messenger of the goddess → Xi-wang-mu, and these ravens brought her food. The legend also tells how the celestials engaged in tournaments and competitions: the suns prepare for combat in the guise of three-legged ravens, but retreat as soon as → unicorns lay on a duel, or a qi-lin tries to swallow them up.

Ravens are supposed to be very pious birds; and they raise burial mounds to those men who are particularly distinguished for their xiao. There are also 'divine' ravens who live in temple complexes and are fed by visitors. When ravens pick up food in the shadows, they are supposed to become pregnant, and then they spit out their young.

The croaking of ravens is variously interpreted depending on the hour when it is heard. According to one text, croaking in the evening, from eight to ten o'clock, is a good sign; but if it is heard between ten o'clock and midnight it is a harbinger of death. In general, the croaking of ravens is held to be unlucky.

If a woman's hair is described as 'raven hair' this means that it is black and beautifully lustrous.

The raven, as an ugly black bird, is contrasted with the auspicious → magpie in the saying 'Better an honest raven than a deceitful magpie.'

A 'fire raven' (huo ya) serves Wen yuan-shuai, one of the gods of smallpox.

Red
hong

紅

Even in prehistoric times, red seems to have been regarded as a 'life-giving' colour: evidence from burial sites suggests that cinnabar or red chalk was interred along with the corpse. Red is the colour of the summer, of the South and also of the ancient realm of Zhou (c. 1050–256 BC). This 'Red Age' had red clothing, red tassels on the → hats of officials, red seal-cords, horses, flags, sacrificial animals, etc., etc.; and it all began with the appearance of the Red raven. This ancient stratum of popular belief is not exhausted yet – cf. the presentation of communism as the 'rule of the Reds' (Feng You-lan) and of the 'Red Guards' as the shock-troops of revolutionary unrest.

On the Chinese stage, a red-faced man is a holy person, often the god of war → Guan-di. Of the three gods of good fortune, the one who confers high office and riches wears a red robe; the one beside him, dressed in → green, blesses a family with children, while the third, who gives long life, is dressed in → yellow or in white. Thus, red is also held to be the colour of wealth.

Until the 19th century, concubines were not allowed to wear red skirts; only when the concubine went for the first time to the husband, did the chief wife give her a red garment to wear.

'Letting red fall' is, as one would expect, the act of deflowering a virgin, who then loses 'virgin red'.

One still hears the proverb 'Red face – unhappy fate' meaning the early demise of a husband who is sexually plagued to death by an over-demanding wife. 'Old Reddy' (*hong lao*) was a vulgar way of referring to rank-and-file soldiers; and 'red contract' was a document officially stamped in red, authenticating a legal or business deal, e.g. the sale of a slave. In the 14th century, a 'red register' was drawn up, listing all the wine producers in the country. The 'red heart' is the centre of the target; 'red lotus' is a late-cropping brand of rice.

'Red' can also mean 'naked'. For example, a 'red child' is a naked baby – not one with red hair! (A red-haired child, believed to be a bastard, was often exposed in ancient times.) A 'red spot' was painted on a child's forehead on the 14th day of the 8th month, to protect it against diseases. Grown women also had a red spot painted on their cheek as a beauty spot. When one prayed for divine help or guidance in a temple, it was customary to bind a 'red cord' round the neck of a statue or part of an altar. The 'Red Eyebrows' were a group of rebels in the 1st century AD who painted their eyebrows with an indelible red so that they could not desert their cause. The Taoist sect whose members specialise in exorcism are known as 'Redheads', in contradistinction to the 'Blackheads', who conduct funeral services.

Since red and green are the colours of life, their combination is especially significant. In one novel we read that many a girl is as red as → peach-blossom and ripe for love, while others are as green as → willows and can only be pitied. (But we must remember that 'pity' is a word that men often use when they are describing their feelings for young women.) Very frequently we hear of girls who have red skirts and green stockings, which means that they are very young. The phrase 'Red lamps – green wine' describes the way of life in low pubs. Painting may still be referred to as *dan-qing*: in this compound, *dan* = cinnabar and *qing* is a very old colour word which can mean anything from dark blue (the blue of the sky) to grey and green. 'Red and green' is the symbolic formula of Chinese painting. 'Red and white' is a phrase referring to marriage and funeral ceremonies. And finally one speaks appreciatively of the red lips and the white teeth of a beautiful woman.

Ren

This word denotes a specific state of mind, which we might render in somewhat basic fashion in English as 'to forbear', 'to endure': to put up with something which one would rather do without, in order to avoid something worse. There is a story about an old man who was once asked how he managed to live so happily in one house with his wife, his children, his daughters-in-law, his sons and all their wives, etc. He answered with the one word: *ren*. There is an old proverb which says: 'Forbear, forbear, forbear, pardon,

pardon, pardon' (forbearance ranks higher in the Chinese scheme of things than forgiveness).

Rhinoceros
xi-niu

The rhinoceros was native to China but has long been extinct. The horn is one of the lucky symbols associated with the → scholar. It is the emblem of the 'sound character' which a good scholar ought to have. The horn was also popularly supposed to have the property of identifying poison in a liquid.

A belt made of rhinoceros hide is impermeable. According to legend, such a belt was used by → Cao Guo-jiu, one of the eight → Immortals, when he crossed the path of the dragon kings who lived under water.

Rhombus
ling-xing

The rhombus is one of the → eight lucky symbols. It is said to symbolise a sound state of affairs in the country and its government, but some sources say it is an emblem of victory.

As in Europe, the reduplicated rhombus (*fang-zheng*) is supposed to ward off evil spirits, demons and so on. The figure is often seen on walls.

Rice
dao; mi 稻米

Rice, a staple food of the Chinese people, is cultivated mainly in South and Central China. In the North, there is a higher proportion of farinaceous crops and foods.

Its status as a useful plant goes back to the dawn of Chinese history: the mythical → Emperor Shen-nong is supposed to have performed the solemn ceremony of planting the first rice every year, and before the close of the second millennium BC there were extensive irrigation schemes along the Yangtse for the rice-fields. Here too, cosmological considerations were borne in mind: a rice field had to be proportionate in size with human dimensions if large areas of wet paddy-fields were to be regulated and held to the proper depth.

Among the Li-su (a minority in Yunnan) there is a legend that the → dog brought rice to mankind, but, as he had to run through water, he lost most of the grains on the way, and only the tops of the stalks showed. In another South Chinese legend it is the → rat that is the bringer of rice.

In olden times, rice was the food of the upper classes. Rice was also laid in a dead person's mouth. Even nowadays, rice bowls should not be heaped with rice: that should happen only in the case of the rice offerings made to ancestors. Wasting rice, whether by throwing it away or leaving it in the bowl, was gravely frowned upon, and whoever did it

could expect to get smallpox or be struck by lightning.

The flippant way in which rich people treat even important things like rice is illustrated in a parable: asked where rice came from, a rich man said, 'From the mortar,' and, when pressed for a better answer, 'From the sack.' He had no idea that peasants worked hard to produce it. Today, rice is occasionally used as a means of warding off evil spells, and in sacrifices.

When trying to cure those possessed of evil spirits, the Taoist Zhang Lu made a habit of asking for five measures of rice, a custom which gave its name to the religious and political sect of the 'Five-Measure-Rice-Taoists' (*wu-dou-mi*).

Irrigating and weeding rice-fields

Riches, God of 財神
cai-shen

The god of riches is represented sometimes as a single being, sometimes as a dual being, sometimes as a group of deities. As a *mixta persona*, the being on the left is the military god, the being on the right is the civil god (cf. the Emperor's governors). The two beings who figure in the dual god of riches are not always the same, however. Sometimes we find → Guan-di, the just and upright warrior, and Bi-gan, the loyal minister; then again, it is Guan-di and Yao-wang, the 'King of medicine' (probably the god Bhaisajyaguru, of Buddhist origin). The two → He-he (the Heavenly Twins) are also venerated as gods of riches,

The military god of riches with his civilian counterpart

especially in the province of Anhui, though usually in a subordinate capacity to a main deity.

Other texts again recognise five gods of riches (→ Good luck, five gods of) who were really five brothers: their names are not given. What mattered, apparently, was to get rich: exactly who provided the riches was less important. If there was some doubt as to who the god of riches was, the same went for the day set aside for his worship. In most regions, sacrifice was done to him on the 2nd day of the new year, but some sources add the 5th. An ancient Peking tradition has it that the god of riches visits the supreme lord of all the gods on the 2nd and the 16th days of each month, in order to report to the 'Jade Emperor' (Yu-huang) on what people on earth have been doing. Their prospects, auspicious or otherwise, for the coming days can then be apportioned.

Riding
qi-ma   騎馬

The Chinese seem to have learned how to ride horses from their northern neighbours. Riding brought with it a change in men's garb from the flowing garments formerly worn (and retained till much later by civil officials) to trousers. The use of the verb *qi* is also a late development; earlier, one spoke of 'mounting a horse'.

A picture showing an → official on horseback, accompanied by a man who holds a → canopy over him, while eight other persons stand round him, is a reference to Liang Hao (913–1004), who was actually 84 years old when he came first in the final civil service examination.

Sitting on a horse facing backwards was not considered, as it was in Europe, a punishment or a silly caper: China's most famous poet, Li Tai-bo, rode in this fashion – and on an ass, into the bargain, i.e. on a mount used by only the poorest of the poor.

'Riding' as a metaphor for sexual intercourse is known from usage in Europe and Japan, but is not in common use in China.

Hunting in Ming times

Ring
huan

環

Like the wheel, the ring symbolises permanence: what is lasting and not subject to decay. Among the Yao people in South China, the ring is the emblem of betrothal and of love: and this is not unknown elsewhere in China. The Chinese word for 'ring' – *huan* – is phonetically identical with the word for 'to return'.

River
he; jiang; shui

河 江 水

The three great rivers of North China symbolise the first three Chinese dynasties: the Lo symbolises the Xia Dynasty, the Huanghe the Shang Dynasty, and the Wei the Zhou Dynasty. It was believed that when the water in a river changed colour – e.g. turned red – this was a bad omen for the dynasty. On the other hand, when the Huanghe (the Yellow River) turns clear, it is a good sign: this happens, so they say, only once in a thousand years, and lasts only for a day.

The mythical ruler Yu – the great Yu, the founder of the Xia Dynasty, to whom heaven entrusted the 'Nine Divisions of Hong-fan', i.e. part of the 'Book of Writings' – subdued the waters and tamed the rivers. So it was fitting that a dragon-horse should arise from the Yellow River and present him with a diagram of the river (*he-tu* – a magic → square). In the same way, a → tortoise brought him the 'Lo-shu' book from the river Lo.

All rivers have their patron gods, and one must not forget this. In ancient times, human sacrifice was made to them; in later times, this was replaced by ritual sacrifice in the temple. A celebrated legend tells how, after a breach in a dam, the river overseer had a boy thrown into the waters of the Yellow River, as instructed in a dream. Thousands of workers then had to shovel earth over the breach. But suddenly a giant hand rose from the middle of the flood, and everyone fell to the ground in awe. The boy was elevated to the status of river-god.

Stories about heroes who dive into the water to fight with the river-god are known in various parts of China. In modern folklore the dragon-king is supposed to dwell in big rivers, and to expect sacrifices. Drowned people are very dangerous: they cannot be reborn until they have found 'substitutes', so they lurk near rivers looking for bathers whom they then drag down in the water.

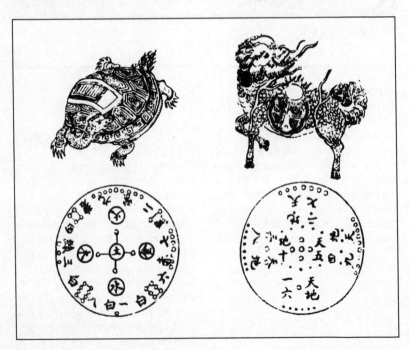

The magic squares he-tu *and* lo-shu

Rosary
nian-zhu 念珠

The rosary came to China along with Buddhism. It consists of beads, usually of wood or kernels, which are decorated in various ways. No fixed number is laid down, the usual rosary has 108 beads – i.e. 100 for 100 separate prayers, and an additional 8 in case your arithmetic has let you down. This number is otherwise explained as being composed of the → 12 months, the → 24 divisions of the year, and the → 72 five-day divisions: this makes 108 a sacred number.

One often sees elderly Chinese with strings of stone or wooden balls in their hands. These are meant to keep the fingers supple – or to help one's thoughts to wander.

Rose (Red)
qiang-wei 薔薇

In China, the rose enjoys nothing like the prestige it has in Europe. It is indeed an emblem of youth, but not of love.

It is also the plant which can stand for all four → seasons.

Rose and herb of immortality

S

Sack
bu-dai 布袋

Sacks made of leather played an important part in ancient Chinese life. They were used, as in European classical antiquity, as containers for wine. Criminals, especially those guilty of political offences, were often sewn into leather sacks and either drowned or beaten to death.

The 'god of sacks', Di-jiang, who lived on the celestial mountain, had neither eyes nor face, but six feet and four wings. He sang and danced, and resembled the Primeval Being who had no limbs, or the Primeval Chaos which was also imagined as an inchoate mass. For these reasons, the popular name for a sack was *hun-dun* = chaos. Nowadays, meat-balls wrapped in dough and boiled in water are also called *hun-dun* (the Cantonese pronunciation is *wan-dan*).

A popular figure in folk-art is the monk bearing a sack. He is supposed to have died on the 3rd day of the 3rd month of 917, in the monastery of Yue-lin in Zhejiang Province; but after his death he was seen by many, and is regarded as an avatar of Maitreya (Mi-lo). Although his sack was heavy, only a child could carry it. Once, a monk saw him taking a bath, and noticed that he had an eye on his back. Ashamed that this was no longer a secret, he gave his sack to the monk who had discovered it.

Saddle
an

An = saddle is a homonym of *an* = peace; and it is often depicted together with a vase (*ping*), which is in turn a homonym of *ping* = rest, quiet: so such a picture expresses the wish that the recipient will have peace and quiet. For more than a thousand years it has been the custom in China to place a saddle at the main gateway of the parental home before the bride and bridegroom entered it. The bride was then expected to step over the saddle in token of her wish to bring only peace and concord to the house. In the Middle Ages, this custom seems to have been observed among China's neighbours to the north as well.

Sago
xi gu mi   西 谷 米

The sago palm grows in South China. A kind of flour is made from its sago. Formerly, men who lived on the South China coast were often on the high seas for long periods. Young wives used to tie their husbands' kneebands or handkerchiefs to a sago tree to which they then prayed that their loved ones would soon come home safely. Similarity in sound may play a part here: *guang-lang* = sago and also = '(arrival at) coastal customs point'.

Sash (Belt)
dai   帶

In olden times, → officials wore a leather belt with a metal buckle. The Middle Ages saw a change in both style and material. On the modern stage, actors playing officials wear a belt which looks like a wooden hoop. The word for 'belt' (*dai*) can also mean 'to take along with oneself': so, a picture showing an official entering a palace along with his son,

A toggle in the form of a mushroom

expresses the wish that both father and son should become high officials. Even today, it is customary among the Mongols for a man who has been having intercourse with a girl, to give her a belt when he is leaving her. If the girl turns out to be pregnant she is 'married by means of the belt', and henceforth she will take the name of her lover, as will her child.

In South China, sashes are often worn in preference to belts, and are made out of cloth rather than leather. At wedding ceremonies, 'exchange of belts' symbolises the marriage. This corresponds to the old Chinese custom of the 'girdle-cloth' which the mother fastened to a bride's girdle when she was moving into her husband's house. She removed it in the marriage bed, and it was subsequently returned to her mother to be washed (i.e. it should be bloody!). Here also, the act of touching the girdle signifies the consummation of marriage.

If a man wanted to take such useful things as a → fan or a writing → brush along with him, he fastened them to a cord which ran through his belt or sash and was secured by a toggle. These toggles were in use until the beginning of the 20th century and are often very fine examples of the Chinese miniaturist's art.

Sceptre
ru-yi   如 意

The Chinese sceptre has nothing to do with the → insignia of a ruler. It embodies the notion of 'according to wish' or 'what one wants' (*ru yi*), and it is often given to old men in token of the wish 'May everything go as you wish!' The *ru-yi* is finely carved

from wood or jade, curved in shape and fitted with a kind of head.

The magic sceptre which makes wishes come true figures often, but not exclusively, in Buddhist graphic art. Together with the writing → brush symbolising the → scholar or → official, and a silver → money-shoe, the sceptre completes a picture which may be interpreted as wishing the recipient professional and social success and advancement.

The lover of the notorious Empress Wu of the Tang Dynasty was known as Ru-yi Jun = 'Master Gets-what-he-wants', no doubt because of his famed sexual prowess. Formerly at → marriage ceremonies, it was customary for the family of the bridegroom to present the bride's family with a sceptre, in earnest of the wish that → married bliss might ensue.

Sceptres are to be seen in many Chinese paintings – held by a boy riding on an → elephant, in the hands of the → He-he (when these appear as the aged → Luo-han), or

The head of the sceptre: 'As you like it'

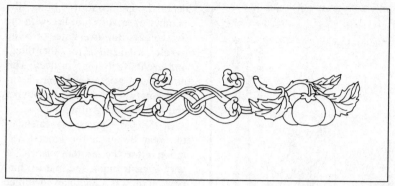

Sceptre and persimmon: 'May everything go according to (your) wish!'

in combination with → persimmon, → peach, and → plum, or against the background provided by a → meander design.

Scholar
shi   土

The scholar belongs to one of the four → callings. He is symbolised by the eight → precious things. Kuixing, the god of literature, was originally a scholar. He is portrayed with a blue face. The old word for → blue (*qing*) symbolises the scholar blue with → cold, bent over his studies in the light of the 'blue lamp' or the even more economical → glow-worm.

Ever since the days of → Confucius, the literati, the philosophers, and the scholars in official posts, have ruled China; nor were they ever less than attentive to the interests of their class. Even poor scholars were respected by ordinary people, once they had passed their examinations.

'As soon as they were appointed to office, many scholars allowed themselves to be corrupted by rich merchants to whom they then extended unique privileges and monopolies. But they never allowed the privileges of their own class to be eroded: these were inalienable. The scholars formed a closely knit group equipped with an education, a culture and a system of monopolies which they inherited and passed on to their successors. Their ideology was Confucianism, and their catechism was the Confucian Classics' (Erwin Wickert).

As late as in 1942 Mao Ze-dong could criticise his own prejudices in public: 'I could wear the clothes of other intellectuals, as I assumed they would be clean. But I was hesitant to don the garments of workers, peasants and soldiers, as it seemed to me they must be unclean.' Sixteen years later, at the 7th CPC Congress, Mao was praising the first → Emperor, when Lin Biao interrupted to point out that the Emperor had, after all, burned the → books and buried scholars alive. Mao

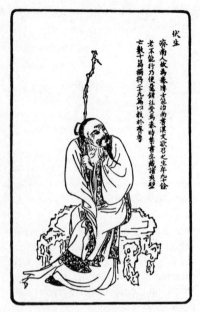

The Confucian scholar Fu-sheng, who as a nonagenarian was active in restoring ancient texts, during the Han Dynasty

decreed, in order to bring the number of seasons into line with the five colours, the five states of being (→ elements) and all the other things and events that come in fives. This fifth season was a short one, interposed between the end of summer and the beginning of autumn.

In the old Chinese → calendar, the year began at the second new moon after the winter solstice. In very ancient times, the first or third new moon was sometimes identified as the beginning of the new year. In our Western scheme of things the seasons begin immediately after the relevant solstice or equinox, but in China there is a gap of up to two months. This has to be borne in mind when we read, for example, that the → plum-tree 'blossoms in winter' – winter, for the Chinese, ended in April or even in May.

answered: 'So what; he buried 460 scholars, we've buried 46,000.' One-upmanship in 'Cultural' Revolutions? Some modern scholars have tried to show that the burying alive of scholars is a later story put about when the first Emperor had come to symbolise the cruel and bad ruler.

See also Bo-shi, Fox, Xiu-cai.

Seasons
si-shi 四時

The Chinese divide the year, as we do, into four seasons; though there was a period in the Middle Ages when a division into five seasons was

The rose as the symbol of the four seasons

The *Yue-ling* treatise ('Ordinances for the Months') lists the months with their correspondences: the animals that reappear, the plants that must be sowed or planted or which are then in bloom, the stars that the farmer must observe before he chooses a day for this or that job, and also the rituals to be held in the imperial court. Requirements were meticulously set out: ritual music must be in one of the five → tones; if the season was spring, → green garments must be worn as green is the colour corresponding to spring, etc. Even executions were to be carried out in autumn only, as the colour corresponding to autumn was white, the colour of dying and death.

Flowers portrayed in a picture identify the season: thus, the → plum-blossom symbolises winter, the → peony indicates spring, the → lotus summer and the → chrysanthemum winter. In China, the rose plays nothing like the part it does in the West, but it is recognised as the plant for all seasons, perhaps because, at least in the South of the country, it blooms all the year round.

As in Europe, human life is compared to the four seasons: up to 15 years of age we are in the spring of life, from 16 to 29 in its summer, from 30 to 39 is our autumn, and from 40 to 50 or even 60 our winter. Interestingly enough, the Chinese reckon human life from the moment of conception – i.e. a newly born child is already a year old.

Seven
qi   乙

When a Chinese speaks of the 'seven stars' (*qi xing*) he means the → sun, the → moon and the five → planets. This is an Indian or Near Eastern concept which took root in China. The idea of a seven-day week, though known, never caught on until the introduction of the Gregorian calendar in the 20th century.

Qi xing may also refer to what is called 'the Plough' in the West – i.e. part of the constellation of Ursa Major (→ bear). The 7th day of the month in the old lunar calendar is the day of the waxing half-moon, and on the 7th day of the 7th month is held a festival which is one of the biggest events in the Chinese year, especially as far as women and → girls are concerned (→ Spinning Damsel and Cowherd).

As an uneven number, seven is a *yang* number, but in numerology it is associated with women as a *yin* element. This is because the rhythmic development of the female organism appears to be based on the number seven. At seven months, a baby girl gets her first teeth which she loses when she is seven years old. At 2×7 years = 14 'the *yin* path opens' (i.e. onset of menstruation). Finally, at 7×7 years = 49 the menopause ensues.

Analogously, the male organism is supposed to develop in factors of eight.

Seven is of particular significance in the cult of the dead. The term *zuo qi* = 'make seven' refers to the seven-day periods following a death, during which the soul of the deceased gradually severs itself from this world and from its relatives. On each seventh day certain sacrifices are made and ritual ceremonies held, often with the participation of Buddhist monks who recite sutras. The whole process takes 49 days: by then the soul of the deceased has made its way to the world beyond.

Seventy-two
qi-shi-er

In ancient Chinese texts, the → nine provinces of the → earth are combined with the → eight → heavenly directions, or the eight → trigrams. Seventy-two weeks of five days each, give 360 days – i.e. slightly more than a solar year.

The mythical → Emperor Yao was said to have been 72 inches in height and to have ruled for 72 years. The founder of the Han Dynasty is supposed to have had 72 black marks on his thigh – an auspicious sign! We know that Confucius was 72 when he died; and he is said to have had 72 disciples (as Jesus is said to have sent 72 disciples forth into the world, one for each name of Jahweh).

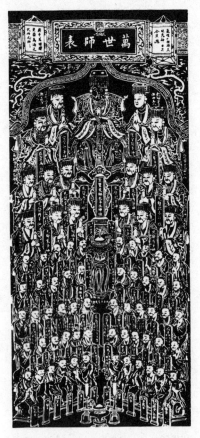

The seventy-two disciples of Confucius (stone rubbing)

Sex
se

An appendix to the celebrated *Yi-jing* ('Book of Changes') contains the sentence: 'Male and female mix their essential forces (*jing* = seminal fluids) and the → ten thousand beings arise': a surprisingly unadorned way for Chinese to convey information. True, Confucius, a thinker who is of unsurpassed authority for the whole spectrum of Chinese family and sex life, is supposed to have said: 'Eating and sex (*se*) are given by nature.' He was, of course, referring to matrimony only. Later Confucianism went so far as to recommend husbands not to hand things directly to their wives: they should lay things down so that the wife could then pick them up. That is to say, all bodily contact should be avoided in formal encounter.

The enormously rich sexual imagery conceived by the Chinese and expressed in their language goes to show that their sexuality and erotic impulses have certainly not been suppressed – rather, they have been expressed obliquely in more or less refined form. (See Beauty, Marriage, Married Bliss, Nakedness, Open.)

Post-Confucian thinkers distinguished between *se* (which normally means no more than 'colour') and *yin*, which implies an excess, an overflowing, and which may be translated as → fornication or lewdness: that is to say, the word implies both sexual freedom and sexual excess. A 19th-century writer who was also a pious Buddhist wrote: 'Of the three forbidden things in human life, sex takes first place; it generates sin and blame in ten thousand ways. Worst of all these ways is fornication (*yin*). The gods see it even when it takes place in a dark house.'

The Utopian socialist Kang Youwei (1858–1927) saw these matters in a different light. He made a strong plea for 'love-contracts' valid for a given period (*jiao-hao zhi yue*). This period should be not more than a year, not less than a month; the antiquated terms 'husband' and 'wife' were to be discarded, and 'love-contracts' for life were not to be allowed ('*Da Tong Shu*' = 'The Book of the Great Equality', 1902). This Utopia came to nothing, however; and today men and women who have sexual relations outside of the marriage bond are quite likely to land in a re-education camp.

Shadow *ying*

A man's shadow is similar to his → soul; and there is a story about a man who died when he was frightened by his own shadow. The spirits of the dead have no shadows. Another old story tells how a man of ninety married a wife and died after one night. A son was born, and, as his parentage was in doubt, the matter was taken to court. The judge ruled: if the boy is the son of the old man, he has no shadow.

A 'shadow wall' is a short wall built directly behind the main entrance to keep out evil spirits. The point is that spirits can only move in a straight line and are therefore unable to make a diversion round the 'shadow wall'.

Shan-xiao

The *shan-xiao* are mountain spirits which look like → monkeys or small men and which are found only in Central and South China. Their counterpart in North China is the → fox. Often they have only one leg, they live on crabs and dwell in trees. They are also black and hairy. They try to find out the name of anyone who comes across them, so that they can harm him. Like other → ghosts they can be scared off by fireworks.

Sheep
yang

The sheep is the eighth creature in the Chinese → zodiac. It is the emblem of filial piety (→ *xiao*) as it kneels when being suckled by its mother. Because of the phonetic similarity, however, it can also symbolise → *yang*, the male prin-

Three sheep (or goats) in the sunshine

ciple. Sheep were, on the whole, less important for the Chinese than for the nomads of Tibet and Mongolia, who believed that if sheep-bones were sown at the onset of winter, lambs would be born from the earth in the spring. Normally, no distinction was made between sheep and goats, though the latter are sometimes called 'mountain sheep'.

A 'sheep's-eye-ring' (*yang-yan quan*) is a sort of condom, which is covered with hair like a brush, and which is supposed to be made from the ring of muscle round the sheep's eye. Before use, it must be softened in warm tea.

Shoes
xie

Shoes symbolise concord and harmony (*xie*). In South China, however, the Chinese character written above is pronounced *hai*; and shoes then symbolise the wish for a son (*hai*). 'Lotus-shoes' are small shoes for women with bound feet, and also symbolise the wish: '(May you) bear sons one after another.' At → marriage ceremonies in Central China, the bride and bridegroom exchange shoes, thereby expressing the wish that both (*xie*) may live together to a ripe old age. The same sentiment can also be expressed by means of a picture showing a shoe (*xie*) and a copper (*tong*) → mirror: i.e. both (*tong* + *xie*) should grow old together. The 'iron shoes' which occur in West Asian myth are found also in

Chinese legend: 'He journeyed so far that even (his) iron shoes gave way.' Master Mou, an adept in Shaolin techniques of boxing, wore iron shoes for five years and developed a strange gait.

Silk
si 絲

Silk has been found in graves dating from as far back as the second millennium BC. An old legend credits the wife of the mythical Emperor Huang-di with its invention. Chinese silk was carried along the 'Silk Road' across Central Asia to India while → Buddhism was imported into China along the same route.

In ancient times, various types of caterpillar were used to produce silk, but in modern times virtually only one type has been used – the silkworm, which is nourished on mulberry leaves. Until modern times, again, the whole process, from feeding the silkworms to weaving the finished product, has been in the hands of women. There is a goddess of silk-making, the so-called 'third aunt' (*san gu*); but more usually 'Horsehead-woman' (*ma tou niang*) is venerated as the patron goddess of the craft. She is said to have been a young woman who made fun of a horse's hide which had been left to dry in the yard: suddenly the hide came to life and enveloped her. In this way she became a goddess.

Silkworm
chong 虫

Various sorts of caterpillar were used to produce silk among the non-Han minority peoples in South China in the very earliest times; but for a very long time now the Chinese have preferred the silkworm to all other kinds.

While the Chinese peasant concerned himself with his fields, his wife looked after the silkworms. An ancient rule stipulated that all girls over 15 years of age should rear silkworms. In many regions it is possible to have as many as four or five crops a year, though this involves very intensive labour. The women have to pick the leaves of the mulberry trees, which are best sited as close as possible to the house, and use them to feed the silkworms in their special containers several times a day. At the right time, the worms have to be killed by immersion in boiling water, and then begins the work of spinning and weaving. April is the usual month in most parts of China for all this activity to start.

According to one legend, more than a thousand silkworms were buried along with the wife of King Ho-lü.

Chinese silk was taken to Syria by traders and woven there into the sort of garments that Romans liked to wear; these were then sold to Rome, and the Chinese were well aware of the value of this commerce. So they prohibited the export of silkworms, and did all they could to keep the method of using them a secret. And

Gathering silkworms and placing them on special shelves

indeed it remained a secret until a monk concealed a few silkworms in his pilgrim's staff and introduced them to the West.

The word *chong* is also used for adopted children. Normally, a Chinese family would adopt only children who were related to themselves in some way, but occasionally male children from orphanages were adopted. In coastal areas, adopted sons of this description were often given the dangerous jobs to do, while the sons of the family were given softer jobs at home.

Sir/Mr
xian-sheng 先生

Xian-sheng is the form normally used when you are addressing a man whom you do not know very well and who is not related to you. A

Taoist and a geomancer can be so addressed: and it is a polite way of addressing one's teacher. But as far back as in the 8th century, it was the courteous way of addressing a prostitute: it still is.

Six
liu

No particular significance is attached to the number six in Chinese number mysticism. There are 'six bodily parts' – the arms and the legs plus the head and the trunk. There are also 'six directions' – the four quarters plus 'up' and 'down'. The ancient Chinese Encyclopaedia of Lü Bu-wei speaks of the 'six rivers' and the 'six great kings'. An earlier school of cosmology sought to combine five ('heavenly') things with six ('earthly') things: thus, to the five

Six-footed horse

cardinal virtues were opposed the six affects: anger and joy, pain and pleasure, love and hate.

Shi Huang-di, the first → Emperor, is said to have based his rule on the number six (thus, 36 provinces), while the mythical → Fu-xi seems to have preferred eight, and the Former Han who followed Shi Huang-di opted for nine.

these old people were immured. A related legend has to do with a tricky question which neither the → Emperor nor his minister could answer: to everyone's amazement, however, a certain young man came up with the answer. Asked how he was able to do this, he confessed that he had indeed buried his father alive as required but had left an opening in the cave wall so that he could feed the old man – who had given him the correct answer. The Emperor promptly abolished the custom.

In the time of the 'Three Kingdoms' (220–65) and thereafter, certain years were deliberately chosen for popular uprisings as they were the initial years in a new cycle of 60. In at least one case, however, that of the rabble-rouser Zhang Jio, the new year brought him not a new beginning but his own end.

Sixty
liu-shi   六十

The ancient Chinese → calendar was modulated by series based on → ten and → twelve: combining these gave 60 as a common unit. After 60 days – or 60 years – a new cycle began. From this arithmetical fact it was deduced that human life should correspondingly last for one cycle. Until modern times there persisted a legend that people who had reached the age of 60 should be buried alive. The custom seems to have been particularly prevalent in the loess areas of North China where caves are still to be seen in which

Smoke
yan   煙

Smoke is a symbol of transitoriness: it rises quickly and disperses just as quickly. It is a favourite theme of the great Tang nature poets: for example, Wang Wei:

Sun still sinking over the ford
Up from the village a single fire's
    smoke.
(Tr. G. W. Robinson, Penguin
    Books, 1973)

Far away, single characters are painted by smoke on the sky, mysterious words in code.

In certain metaphors for brothels ('Smoke and Blossom Camp', *yan-hua zhai*) and prostitutes ('Flowers of Smoke', *yan-hua*) Chinese has created memorable emblems of brief and transitory pleasures.

Snake
she

The snake is the fifth creature in the Chinese → zodiac. It is one of the five → noxious creatures, and is regarded as clever but wicked and treacherous: and treacherous people are said to have a 'snake-heart'. Formerly, snakes were objects of worship, especially along the great rivers of China, as river-gods were often imagined in the form of snakes. For example, the god of the Yellow River was a small golden-coloured snake with a square head and red dots under the eyes. This snake-god was very fond of theatrical shows which were laid on in order to keep him in a good mood. Some snake-gods demanded the sacrifice of a young → girl on a certain day each year – until a hero disguised in women's clothing could come along and kill the snake.

As in West Asian myths, snakes could make gifts of → pearls or other jewels. One well-known legend tells how a youth rescues a snake which rewards him with precious stones; but then the Emperor expresses a wish for snake-liver, and the youth asks his snake to donate its liver. This is going too far, and the snake swallows him up.

Snake-liver is even today much sought after for its medicinal properties. A lot of snake-meat is eaten in Taiwan, as it is supposed to be good for the eyes. Snake fat, on the other hand, is very dangerous stuff: if a man eats it, his penis will shrivel up and never be much use to him again.

Snakeskin should not be thrown away: keep it – sooner or later, it will bring you riches. Dreams about snakes are interpreted in various ways. It is lucky to dream that a snake is chasing you. A dream about a → black snake presages the birth of a daughter; one about a whitish-grey one, the birth of a son. In Taiwan, dreaming about a snake means you are going to lose wealth, and if the snake coils itself round you

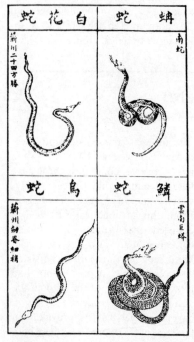

Pictures of snakes in medical books

it presages major change of some kind in your life: here the image of the snake sloughing its skin is connected with the notion of change in general. When a man dreams about one snake by itself, it means that he's going to get a new girlfriend.

Snakes are supposed to be very sensual creatures, and since they are apparently very attracted to the smell of women's underwear they can be caught in this way. So it is not surprising to find the snake identified symbolically with the penis. However, a snake with a triangular head is a *female* symbol – a caveat not to jump to indiscriminate conclusions in the field of psychological imagery!

Snake-demons with human heads are supposed to occur in the province of Guang-xi. If one of these demons calls you by name, it is best not to answer! In the same province, it is said that there are snakes so big that they can swallow an → elephant. However, as the word for elephant (*xiang*) is phonetically identical with the word for 'minister', this is probably a reference to the above-mentioned tale of the snake which swallows its rather too ambitious benefactor, who has in the meantime become a minister.

'White Snake' (*bai she*) is the heroine of a very popular folk-tale, which has been used as a basis for several films. She is a snake, but she has turned herself into a beautiful young woman: she marries the young man she has fallen in love with, and makes him rich. The young man, however, lets himself be persuaded by a Buddhist monk that

his wife is an evil creature, although by this time she is expecting his child. The monk allows the child to be born, but then has her confined to a pagoda which stood until recently on the West Lake, near Hangzhou. When the son has grown up to be a celebrated → scholar, he visits his snake-mother, and duly venerates her.

Sneezing
pen-ti

We say 'Bless you!' to someone who has just sneezed; and in the same way, in China, when a child sneezes they say 'Thousand years (i.e. may you live!).' In Han times there was a booklet on the meaning of sneezing and of buzzing in the ears, but unfortunately this has been lost. If a Chinese can't stop sneezing, he says: 'Someone is saying (bad) things about me.' He should then spit and repeat a stock phrase which runs in translation something like this: 'Good people like me: if bad people are gossiping about me may their teeth fall out!' Conversely one might say: 'If you think about someone he'll sneeze.'

Snow
xue

Snow is connected with old age and with the god of transitoriness (the 'Old Man of the Northern Dipper'). A short poem by Liu Zong-yuan

(773–819) is entitled *jiang xue*, i.e. 'the snowy river': its last line runs:

Only the old man in the straw
mantle sits alone in the boat
and fishes alone in the cold water
of the river.

Other lyricists of the Tang period compared driving snow-flakes with falling → pear-blossom.

When Chinese children make snowmen they have someone quite specific in mind – Mi-lo, the Buddha of the future, who is also known as → Fat-belly Buddha.

Softness
wen rou　温柔

'Warmth and softness have always been better than strength and hardness' says the Chinese proverb. From the life-cycle of the human being – soft and weak at birth, hard and stiff at death – Lao-zi deduced that the weak and soft are related to life, in a different way from the way the hard and strong are.

Brothels are often described as 'lands of warmth and softness' (*wen rou xiang*).

Son
zi　子

The dearest wish of every Chinese has always been to have a son, and this remains true even today. State 'family planning' requires parents to have not more than one child; and something of a crisis does ensue if this child turns out to be a girl. Whatever state legislation has to say on the subject of equality of the sexes, it remains a fact that a son is more valued than a daughter.

The Chinese word *zi* does not always mean 'son'. Affixed to a family name it means something like 'master'; e.g. Kong-zi = Master Kong = Confucius. A cultured young man of outstanding gifts is often called a *cai-zi*. One might expect *zi-di* to mean 'sons and younger brothers' (the literal translation), but in fact it refers to gentlemen who visit brothels. Thus the roué *cai-zi* has his female counterpart, the beautiful *jia-ren*.

Soul
hun; po　魂魄

The Chinese believe that two souls inhabit the human body. One of these – the *po* – is the sentient or animal soul which gives life to the human being. This soul lingers at the grave of the deceased for some time, and if the funeral arrangements have not been entirely as they should be, the *po* can cause a lot of trouble even to its own erstwhile relatives: it is essentially animal-like and fails to recognise them.

The other soul (*hun*) confers personality on human beings. It lives for a long time after death and is much concerned about those it leaves behind – on condition that they make proper sacrifice to it. If this duty is neglected, the *hun* is driven by hunger to steal sacrificial

A soul being interrogated by a tutelary deity in the presence of Guan-di

offerings made to others; it may then harm its relatives, and can be used by magicians who feed it and manipulate it for their own ends. In certain circumstances, it may even be elevated to divine status. The *hun* enters the human body at some point in the month following birth; and this may be one reason why abortion does not rate as a sin in China. The *hun* does not survive cremation, and the official blessing given to cremation in the People's Republic may well be seen as part of the drive to eradicate ancient 'superstitions'.

Buddhists on the other hand have always sanctioned cremation. They believe that after passing through several purgatories in which it is punished for its sins, the soul reaches a dark room where it has to look for a skin. According to the type of skin it finds and puts on, the soul is then reborn as a man, a woman or an animal (→ hell).

The 'soul-tablet' is a wooden tablet with the name of the dead person inscribed on it. It becomes 'alive', i.e. the locus of the soul, when it is smeared with blood from a cock's-comb.

Sparrow
ma-que 麻雀

The 'hemp-bird' rates as the most sensual of all the birds; and so, eating its flesh is supposed to increase sexual potency. It symbolises the penis. According to the old peasant calendars, when the warm weather is over, the sparrows dive into the sea or into the river Huai, where they spend the winter in the guise of oysters.

It is also said of the sparrow that it would rather die than be found wanting in honour. 'Sparrow-school' is a South Chinese term for mahjong players.

Spider
zhi-zhu

The spider is a creature of good omen. Sliding down a thread from its web, it symbolises 'good luck descending from heaven'. In one of the Central Chinese dialects the spider is called *xi-mu* = '(the one)

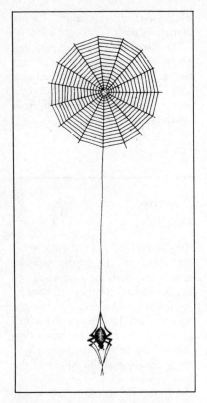

Spider on a thread: joy comes down from heaven

across a lot of girls bathing in a lake. He takes the clothing belonging to one girl, and then sees how the other girls fly up to the sky clothed in feathers – all except one: she becomes his wife, bears him a son and contributes to the house-keeping by doing some weaving. One day, the child finds her robe of feathers hidden away; the mother puts it on and flies away to the sky. One of the cows, moved by her master's plight, tells him to slaughter her and use her hide to follow his wife into the sky. He does this and meets his wife again, but they are so happy in their connubial bliss that they quite forget to do their work. The god of heaven orders that they should meet only once a month thereafter. This verdict is entrusted to a magpie for delivery – but the magpie gets it wrong and tells them that they can meet only once a year.

Their meeting is on the night of the 7th day of the 7th month, the annual feast of young girls, and a giving joy to a mother', as it betokens the return of a son from far away, or the visit of a guest.

Spinning Damsel and Cowherd
zhi-nu, niu-lang

牛 郎 織 女

A favourite Chinese myth – and one of the best-known outside China – is the story of the cowherd who comes

Spinning Damsel and Cowherd

day on which rain should fall, so that we cannot see the meeting of the happy couple.

Spirits
shen 神

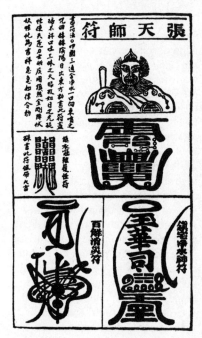

'Letters' to the spirits

Like gods (who are also *shen*), spirits are always concrete and palpable manifestations – whether we are thinking of the → souls of dead ancestors, the patron gods who look after the fields and roads and bridges (the so-called 'tree and stone' deities), the → river-gods hungry for a human sacrifice, or the → Immortals. In Chinese thinking, the boundary between this world and the world beyond is much more elastic than it is for us, and belief in ghosts and spirits is taken more seriously.

The basic distinction here is that between *shen* and *gui*. *Shen* are benevolent spirits: they include the spirits of male ancestors in the direct line who will do good as long as they are well treated. *Gui* are spirits who are helpful to their own families (i.e. they behave as *shen*) but may be the very opposite (i.e. behave as evil → ghosts to non-family).

The spirits of the dead come in for special veneration at the → feast-day of the 'Pure Lucidity' (*qing-ming*). In earlier times, the whole family went out to the ancestral graves, tidied them up, and placed small offerings to the spirits on them. It was believed that, immediately after death, the *hun*-soul was already a good part of the way from the house to the grave. It was for this reason

that the street in *Qu-fu*, connecting the grave of → Confucius with the → Hall, was called *shen-dao*, the 'Way of the Spirits'.

All *shen* once lived on the earth as mortal men. During their life-time – in some cases, after it as well – they did good deeds, and they died without leaving a son behind them on earth. Confucius had a son, who did not become a deity.

The spirits of hanged and of drowned people (*shui gui*) are dangerous. Of them it is said that they cannot be reborn until they have provided themselves with a 'representative' or 'proxy' – that is, until they have arranged for another man to be hanged or drowned at the same place.

The word *shen* is also used for anyone who is particularly skilled in, good at some art or craft: thus, *shen nü* ('god-girl') is a prostitute. The word *xian* = holy man, saint, is used in similar fashion. A 'god-staff' (*shen gun*) is a shaman (male or female). A female shaman can also be described as a *shen-tong* = 'god-boy'. Taoist gods and popular deities are usually represented as wearing the robes of an → official; goddesses are depicted in the clothing that the wife of such an official would wear. It is often difficult to be sure exactly what sort of god is being addressed or depicted. Apart from → Buddha himself, Buddhist gods are always decorated in various ways, and are equipped with emblems which make it easier to identify them.

In ancient times, a question might be put to the → oracle by carving the words on a bone and throwing it into fire; the answer came from the world of the spirits. The cracks made in the bone by the heat were seen as a kind of script which adept priests of the oracle could interpret.

Periods of deep philosophical insight coupled with a rational ordering of society and the natural environment were followed by periods of rank superstition. This happened, for example, in the case of the Western Han Dynasty (206 BC–AD 24). The court was then virtually ruled by shamans and magicians (*fang-shi*). 'The atmosphere was thick with gods and spirits' (Richard Wilhelm).

Spitting
kou-shui　　口 水

Chinese has various metaphors for spittle: 'jade-spring', 'jade-sap', 'jade-drop', 'gold-drop'. Spitting three times on the ground corresponds to saying 'touch wood'. Spitting can do a lot to keep one out of harm's way, probably because → ghosts and evil → spirits are rendered incapable of further metamorphosis if they have been spat on. If there were grounds for believing that a child was really a demon, everybody spat on it.

To this day, every house has its spittoon.

Spoon
shi　　匙

Had an ancient Chinese wished to know how to use a spoon, he would have found no help in the 'Book of Rites' (*Li-ji*), where it is not even mentioned. He would, however, have been instructed in the use of → chopsticks, and also in the use of the hand (previously washed, of course).

The sole female among the eight → Immortals, → He Xian-gu, has a bamboo spoon as her emblem. Like other household articles the spoon was formerly made from bamboo. Nowadays china spoons are usual.

'Spoon and pan' is a popular expression for penis and vagina.

Spring
chun

The spring of the year is the season in which the male element (→ *yang*) is in the ascendant. Nature and men become fertile: and so we speak of 'spring feelings' (*chun-qing*) or 'spring colours' (*chun-se*), where the word *se* has strong sexual overtones.

'Spring pictures' (*chun-hua* or *chun-tu*) are erotic pictures which are often bound up in book form (*chun-ce*). It was customary for couples to look at these pictures in the evenings. The Chinese do not regard this sort of thing as pornography, but rather as a form of instruction by means of which a virgin can be introduced to the 'Art of Love'. The Japanese have similar books, which they call 'pillow-books'.

Looking at 'spring pictures'

The great Ming painter Qiu Ying was celebrated for his 'spring pictures', which were often imitated. Then there is a special form of mirror, known as 'Spring Thoughts Mirror' (*chun yi jing*), on which are painted southern scenes and scenes from erotic plays, such as 'The West Chamber' (*Xi xiang Ji*). 'Spring medicine' (*chun-yao*) is nowadays usually a hormone preparation. Instead of pictures, small figures made from → jade and ivory were formerly given to princes of the royal family before their → marriage. Often these figures had moving parts and could be used to simulate a couple engaged in sexual intercourse. 'Spring Palace' (*chun-gong*) is a metaphor for erotic films, but may also refer to curiosa such as clocks which show a different picture every hour, or → walnuts with pictures painted inside the nut. 'Just one spring breeze' is a metaphor for a one-night stand.

The titles of two famous books, 'The Spring and Autumn Annals' (*Chun-qiu*) and 'Spring and Autumn of Lü Bu-wei' (*Lü-shi chun-qiu*) refer to historical chronicles based on the yearly cycles.

The 'Spring Place' (*chun chang*) in ancient China was situated outside the east gate of the capital. Here, an → ox (*shun niu*) was sacrificed to the god of seed-time and sowing (Goumang). The eyes of the ox were stored in the imperial medicine chest for use as an ophthalmic specific.

Spring (Fountain)
quan

Because of the loess which covers North China, all the rivers and springs in that area are yellowish-brown. In South China, however, clear springs are found, and these provide, along with wells, the main supply of drinking water. Statues of gods were often erected at spots where springs once appeared. In ancient Japan, too, small wooden shrines used to be built at such places. The Chinese word for 'spring' can be written with two components – the water radical plus a phonetic element meaning 'perfect', 'complete', and it is semantically connected with the concept of 'origin'.

Square
si-fang xing 四方形

In the ancient literature we learn of the 'River Plan' (*he-tu*) which is said to have emerged one day from the waters of the Yellow River. This 'plan' had → nine fields, to which corresponded the nine rooms of the *Ming-tang* – a religious temple known as the 'hall of light', which had *inter alia* an astronomical purpose. The nine rooms again seem to correspond to a series of nine 'planets' enumerated according to the Indian tradition as: Sun, Moon, Mercury, Mars, Venus, Jupiter, Saturn, Rahu and Ketu – the last two being invisible 'counter-worlds'

postulated in Indian astronomy. Another ancient scholar says that the 'River Plan' was identical with a → chessboard, which ties up with the cosmic significance with which the ancient Chinese invested the game of chess. Recent research has proved beyond reasonable doubt that the 'plan' was a magic square.

A 'Book of the River Lo' (*Luo-shu*) is often connected with the 'Book of the River He'. This too seems to have been a magic square based on nine.

Step of Yu
Yu bu

This is a ceremonial dance-step, invented, according to legend, by Yu, one of the mythical → Emperors, who is supposed to have subdued the Great Flood. While doing so, he is said to have taken on the form of a → bear and danced in this measure. The step is first mentioned in texts dating from the 2nd century BC, and it is still practised today by Taoist priests in their sacrificial ceremonies. Taoists can use this step to kill snakes and catch spirits; and it is also said that a certain kind of bird (*zhen*) uses this technique to break open stones, out of which it then drags snakes.

禹

克勤于邦　烝民乃粒
儆戒在朕　股肱元首
愿諧好言　九功由立
不伐不矜　振古莫及

Emperor Yu

Stone
shi　　石

Like → mountains and rocks, the stone is a symbol of → longevity. Pictures given as presents to older people often have stones in them. A picture showing a stone or rock jutting up out of the sea is usually a representation of the paradise in the Eastern Ocean (→ islands), of which a poet wrote: 'Life like the Mountain of the South and good fortune like the Ocean of the East.' The 'Birthday of the Stone' (*shi*) is on the tenth (*shi*) day of the year. People in either of whose names the word *shi* = stone occurs, never use appliances or equipment of any kind made of stone.

A cult involving stones as sacred objects was known in various parts of China. In general, prayers were made to these stones for → rain: if rain still did not fall, the stones were beaten. Then again there were stones on which women who wanted a son sat. In a temple in Sichuan province there was a stone with five openings in it; women who wanted to have children bought small stones which they tried to throw into one or another of these holes. If the stone went into the topmost hole, it was a sign that riches were coming the woman's way; a stone into the bottom hole meant that she would get honoured status. A hit scored on the left-hand hole presaged the birth of a son, on the right hand one a daughter.

'Master Stonehead' is a patron god of children in Taiwan. Women pray to him for sons who are as strong as stone. If a son is born, the mother makes sacrifice four times a year to Stonehead, until the boy is sixteen years old.

Stones erected at street corners or in front of buildings bearing the inscription 'The stone dares to stand guard' (*shi gan dang*) refer to → Taishan, and the belief associated with him, that his stone can drive off demons.

Stone and orchid

Official buildings often have stone lions in front of them. Stone seals grace the desk of the → scholar. 'Stone Drums' – i.e. stones which look like drums – suddenly begin to sound when rain or war is imminent. In Korea and often in South China 'stone fights' were held between villages at → New Year. In Taiwan, they were usually held on the 5th day of the 5th month. They were supposed to promote fertility and keep epidemics away.

Su 酥

Su is a specifically Chinese drink which is made from → milk. The word has now acquired adjectival force and is used in the meanings 'smooth', 'soft', 'delightful'. The body of a sixteen-year-old girl may be said to be 'like *su*'. The word is often used to describe the female breast.

Sulphur 硫磺
liu huang

Sulphur is used to ward off the five → noxious creatures which threaten people's lives on the 5th day of the 5th Chinese month. Above all, it can force women who have assumed the form of → snakes to revert to their real shapes (a reference to the famous novel 'Madame White Snake'). At the feast of the summer solstice – which is also a day when → ghosts and demons are active – powdered sulphur is rubbed on the ears and noses of children to protect them. For the same reasons, sulphur is put into coffins. If sulphur is rubbed on the body of a pregnant woman, an unborn girl in her womb is changed into a boy.

Sun 日
ri

The sun is an embodiment of → *yang*, the male principle. It is associated with the East where it rises and with the spring when its power begins to make itself felt. It is also a symbol of the → Emperor.

Emperor Wu of the Former Han Dynasty was born after his mother had dreamt that the sun was entering her body. One of the oldest solar myths is to be found, according to Marcel Granet, in the fragments that

Phoenix and sun

remain of the oracle-book known as *Guei Zang*. This myth concerns Xi-he, Mother of Suns, who rises up in the hollow mulberry tree which is the residence of our sun, and who stands in the valley of the sunrise (the East). Her issuing forth and her disappearance cause 'darkness and light' (*hui ming*). According to one myth, there were once ten suns – the sons of Xi-he – which threatened to scorch the earth until the heroic Hou Yi shot down nine of them. A different version of this myth gives the god of thunder the credit for destroying eight of nine suns: though some sources say that these eight were removed by the young god Er-Lang, who crushed them with a mountain.

The aboriginal inhabitants of Taiwan say that there were once two suns: one of them was shot down, and became the → moon. Among the minority peoples of South China, it is believed that there were originally twelve suns, ten of which were shot down by the sun-hero: the two that were left became our sun and moon. Another myth current in the same area of South China says that in the beginning when it was dark on earth, the → cock induced the sun to come forth (the Japanese had a similar myth).

Elsewhere, we find stories of how the sun went backwards or even stood still (cf. parallels in the Old Testament).

A three-legged → raven is supposed to live in the sun, though its place is taken in some versions of the myth by a → toad. From the way in which eclipses were explained, we can see that the sun was associated with the husband, the moon with the wife. A solar eclipse was taken as a

The Mountain of the South, the moon, the sun and pine-trees: 'Good luck and long life!'

sign that the Emperor himself was being occulted – i.e. he was too much under the influence of the Empress. Lunar eclipses occurred when wives were not duly submissive to their husbands.

Long after Chinese astronomers had identified the true reasons for both solar and lunar eclipses and could predict first the latter and then the former with some accuracy, ordinary Chinese went on believing that a → dog was trying to swallow the sun, and tried to scare off this celestial monster by beating → drums, praying, and firing arrows into the sky.

The sacrifice to the sun was an → ox which was slaughtered early in the morning. A cult involving sun and moon worship can be discerned in the rites of certain secret societies – e.g. the 'Sect of Devil-worshippers and Vegetarians' (13th century, i.e. late Song). According to Wolfgang Bauer, these traces of sun worship and worship of the light show the influence of Zoroastrianism and Manicheism which were introduced into China in Tang times. Among the lower classes, sun worship joined forces with the lucky colour → red, to find ideological expression in popular uprisings – right down to Mao Ze-dong, whose teachings were compared to a 'red sun'. The victorious power of the sun and of the revolution imbues the national anthem of the Chinese people – 'The East is red, the sun ascends.'

A picture showing the god of good luck with his hand on the sun, can be interpreted as meaning 'May you rise in rank (as an official) in as short a time as possible.'

Swallow
yan

As in European antiquity, so too in China the swallow was the harbinger of spring. The popular belief was that every spring the swallows returned from their hiding place in the sea where they had spent the winter as → mussels.

Particularly when it has built its nest in the eaves of someone's house, the swallow symbolises success, happiness and children. Swallows which make their nests of mud also build city walls, according to popular belief, fill in violated graves and complete statues of gods. In pictures showing the → five human relationships, the swallow symbolises that between elder and younger brother. When a swallow builds its nest on a house, it is a sign that someone in the house is soon going to get married.

The dried nests of a species of sea swallow that lives in the Indian Ocean are a much prized and very expensive article of → food. They are made from a particular kind of seaweed which is supposed to increase a man's vital energies.

Swastika
wan-zi

The swastika is one of the oldest symbols in both India and China. In the Indus culture of Mohenjo-Daro (2500–1500 BC) it was used mainly as a symbol of good luck; in China,

Five swastikas, five bats and the character meaning 'longevity'. That is, five-fold fortune and happiness, and a long life

it was interpreted more as an emblem of immortality.

The swastika can be angled clockwise or counter-clockwise. The former is the 'seal of the heart of Buddha' and often to be seen on the breast of statues of Buddha.

In China, the symbol was a very old form of the character *fang*, meaning the four regions of the world. From about AD 700 it has

Swastika motif in decoration: ten thousand years of luck

been used to mean → ten thousand (*wan*), i.e. symbolising infinity. This meaning is implicit in the emblem's use as a decorative motif, often far removed from the original shape, in printed fabrics.

Swing
qiu-qian

At → New Year and in the spring (often round about the 4th day of April) swinging on rope swings was a popular amusement, especially among young women. Swinging had a religious connotation, and symbolised a prayer for → longevity (*qian-qiu* = a thousand autumns). In some parts of South China and Thailand, and in Korea, the activity was connected with the 5th day of the 5th month, i.e. according to our calendar, with the summer solstice. At this turning point of the year, the to-and-fro motion of the swing may symbolise the annual progression of the sun along the ecliptic. However, there is no textual authority for this.

It was the only Chinese feast-day on which young → girls could enjoy themselves in the open air.

Sword
da dao

A demon-slaying sword is the attribute of → Lü Dong-bin, one of the

Magician with demon-repelling sword

eight → Immortals. Many legends have collected around swords and their magic properties. Among the most celebrated were the male sword Gan-jiang and its female counterpart Mo-ye, which were said to have been forged from the liver and kidneys of the metal-eating → hare of the Kunlun Mountains. And we hear how a pair of carp in ancient Vietnam turned into iron from which two swords were then made.

In dreams, the sword is represented by the → snake, but if a woman dreams of drawing a sword she will give birth to a son. If she dreams of possessing a sword, this is a very lucky omen; but if a man dreams that he sees a sword fall into the water, this presages the death of women.

An ordinary sword can be turned into one that will repel demons by smearing it with the blood of a woman who is pregnant with a male child and uttering a magic formula over it: it should then be forged anew.

T

Tai-ji 太極

The philosophic concept of *tai-ji* is of cardinal importance in Confucianism from the 11th century onwards. Even before then, the term *tai-ji* was used to mean the Original → One, from which there developed first the duality or syzygy → *yin* / → *yang*, then the five permutations or states of nature (→ elements) which generate the → 'ten thousand things'. It was Zhu Xi (1130–1200), often regarded as the greatest Chinese philosopher after Confucius, who made *tai-ji* into the Absolute, the ruling principle of the metaphysical world. Its symbol now became the empty circle partitioned into *yin* (dark) and *yang* (bright). The line between them resembles a capital S. It is popularly believed that a replica of this circle (*tai-ji tu*) can be seen on the placenta at birth.

In the 16th century, the term 'Tai-ji dress' referred to a sexual practice and 'Tai-ji bells' (*tai-ji wan*) is another name for Burmese → bells.

The same word is applied to a form of boxing which is now also known in the West. Its invention is sometimes attributed to Xu Xuanping (Tang Dynasty) but more often to Zhang San-feng: at all events, it has been practised since the 16th century.

The Tai-ji method seems to be a late development from the so-called Shao-lin school of boxing. Its practitioners see themselves as members of an esoteric cult.

The tai-ji, *from which* yin *and* yang *develop*

Tai-shan 泰 山

This is the name of a 'very (*tai*) big mountain (*shan*)' in the province of Shandong. It is one of the five sacred → mountains of China, with many temples on its slopes to which people make pilgrimages and where sacrificial rites are carried out. In legend, the mountain is said to have been thrown into the sea by the eight → Immortals in their fight against the sea-dragon. Nowadays, *tai-shan* is a way of referring to one's own wife; and *tai-shui* (= 'big water') is an expression for a man's mother-in-law.

Formerly, one used to see in front of houses big sandstone rocks bearing the inscription 'The stone of Tai-shan dares to stand guard.' These stones were placed thus to ward off demons and → ghosts.

validated by putting the halves of the seal together. Private documents were not only sealed but also signed and marked with a finger print. Chinese seals are of wood, ivory or jade, and are often beautifully decorated. Loss of a seal could be a very troublesome business; for example, if one wanted to get money from the bank, a signature by itself was not enough – it had to be accompanied by the correct seal impression.

Until quite recent times, every Chinese house had a plaque giving the names of the family dwelling therein. In earlier times, this plaque also specified the names, sex and age of all persons belonging to the family.

A citizen going on a journey had to get a pass from the authorities specifying his destination and the reasons for his journey.

Tally
hu-fu 虎 符

In olden times, any → official who was going to war or to a post in a city remote from the capital, was given a distinguishing tally by the → Emperor, consisting of half of a bronze figure of a → tiger. An envoy sent to this official by the Emperor would then carry with him the other half as a means of identification. The figure thus divided was not always of a tiger: sometimes a fish was represented. In later times, official documents were sealed and then cut through so that a document could be

Tao-tie

A kind of mask which is usually found on bronzes dating from more than two thousand years ago. It is also found in association with other artefacts, and presents researchers with something of a puzzle. The word *tao-tie* is supposed to mean 'glutton', but this throws no light at all on the object as represented. The mask is often furnished with antlers, sometimes again with a tiger's head. One theory is that it represents two animals in profile.

Taro
yu-nai 芋芳

Taro is a tuberous plant usually cultivated in wet-fields which seems to
have been brought to China from
Polynesia. It is now grown largely in
South China. In Fujian province, it
is supposed to be eaten ritually at
the feast of the 15th day of the 1st
month, in order to get – or keep –
good eyesight. In Anhui it is sacrificed to the god of riches on the 4th
day of the 1st month, as *yu-nai* (=
Taro) sounds very similar in the
Anhui dialect to *yun-lai* = 'good luck
(or wealth) is coming'.

Tea
cha 茶

The West European word 'tea' (*Tee*,
thé, etc.) is derived from *ti*, the
Fujian dialect pronunciation, while
the Turkish word *çay* is derived from
the North Chinese pronunciation,
beverage which is now the standard
and typical drink of China and Japan
was brought along with Buddhism in
the 3rd century AD, presumably by
monks from Assam. Soon there were
two main areas of cultivation – the
province of Sichuan in West China
and the central Chinese provinces
south of the Yangtse. Its commercial
value and importance increased to
such an extent that from the 8th
century onwards it was a government
monopoly, and good horses from
Mongolia were paid for in tea. To
begin with, only 'green' tea was in

*Wild tea and bird: 'Long life in the radi-
ance of spring'*

general use, i.e. the dried leaves
were used without further preparation. The rolling process still in
use today is a later innovation. For
centuries tea was sold in the form of
pressed balls or slabs, with flour as
an additive. This is still the custom
in Tibet and in parts of Mongolia,
where tea in block form contained,
in addition to flour, ginger, onions,
salt and animal blood; the 'tea' was
eaten as a soup and regarded as a
staple foodstuff. In China, tea was
prepared in this way (without the
animal blood) until the 11th century.
It was only from the 15th century
onwards that tea began to be
enjoyed in and for itself; probably
the influence of contemplative

Buddhism played a part here.

So-called 'red' tea is the typical black tea known in Europe. According to legend, it was invented in Tang times by Lu Yu who was found as a baby in the water and raised by monks, though other legends tell us he slipped out of a bird's egg. Many potters give you a clay figure of this tea-god as a bonus if you buy ten teapots. In general, however, it is green tea that continues to be drunk in China.

Ten Heavenly Stems
tian-gan 天 干

The cycle of Ten Heavenly Stems coexisted in early Chinese thought along with the cycle of → Twelve Earthly Branches (→ zodiac), and it is frequently mentioned in the oldest texts. The signs in the cycle of ten are known as *gan* and are arranged over a rectangular coordinate system giving the 'Heavenly Stems' (*tian-gan*). The signs in the cycle of twelve are arranged in a circle, and are known as 'Earthly Branches' (*di-zhi*). The cycle of twelve is based on the number six. Combination of the two cycles gives the great cycle of → sixty years, which is the Chinese equivalent of our century.

The individual ten signs (*gan*) have so far proved indecipherable. It has been suggested that they may refer to an early ten-day week, but there is no evidence for this, and it is in any case unlikely, as, very early on, the Chinese → calendar was geared to the phases of the → moon, which precluded runs of thirty days.

Ten Thousand
wan 萬

'From one comes two, from two comes three, from three come the ten thousand things' was Lao-zi's pithy way of summing up Chinese

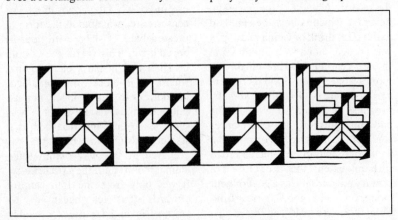

The sign for 'ten thousand' written as a meandering watercourse

cosmology. Chinese has words for 'hundred thousand' and for 'million', but in everyday language 'ten thousand' is used as a kind of upper limit, denoting whatever is or should be plentiful. The → Emperor was addressed as 'Ten thousand years of life' in token of the wish 'May Your Majesty live for ten thousand years!' With protocol in mind, the Crown-prince was addressed as 'Thousand years of life'.

At all times, 'ten thousand' has been an effective symbol for → immortality, taking various forms such as a → swastika, a scorpion or a meandering watercourse. A picture showing a → sceptre against a background of the meander design (*wan*) can be interpreted as 'May the ten thousand (*wan*) things (= everything) go according to your wishes!'

on which it stands have cosmological significance. 'The → heaven covers and the → earth bears' we are told in ancient texts. The terrace is usually in the form of a rectangle or of a → square (*fang*, even number, female), less frequently in circular form (uneven number, male). The rice-fields rise uphill in terraces, and water flows from terrace to terrace downhill. The use of a flat-topped terraced structure for sacrifices, for ceremonial feasts and for entertaining guests goes back to very ancient times.

The 'Moon Terrace' (*yue tai*) is what we prosaically call the 'platform' at a station!

Tendril
man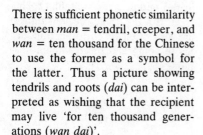

There is sufficient phonetic similarity between *man* = tendril, creeper, and *wan* = ten thousand for the Chinese to use the former as a symbol for the latter. Thus a picture showing tendrils and roots (*dai*) can be interpreted as wishing that the recipient may live 'for ten thousand generations (*wan dai*)'.

Terrace
tai

In Chinese architecture, the roof covering a building and the terrace

Thirteen
shi-san

The Chinese developed two numerical cycles – the Ten Stems and the Twelve Branches, and by definition each of these excludes 13. The number appears in Indian number mysticism in an 'unfavourable relationship' to other numbers (this is because the Indian year was originally divided into 12 lunar months, which meant that at the end of the lunar year a 13th month had to be intercalated; significantly, this month was called 'Lord of Troubles'). The expressions 'Thirteen Points' or 'Thirteen Tai-bao' are used as expletives. *Tai-bao* was originally a title given to a high → official at court; it came to mean a big-time crook.

Thirty-six
san-shi-liu

Shi-huang-di, the first Emperor, built up his → Middle Kingdom on the basis of the number six: he squared six to get his 36 provinces, and his retinue consisted of 36 carriages.

The 36 provinces formed the centre of an earth which was imagined as a flat square, round the edges of which there lived 36 'barbarian' or foreign peoples; each side of the square was coterminous with nine of these peoples, or, as the Taoist philosopher Huai-nan-zi (179–122 BC) worked it out, 10 in the West, 6 in the East, 13 in the South and 7 in the North. Either way, the figure of 36 was arrived at, as logic demands.

Legend has it that in the Tang Dynasty (618–907) 36 scholars were magically done to death by the Taoist high priest and then deified as gods of plague.

A South Chinese tradition says that towards the end of the Ming Dynasty (*c.* 1644) 360 scholars in the province of Fujian committed suicide rather than submit to the incoming foreign Manchu Dynasty. They were deified as gods of plague. As part of their ceremonial cult, a boat is elaborately decorated and then pushed out to sea: this is supposed to keep epidemics at a safe distance.

Three
san

Like all uneven numbers, three is masculine and a very important number in Chinese thought. From the basic trinity of → heaven, → earth and → man (*san cai*), a multitude of trinities are derived. For example, early Han speculation distinguished three successive historical periods having the properties of 'loyalty' (*zhong*), 'respect' (*jing*) and 'refinement' (*wen*) and corresponding to the 'First Three Dynasties' – Xia, Shang and Zhou.

According to the 'Book of Rites' (*Li-ji*), man, by virtue of his intermediate position between heaven and earth, corresponds to the number three. Bhaisajya, Sakyamuni-Buddha and Amitabha (the Buddha yet to come) are seen as the 'three precious things' (*san bao*); and these are often represented together in Buddhist temples, with → Buddha in the middle and Amitabha to his right. But the 'three precious things' are also often taken to be Buddha, his teaching and the community of monks.

The three wishes: happiness or good fortune (a child with a peach and a bat), long life (the god of longevity) and riches (deer)

Confucianism, Taoism and Buddhism are seen as the 'three teachings' (*san jiao*) and they are summarised in the expression 'The three teachings are one.' This claim tends, however, to obscure the fact that, as state religion, Confucianism was in a very different position from the other two. It is true, though, and the expression underlines it, that all three religions have a part to play in human life: Confucianism is the religion of filial piety (→ *xiao*); popular Taoism has to do with the individual's position in the community, with whose ceremonial purification it is charged; finally, Buddhism is a way of looking at death and at the meaning of life in general. Buddha, for example, should not be pestered with trivial complaints and desires: what he has to decide is whether a man should be reborn on the same level or as an animal, and whether a spirit should suffer in purgatory or go straight to paradise.

The Buddhist canon is divided into 'three baskets' (*tripiṭaka*). The tree plants which symbolise long life – the bamboo, the pine and the plum-tree – are very commonly lumped together as 'the three → friends'.

For hundreds of years, the 'Three Character Classic' (*San zi jing*) was the book from which Chinese children first learned their written Chinese. It was a work inculcating Confucian morality and consisting of simple sentences each of which had three characters. In Taiwan one has to be careful nowadays about using the title *San zi jing*, as it can be taken as a very coarse expletive meaning '(I) fuck your mother.'

'The three teachings are one'

The 'three oppressed things' (*san ya*) are three creatures which we do not eat: the wild duck, since it symbolises marital love; the → dog, because it serves its master faithfully; the black → eel, because it symbolises the fidelity and devotion which should exist between ruler and subject.

The 'three *yangs*' (*san yang*) are the three months of spring, in which the male element (→ *yang*) comes more and more into its own. The idea of spring is associated with happiness and success; and the three are pictorially represented as a sheep (*yang*) or as a group of three sheep. The vagina is sometimes referred to as a woman's 'third eye'.

Village elders and city fathers used to be called the 'three old worthies'. In such titles, the number three is used 'as the standard emblem of any arrangement embodying hierarchical organisation' (Marcel Granet).

Thunder
lei

Thunder and lightning are mentioned in very early texts: 'Thunder is the sound of → fire, and it is the laughter of heaven' (Huang-di Neijing). Elsewhere, we are told that thunder is the anger of the god of heaven: when thunder rolls, one should sit fully clothed, wearing a hat, and taking care not to be flippant.

Thunder was sometimes represented as a drummer, equipped with a number of drums. He began to beat his drums in the 2nd month of the Chinese year (→ dragon) and laid them aside in the 2nd month of autumn.

In later texts, thunder is represented as a beast with the head of a pig or an ape, with horns and with claws on his hands and feet, and with

The god of thunder

large wings which were of flesh, not of feathers. He had red hair. When the thunder-beast comes into contact with a pregnant woman (i.e. when she is struck by lightning) it can no longer rise up, and falls back to the ground. Then we can see what it really looks like. Just as dangerous for it is contact with a chamber-pot.

Thunder travels about in a chariot drawn by the → spirits of the dead. One story tells how lightning was about to strike a woman who had failed in her pious duty towards her aunt. She, however, covered her head with her blood-bespattered stocking, and the thunder-beast fell helplessly to earth. It looked like an eagle. People who eat pork and fish together are more likely than others to be struck by lightning.

Tiger
hu

The tiger is the king of the wild animals. In ancient times, sacrifice was made to it because it devoured the wild pigs which laid the village fields waste. It is a → *yang* creature, a bearer of the male principle; and for this reason, a white tiger symbolised autumn and the West (West is associated with the female principle → *yin*). The tiger is also a symbol of courage and bravery, as it can drive off demons. This is why we find stone figures of tigers on graves. More than one god is depicted riding on a tiger, and some pictures show a boy doing the same thing: this is a reference to a certain paragon of

Tiger with bamboos: the positive hero (naturalistic)

Tiger amulet: the guardian of the treasure (stylised and ornamental)

filial piety (→ *xiao*) who rode a tiger to divert it from his father.

The tiger was so much feared that its very name was taboo, and people referred to it as *da chong* = 'big insect', or 'King of the Mountains'. Instead of systematically hunting it to extinction, several provincial governors begged the tigers to go into the hills and stay there: and legend has it that the tigers actually agreed. There are other instances of tigers obeying the voice of authority, as in the well-known tale of the old lady who took the tiger to court because it had killed her son and she was now starving to death. The competent official ordered the tiger to appear before the court, whose verdict was that the tiger should provide food for the woman till she died. It was believed in South China that members of the minority peoples could turn themselves into tigers.

The tiger is the third sign in the Chinese → zodiac. A tiger depicted on the door-post is a guard against demons, and small children are given 'tiger-caps' to protect them. 'White tiger' is a rude expression for a woman. 'Tiger step' is one of the thirty positions in sexual intercourse, and 'tiger' (*hu-z*) is a chamber-pot, as this is made of clay or porcelain in the form of a crouching tiger with its mouth open.

Tile
wa   瓦

Kilns were usually sited outside towns because of the smoke. After a certain period of use, kilns had to be shut down and started up somewhere else. Abandoned kilns were often used as dwelling-places by very poor couples, or by people who for one reason or another were not allowed to settle in a town. Thus, 'tile-kiln' (*wa-zi*) came to mean 'place of pleasure', especially a brothel. But the word was also explained as referring to a place where one could have → sex by the hour as cheaply as buying tiles.

A 'tile-man' (*wa-ren*) was a middleman in country districts who estimated the likely yield of a harvest from the standing ears. A *wa-la* (written in part with the character for 'tile') is supposed to be a fish found in the far-off western sea, whose eyes are dark as long as it stays there, but bright if taken out of the water. Symbolically, this expression has come to be used for someone who weeps crocodile tears. Singing girls are also sometimes called *wa-la*, because the love they proffer is false.

Toad
ha-ma   蛤蟆

The three-legged toad is a → moon symbol, just as the three-legged → raven is a sun symbol. And, because the toad lives to a considerable age, it is also a symbol of → longevity. People said that it could swallow the moon (in an eclipse); so it also stands for unattainable wishes and desires. According to an ancient tradition, the toad is the transformed → Chang-e, the wife who stole the elixir of immortality from her husband, and fled to the moon where she was turned into a toad.

Ordinary toads are, it was said, a cure for boils, and they should be eaten by sufferers. A toad which is → ten thousand years old (it is then known as 'flesh-mushroom') should be caught on the 5th day of the 5th month, and then dried. If you scratch the earth with a toad's leg, a spring gushes from the spot. It was also believed that the toad could make you invulnerable (→ frog).

Among the Tanka, a South Chinese minority people who live on boats, the following interesting ceremony is held on the 15th day of the 8th month (a full moon) in honour of a newly-wed couple: a → cinnamon tree is placed at the door of the bridal bedroom, with a toad and a → hare under it. The bridal bed is curtained off: candles burn beside it. This space is called the 'Toad Palace'. An old woman acting the part of → Xi-wang-mu, Queen Mother of the West, steps onto a platform towards the front of the of the → marriage is full of lunar symbolism.

Tobacco
yan

Tobacco arrived in China via the Philippines. It was in the province of Zhejiang that it first caught on. The oldest Chinese word for tobacco was an attempt at a phonetic equivalent – *dan-pa-gu*. Then *yan* meaning 'light yellow' (because of the colour of the dried leaves) came to be used: *yan* is also the ordinary word for → smoke. A metaphor for tobacco is 'Thinking-of-each-other Weed'. This comes from a story about a man who was so desolated by the death of his wife that he visited her grave every day. One day, a plant grew up out of the grave which turned out to be a tobacco-plant – he smoked the leaves and got over his bereavement. Virtually the same story is told about the opium poppy.

Tones
sheng-yin

The → five notes (tones) of the old Chinese scale symbolised happiness, war, drought, water and unhappiness, in that order. A sage could assess the condition of a state by listening carefully to its → music.

According to legend, the Yellow Emperor (Huang-di) ordered Ling-lun to prepare pipes giving a musical scale. Ling-lun took bamboo canes from the Yue-xi valley and decided

The Immortal Liu Hai with the three-legged toad

boat. In front of her she has an assortment of lucky objects – ground-nuts, gourd seeds, cinnamon cakes, tea, wine, etc. When all the members of the family are assembled, the bride and bride-groom appear in their wedding garments and stand in the moon-light. Then they enter the bridal chamber (the 'Moon Palace') and pause at the 'Gate of the Moon-hall', i.e. before the bed. The old woman utters her final words of wisdom and leaves; the couple embrace each other and kiss, and are then led to the 'Toad Palace' (the bridal bed). Originally, this was a lunar festival, pure and simple, which was celebrated all over China on the same day. The ritual re-enactment that the tonic of the scale should be *huang-zhong* – the 'Yellow Bell'. 'He blew on it and said: that is as it should be. Then he cut the twelve pipes. As he heard the male and female → phoenix singing at the foot of the Yuan-yu Mountain, he distinguished between the twelve keys. Therefore it is said: the tonic of the "Yellow Bell" is the base-note of the whole-tone scale and of the scales derived from it' ('Spring and Autumn of Lü Bu-wei' tr. Richard Wilhelm). In this myth we find a reference to the sexual dance of the pair of phoenixes, and also to the → mouth organ which used to accompany such dances and whose pipes were arranged to look like a bird's plumage.

Tongue
shetou　　古 頭

Recent excavations have yielded male figures with outstretched tongues; and one text tells of a ghost in South China whose tongue reached down to the ground. There is also a relief dating from Han times which shows a man with his tongue sticking out. The significance of the outstretched tongue is not quite clear. One text seems to suggest that it is a way of poking fun at someone else's misfortunes.

The tongue of a young girl may be symbolically described as 'fragrant tongue'.

Tooth
ya; chi　　牙 齒

The → Immortals in the realm of Uttarakuru have teeth which are 'faultlessly placed, with no gaps or irregularities, brilliantly white with fine shading recalling bright jade'; such teeth are characteristic of female → beauty.

Among some of the non-Han minority peoples in South China, however, it was the custom to knock out one of a young woman's front teeth, while other tribes blackened the front teeth – an embellishment which owed not a little to their enthusiasm for chewing betel-nut. Dreaming about losing a front tooth was supposed to presage the imminent death of one's parents. Normally, teeth were cleaned only in the morning. Only in one text is cleaning them in the evening recommended, and this may have something to do with sexual hygiene. Grinding the teeth is one way of warding off → ghosts. It was also customary to grind one's teeth on entering a temple.

Tortoise
gui　　

To the Chinese the tortoise has always seemed an enigmatic and highly symbolic creature (→ *ao*). The saying 'It conceals the secrets of → heaven and → earth' is still current in China. In the very earliest references to it, we find its shell compared to the vaulted heaven, and its underside to the flat disc of the earth. Both as a replica of the cosmos and because of the markings on its shell, it was used in very early times in prognostication. It seems clear that the 24 rim-plates of the shell were correlated with the 24 divisions of the agricultural → calendar.

The tortoise is also the hero of many legends. It helped the first → Emperor to tame the Yellow River; and whenever a cultural hero crops up to bring order into the universe, a tortoise is by his side. Emperor Shang-di rewarded it by conferring a life-span of → 10,000 years upon it. In fact, its genuine longevity makes it a natural choice for a long-life symbol. At sacrifices in modern

Stylised tortoise shell design

Taiwan, large tortoises are made out of dough and painted → red. For one such ceremony held on the 13th day of the 1st month 1971 (→ New Year) a 'Long-life Tortoise' was fashioned out of 7,478 lb of glutinous rice!

It also symbolises immutability, steadfastness. A tortoise often crowns a stone grave pillar, and the inscription tablets of the ancient Emperors were supported on stone tortoises. Characteristic of the present 'restorationist' phase in Chinese Communism is the saying 'Chairman Mao altered the courses of rivers and moved mountains, but he could not change the shape of the tortoise'.

But the tortoise is also regarded as an immoral creature. As there are no male tortoises – so ran the belief – the females must mate with snakes. Thus, the tortoise is depicted together with a snake as the creature of the North (→ constellations, → planets).

Tortoise and snake (stone rubbing)

The word 'tortoise' was in fact taboo, and the creature was referred to as the 'dark warrior'. The legend goes that the tortoise and the snake arose from the entrails and the stomach of the 'Emperor of the North' (Bei-di).

A *gui-gong* = 'tortoise-master' is a swear-word meaning 'father of a whore'. A *wu-gui* = 'black tortoise' is a pimp, and 'tortoise' is a graphic metaphor for penis. Exactly why the tortoise should also be called 'King Eight' is not clear. One theory is that it refers to a man who has forgotten the eighth virtue – shame. It is also a very insulting term for a brothel-keeper.

Towel
shou-jin

On social occasions, warm damp towels are handed out, with which the guests wipe their hands and faces. This is refreshing in summer, comforting in winter. On her wedding day a bride may be given a towel (*jin*) to take with her, but this custom has its critics, as towels are apt to remind one of burials where they are used to wipe one's tears.

A woman calls her closest female friend her 'towel-touch'.

Tower
lou

In Chinese literature, the word *lou* rarely means what we understand by 'tower'. Rather, it refers to the upper storey of a private house containing rooms for family use. Pawn-shops in market places are usually of at least two storeys and are known as *lou* as are also the watch-towers in villages (e.g. among the Hakka). The same word occurs in the title of what is probably the most famous Chinese novel of all – the *Hong lou meng*, the 'Dream of the Red Chamber' as it is usually translated – the better to indicate that it is a question of a room in an upper storey.

'Three-storey tower' is a metaphor for the vagina.

Town
cheng

Wherever it is geologically possible, Chinese towns are laid out in the shape of a → square, like rice-fields and army camps. In the design of all three, the laws of → geomancy play a key role: that is to say, they are orientated according to the heavenly directions. In the case of towns, the number → three was taken as basis: this gave a right-hand and a left-hand area, enclosing the palace of the ruler in the → middle. For more than two thousand years, this central palace has been the residence of the town governor.

The 'Empty City Stratagem' (*kong cheng ji*) is a reference to an episode in the novel *San-guo-zhi yan-yi* ('The Romance of the Three Kingdoms') which is a motif in many pictures. Three men are seen sitting peacefully and unconcernedly on the city wall just above the main gate where

Tutelary deity of town, clad as an official

a hostile army is preparing to storm the city. The attackers decide, however, that the town must be very heavily armed indeed if its leaders can sit there eating so unconcernedly, and they abandon their plan. In point of fact, the town was completely undefended.

For the last fifteen hundred years or so, each town has had its own tutelary deity or 'town-god' (*cheng huang shen*). He was also in some measure the patron saint – often a deceased official of the town or a worthy mandarin, deified at popular request via the competent official who would memorialise the Emperor in this respect. It was up to the Emperor to decide whether this or that town deserved a tutelary deity, and to make the relevant appointment: equally, the Emperor alone could promote or demote 'town-gods' already occupying such posts. In pictures, 'town-gods' are always shown wearing official robes.

Often the god is shown discharging another of his functions – judging recently deceased citizens of the town he oversees.

Tree
shu

Ancient Chinese cosmology included the *fu-sang*, the 'hollow mulberry tree', and its counterpart the *kong-tong*, the 'hollow Paulownia tree'. Each of these represented a hollow tree and a mountain at one and the same time: each served as a hiding place for the → sun and as a dwelling place for rulers.

Artists of the Han period often portray a hero tethering his horse to a great tree, which may possibly represent the *fu-sang* tree of the ancient legends. The *fu-sang* tree, so it was said, stood at the place where the sun rose. In it were many birds representing suns. The story goes that the hero Hou Yi (also known as Shen Yi, i.e. the god Yi) shot down all of these suns except one, as the heat of the ten suns was so great that mankind was in danger of being burnt up. Its description suggests that the *fu-sang* tree was something like a mulberry. *Fu-sang* was also the name of a country whose inhabitants kept → deer instead of oxen, in order to have does' milk.

For notes on the trees of China and their symbolic meanings, see the following: Bamboo, Boxwood, Chestnut, Cinnamon Tree, Cypress, Maple, Olive, Persimmon, Pine, Plum, Willow, Wood Oil Tree (Paulownia), Wu-tong.

Triangle
san-jue 三角

The triangle is hardly used at all as a symbol in China; where it occurs, it is a female symbol (→ snake).

Triangles on prehistoric grave pottery have been interpreted by Western scholars as symbolising either the female genitalia (a triangle standing on its apex) or the male member (triangle with apex upwards), but these guesses have not been generally accepted or verified.

In Tibetan Tantrism, a triangle with apex downwards is indeed a female symbol; when the apex is upward, it symbolises → fire, and, following from this, the downward-pointing triangle can also symbolise a fireplace.

of commentary, elaboration and legend. Marcel Granet has described it as 'the cosmos in capsule form', and we may see the 64 hexagrams as covering all human conditions and occasions – a kind of inspired formula for interpreting the world.

According to legend, the system of trigrams and hexagrams was developed by Zhou-gong, the relative and most important political adviser of the first Emperor of the Zhou Dynasty (from *c.* 1050 BC). It is a fact that no object belonging to the Shang Dynasty (which preceded the Zhou), so far discovered, bears any similar design.

Somewhat tortuous reasoning connects the eight trigrams with the five → elements (*wu xing*) and the five directions. The trigrams are often to be found on the garments of celebrated men, such as Jiang-Ze-

Trigrams
gua 卦

The basic forms of the 'Book of Changes' are provided by eight trigrams. The lines forming these trigrams are either whole (male) or broken (female). Each trigram consists of three male or female lines; and according to the make-up, the trigram symbolises heaven, earth, water, fire, dampness, wind, thunder or mountains. The trigrams can be superimposed upon each other, and in this way 8 × 8 = 64 hexagrams are obtained. These 64 hexagrams provide the essential text of the → oracle-book, the *Yi-jing*; the rest of the material in it consists

The eight trigrams, with the yin-yang *symbol in the centre*

ya, the military adviser of the first Zhou Emperors, and the 'Heavenly Teacher' (*tian-shi*), the leader of one of the main Taoist sects. They also appear in a purely decorative function on vessels.

Tripod
ding

Bronze tripods dating from the middle of the second millennium BC have been found. They were probably developed from earlier forms of cooking pot, but they soon acquired special significance as vessels used on state occasions. Indeed, it was believed that dominion over the → Middle Kingdom was connected with possession of the nine tripods. Legend has it that it was Huang-di who introduced this symbol, but in fact as far back as the Zhou Dynasty (1050–256 BC) nine tripods were in ceremonial use to represent the nine provinces.

The three feet represent the three senior dignitaries supporting the Emperor. The loss of even one of these tripods was taken as heralding the end of the dynasty. Today, the tripod maintains its status as one of the good luck symbols (→ precious things).

Twelve
shi-er

The old Chinese year had twelve months of either 28 or 29 days. This system was based on the → lunar calendar, and gave a year of only 354 days. As a result, the calendar was very soon out of step with the seasons, and intercalary months had to be introduced: in every 19-year period, intercalary months had to be inserted no less than seven times. Years with intercalary months were very popular, as officials were then paid thirteen times instead of twelve!

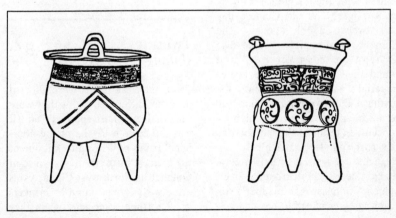

Ceremonial tripods

The mythical Emperor Shun

Two cycles, one based on ten and the other based on twelve, can be discerned in even the earliest strata of Chinese thought. Together, the two generate the cycle based on → sixty. The duodecimal series is correlated with the → zodiac with its twelve signs. The old Chinese day had twelve double hours. The Chinese astronomers were also aware of Jupiter's twelve-year orbit round the sun. There were twelve imperial → insignia, and the mythical Emperor Shun is supposed to have appointed twelve high → officials. In terms of the old doctrine of correspondences Chinese → medicine recognised twelve viscera: lungs, heart, pericardium, liver, spleen, kidneys, gall-bladder, stomach, greater intestine, lesser intestine and a hollow organ.

The pentatonic scales of ancient Chinese music were later supplemented by twelve-tone scales.

Twenty-four
er-shi-si

For the Chinese peasant who wanted to know when he should plant and harvest his staple crops, the old lunar calendar was not sufficiently accurate. For example, before the insertion of an intercalary month, it was often 15 days 'slow', i.e. behind the sun; and immediately after insertion of the intercalary month it was 14 days 'fast', i.e. in advance of the sun. Accordingly, another division of the year was worked out, one depending on the → sun.

The year was divided into 24 equal periods, each of 15 days. This gave a solar year of 360 days, which was astronomically never more than 5 days a year out – a minor discrepancy which could be ironed out by inserting days at certain intervals.

Twins
shuang-tai

Twins differing in sex were allowed to die in ancient China, as they were regarded as 'ghost spouses'; and it was the custom in one of the aboriginal tribes of Taiwan to kill one of the twins at birth. In the province of Qinghai in North-west China, twins are always looked upon as bringers of ill fortune, especially when they differ in sex. However, in another text we are told that the wife of a pious man was blessed at the age of fifty with male twins, allegedly as a reward for his piety.

Two
er   ☰

Two-headed quadruped

Like all even numbers in Chinese, two is female. In ancient times, it was correlated with the → earth, as → one was with the → sun, and → three with → man.

'The One represents unity, which can have no other value, as it is the all-embracing totality. It is a Whole combining One and Two: for in the One all conjunctive and disjunctive aspects, such as right/left, up/down, back/front, circle/square, *yin* and *yang* are cancelled out. This Whole which is at once a Unity and a pair, is recapitulated in all uneven numbers, beginning with Three (which is One plus Two)' (from Marcel Granet's fundamental work on Chinese number mysticism).

Consultation of the → oracle is based on two, i.e. on the binary system. Each of the 64 hexagrams of the *Yi-jing* ('Book of Changes') consists of two superimposed → trigrams.

U

Umbrella
yu san

雨 傘

The umbrella is one of the → eight Buddhist symbols; it corresponds to the divine spleen. Umbrellas were held over dignitaries and, at least among the minority peoples of South China, came to be regarded as symbolic of the rank held by these officials, and of their integrity. In the marriage ceremony an umbrella was held over the bridegroom during his ritual progress to his bride. Placed over the bed of a woman in labour, the umbrella will keep off evil spirits. There is also a story about the spirit of a dead woman which wanted to cross the sea to Taiwan. As the spirit could not do this by itself, it hid in the umbrella of a merchant who was about to make the crossing.

Folding umbrellas have been known in China for over two thousand years. 'Multi-decker' umbrellas were also in use.

Folding umbrella

Unicorn
qi-lin

麒 麟

The mythical *qi-lin* has very little in common with the unicorn of Euro-

Drawing of mythical qi-lin, *incised in stone*

lin brings sons.' The youth often carries a → lotus (*lian*) in his hand: this symbolises the wish that one may go on begetting sons one after the other (*lian*). One New Year ceremony held in the Central Chinese province of Jiangsu, was called the 'Unicorn brings Children' feast. Young people walked about carrying a stuffed figure of a unicorn surrounded by lanterns. They went from village to village performing short theatrical sketches about classical heroes such as Yo Fei (a patriotic general), Shun (a mythical Emperor and supreme exemplar of

pean legend. Certainly it is sometimes shown with one horn, but it can also have two or three. The *qi-lin* is described as an animal with a → deer's body, and this has led several students to conclude that some sort of deer may underlie the legend. More detailed descriptions, however, give the creature the tail of an ox, fishy scales, cloven toes or five toes to each foot, and a horn covered with fur. It is usually white in colour. Along with the → dragon, the → phoenix and the → tortoise it belongs to the 'four supernatural creatures' (*si ling*); it is the 'chief of the hairy creatures'.

It has always symbolised a large family of children. One of the Nan songs in the celebrated *Shi-jing* runs as follows: '*Qi-lin*'s foot – *qi-lin* brings noble sons; *qi-lin*'s forehead – *qi-lin* brings noble kindred' (Karlgren No. 11). Folk art shows a youth riding on a unicorn over the clouds: the inscription runs: 'The *qi-*

Youth on qi-lin *with lotus (*lian*) and mouth organ (*sheng*): the meaning is 'May the* qi-lin *bring (you) sons who will rise in unbroken (*lian*) line from one stage to another (*sheng*)'*

The qi-lin *brings the mother of Confucius a piece of jade on which the destiny of the great sage is set out (16th century)*

filial affection) and Meng Jiang (a woman and a model of conjugal fidelity).

Another legend has it that the *qi-lin* will not step on any living thing, not even on growing grass. Along with the covered horn, this may have contributed to the fact that the creature is also regarded as symbolising goodness. It appears when the land is well governed or when a saint is present. But not always: it depends on the circumstances, and in one of the *Jia-yu* stories (→ Confucius's 'School Conversation Books') we are told that the master burst into tears on seeing a remarkable stag whose right foreleg has been broken. Asked why he wept, Confucius answered: 'The *qi-lin* appears when the prince is wise and judicious; if it appears when this is not the case, it bodes ill. For this reason I am distressed.'

In general, a picture of a unicorn expresses good wishes. The skirts of noble ladies used to be adorned with pictures showing the other supernatural creatures paying homage to the *qi-lin* as to their leader. Scenes showing men riding on a *qi-lin* usually refer to episodes from the novel *Feng-shen yun-yi* (Ming Dynasty).

The expression '*qi-lin* horn' refers to one of the 30 positions of sexual intercourse.

Urine
xiao bian 小 便

In North-west China women wash their faces in urine to improve their skin. The urine of → foxes and of spirits masquerading as foxes is supposed to cure various diseases. Many professional magicians drank it to prolong their lives.

On the day when the bride quits the paternal home, she is not supposed to give in to 'little need' (*xiao bian*) until the evening. Urinating on a statue dishonours it: however, in the great temple of Yo Fei in Hangzhou there was a small statue of Qin Kui (Yo Fei's adversary through whose intrigues the heroic general met his death) which could be dishonoured with impunity. Other expressions for this call of nature are 'to unclasp the hand' (*jieshou*) and 'to cleanse the hand' (*jing shou*).

V

Vase
ping

瓶

'Bottle' and 'vase' have the same written character in Chinese; furthermore, this character is phonetically identical with *ping* = peace, and this, together with the wide variety of plants, flowers, etc., which one can put in a vase, gives rise to a rich field of symbolism. Thus, a picture showing the flowers of the four → seasons in a vase, expresses the wish that the recipient may enjoy peace at all times; while three → halberds in the vase, with a → mouth organ close by, signify '(May you) rise peacefully to the three highest grades!'

Formerly, a special role fell to the so-called 'treasure-vase' (*bao-ping*). Filled with the 'five nourishing fruits' (*wu-guo*) – that is to say, millet, wheat, sorghum and two kinds of beans – it formed part of a fertility rite held during the → marriage

Pine and plum-tree twigs with narcissi in a vase: 'Evergreen life, love, good fortune and peace!'

ceremony. A 'black bottle' was used by magicians to hold → spirits captive. A hot bottle was known as a 'warming-wife' or 'foot-wife'; while 'oil-bottle' was a metaphor for the penis.

In the fields of South China, earthenware urns at least a couple of feet deep are still a common sight. These are the so-called 'bone-vases'. They used to contain the bones of relatives which were dug up two years after burial, stripped of remaining flesh and laid in these jars as their final resting-place. It gives a Chinese the creeps to see a foreigner buying a 'bone-jar' to put in the lounge.

Vinegar
cu　醋

'Drinking vinegar' is the standard Chinese metaphor for 'feeling jealousy'. As a result, in North China the word is avoided like the plague, and if you have to ask for some vinegar at dinner, you say, 'May I have some of the taboo word please?'

It used to be part of the → marriage ceremony to bring a bowl full of vinegar to the bride as she sat in her palanquin; she then held a heated rod in the vinegar till it seethed. The bride then walked ceremonially round her palanquin and entered her future home: in this way, it was hoped, she would never be troubled by feelings of jealousy.

But when someone has a fishbone stuck in his or her throat, a popular remedy is to make the sufferer drink vinegar (or 'eat' vinegar, as the Chinese say: the verb *chi* = to eat is used with tea, wine, etc.).

W

Walnut
hu tao 胡桃

The literal meaning of *hu tao* is 'Hun peach', where 'Hun' is an umbrella word covering all of the peoples and tribes who live north and west of the → Middle Kingdom. Some sources say that the walnut did not reach China till the 4th century AD, though it is attested in Japan at a much earlier date.

Hu-tao is also shorthand for the saying 'Mr. Qin-*hu* flirts (*tao*) with his own wife.' This is a reference to an old story which still provides a plot for stage performances: after many years of absence, a man comes home and sees a young woman picking mulberry leaves for the silkworms outside his house; he begins to flirt with her. When they go indoors they discover that they are married – to each other. In some versions, the woman is made to commit suicide out of shame. Thus, the walnut became a symbol for 'flirt'.

Wash
xi 洗

In imperial China, it was accepted that one should have a really good wash once every five days; and children should be washed as often by their parents. The hands should be washed five times a day with water. Before an audience with the → Emperor, one had to have a bath. A new-born child was washed on the third day after birth. Clothes were often washed in a pool or river, laid on a stone and beaten with a sort of mallet. This mallet was sometimes compared to the penis.

Water
shui

水

Water is one of the five → elements or 'permutations'; it is associated with the North and with the colour black, and also with the → moon which causes the dew to fall at night. Water also symbolises → *yin*, the primeval female principle, the counterpart of → *yang*, the male principle which is the element of fire and of the South. In the old Chinese cosmology, fire and water arise from the 'Great One' (→ *Tai-ji*): 'water moistens and strives downward, fire blazes and strives upward' (Section 1 of the *Hong-fan*). From the sexual union of these two principles the five elements arise, and these engender the → ten thousand things. Thus, water belongs to night as fire to day; sexual activity appertains to the first part of the night, and many expressions denoting sexual intercourse have to do with water.

Water is soft, yielding and pliant, as a woman should be. 'Weak overcomes strong, soft overcomes hard' runs a celebrated passage in the *Dao de jing*. For → Lao-zi water was an exemplar of proper behaviour, by means of which the weak can overcome the strong, just as a woman overcomes a man.

The phrase 'water poured out' refers to a well-known story which has also been turned into a play. Zhu Mai-chen was very poor, as he did nothing but study and never earned any money; so his wife, unable to put up with it any longer, left him and married a well-to-do butcher. Against all expectation, however, Zhu finally passed his state examination and became an illustrious official. One day as he was passing through his native village, his former wife ran out to him and begged him to take her back. Without even

Confucius and his disciples on the shore

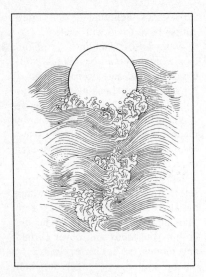

The sun arising from the sea

Water buffalo obeying a child (woodcut c. 1920)

getting off his horse, Zhu poured a jug of water on the ground and said: 'Water poured out can't be put back in the jug.' The wife is supposed to have committed suicide.

The unusual expression 'water and fire' is a scatological expression meaning 'pissing and shitting'.

In Chinese woodcuts and ink drawings water is characteristically shown as waves or as series of quarter, half or three-quarter curves. These can symbolise the sea, a lake or a pond.

Thai-speaking minorities in South China sacrifice a water buffalo at their ritual feasts. They also hold buffalo-fights, in which two animals fight till one is defeated: it is then cooked and eaten by the victorious side.

Many paintings show an old man riding on a water buffalo. This is Lao-zi, who is supposed to have left China in this way. Another favourite motif is a little boy riding on the buffalo – to show that the powerful animal can be obedient to a child.

See also Ox.

Water Buffalo
shui niu   水 牛

The water buffalo is found all over China, but it is most typical of South China, where it is extensively used for ploughing the wet rice-fields.

Waves and whitecaps

Waves
lang 浪

Wavy lines are used in ornamentation to indicate → water; usually these lines are stylised patterns of quarter, half or three-quarter circles in parallel series. This design on the hem of a court garment represents the sea; mountains in the same design represent the → landscape. The wave pattern often represents the tide (*chao*) and can therefore symbolise the homophone *chao* = 'audience' (at court, etc.). That is to say, the wish is expressed that the recipient of such a picture may rise to become an important official at court.

Well
jing 井

A man who wants to → marry but cannot find a bride, is said to be 'looking for a river and keen to find a well'. In erotic literature, the well stands for the vagina. In Fukien Province, the wells are ceremonially cleansed on the 7th day of the 7th month, that is to say, on the day when the heavenly pair of lovers are united, and a joyful feast is held.

If a wedding procession has to pass by a well, it is covered over, as it is often reported that unhappy women have committed suicide by throwing themselves into wells.

The expression 'meeting at the well' refers to a play, whose hero, Liu Zhi-yuan (895–947), marries a girl when he is still a young soldier, but leaves her to marry the daughter of an official. Thirteen years later he meets his first wife at a well, along with a child who turns out to be his son. Thus, we see that the relationship between young women and wells is both deep and extensive – as might be expected, considering that for thousands of years it was young women who had to draw the water from wells.

Nine ears of wheat

Whale
jing-yu

As might be expected, it is only in the southern coastal regions of China that the whale plays any role in Chinese folklore and symbolism. In Taiwan, it was popularly believed that it was the whale that brought → millet-seed to mankind, and the creature was honoured at a special festival. In ancient Japan also there was a cult of the whale.

When Coxinga refused to submit to the Manchus and fled to Taiwan (from which he was later to expel the Dutch) a whale is said to have appeared off the town of Tainan. When Coxinga's dynasty collapsed, the whale too vanished, never to return.

Wheat
mai

It is mainly in the northern and western provinces of China that wheat is grown – i.e. where rice does not do so well. By the ancient theory of correspondences wheat is corre-

lated with wood as permutation, or state of being (→ elements): and also with spring, the colour green and the sheep. Accordingly, wheat was eaten mainly in the spring, along with mutton. 'Grain rescues life' we are told in the ancient 'Book of Odes' (*Shi-jing*). The ear of grain symbolises the clitoris, another term for which is 'wheat molar'.

White
bai

Symbolically, white is connected with the West; so the 'white tiger' is the animal of the West, just as the blue dragon is the creature of the East. White clothing is said to have been worn in the time of the Shang Dynasty (which ended *c.* 1050 BC) as white was the symbolic colour of this dynasty.

In the 7th century, scholars who had not yet been appointed to posts wore white clothes. The earth-god (*tu-di*) is represented as an old man with a white face, as is Guan Ping, the son of Guan Yu (who became the war-god, → Guan-di).

White is also the colour of the autumn, and the emblem of old age. On the Chinese stage, actors with white faces represent men who are not exactly wicked, but who are cunning and treacherous. Another name for these is 'doufu-faces', because *dou-fu* (bean-curd) has a whitish-yellow colour.

When a procession is being held in honour of a goddess, women who want to have a son take a white flower from the vase which is being carried by the escort accompanying the procession. At the feast of → lanterns, held on the 15th day of the 1st month, however, white blossom presages a daughter; those who want sons must take a yellow flower.

One should never wear anything white in one's hair, as this is very unlucky. It is often said that white is the colour of mourning in China. This is not quite correct: the word in question is *su* which means a kind of unbleached sackcloth, and mourning apparel made from it is a brownish-yellow rather than white.

'Pure white' (*qing-bai*) is an expression denoting virginity. Women are regarded as sexually 'impure' during menstruation and after giving birth. Men 'wash and cut themselves pure' when they have themselves castrated.

The 'White Lotus' was a powerful secret society which arose early in the 12th century; the man who was to found the Ming Dynasty came from its ranks. The name 'White Lotus' carries the connotation of another, better and 'purer' world.

Wilderness
ye

The expression *chao-ye* means literally 'Imperial Court and wilderness'; a contrastive pair, consisting of, on the one hand, the capital city, the seat of the → Emperor, and on the other, everything outside the city walls or, simply, 'outside'. Superficially the contrast seems to be the same as that made in English between 'town and country', German '*Stadt und Land*'. But there is a basic difference. *Ye* means 'uncivilised'. A *ye-ren* is a 'wild man', a barbarian, a man who lacks what a Chinese would call 'culture'. It is significant that nature in the raw is hardly ever, if at all, portrayed in Chinese painting; what is *ye* – wild and terrible – is not held to be a fit subject for art. The landscapes we are shown are those modulated by man: humanised or civilised nature. We see roads, here and there houses, people. Even the rivers are in the service of man, as is evident from the fishermen in their boats.

In many Chinese novels, bandits figure as 'people of the greenwood'. As long as there were still large forests in China these bandits were feared; one is reminded of the terrors of the forest as described in German fairy-tales. This is one reason why Chinese travelogues are so monotonous – travellers are only interested in monasteries, temples, places of habitation, roads, and so on: i.e. in the marks that man has made on the landscape which is itself, however beautiful, described in more or less stereotyped set phrases.

Willow
liu

The willow, much valued as firewood, is a symbol of → spring. As spring is the season of erotic awakenings, the phrase 'willow feelings and flower wishes' means sexual desire; 'looking for flowers and buying willows' means visiting a prostitute, 'flowers and willows by the wayside' are prostitutes, and 'sleeping among flowers and reposing beneath willows' is a term for visiting a brothel.

Under the willow-tree

The waist of a → beautiful woman is compared to the willow, her → eyebrows to the curve of willow leaves. A young girl is a 'tender willow and fresh → flower' while a woman who can no longer claim virginal freshness is described as 'faded willow and withered flower'. A woman's pubic hair is 'in the depths of willow shade'.

Furthermore, the willow repels demons. In one novel, 49 children armed with willow twigs score a victory over → ghosts. At the Qingming festival, held on the 105th day after the winter solstice, willow twigs were worn, or one put a willow wreath round one's head. There was a current saying, to the effect that if you failed to wear willow in some shape or form on this feast-day, you would be reborn next time round as a yellow dog.

In ancient China it was customary to give someone who was going away twigs broken from a willow-tree. Thus, a scholar who was being moved to a post in the provinces would receive such twigs from women and friends assembled at the east gate of the capital city.

Wind
feng

In Shang times (up to *c.* 1050 BC) the wind seems to have been venerated as the god Feng-bo, who was represented as a sort of bird, perhaps an original form of the → phoenix. The ancient Chinese had names for → eight different winds, and the

'The urns all overthrown, hairpins and badges of office have disappeared – suddenly a gust of wind blows in. Dust and ashes fly about in confusion' (Han Shan)

wind-rose was represented as a fan with eight radial sections.

Symbolically, wind figures in two entirely disparate sets of images. One of these seems to be connected with the way the wind blows over wide areas of the land: *Guo-feng* ('Wind of the Land') is the title of a special section in the *Shi-jing* ('Book of Odes'), a section which contains some of the oldest folk-songs in the collection. *Feng-shui* is the science of wind and water (→ geomancy), *feng-su* is 'customs and usages', where *su* = general; thus, wind can also be used to mean 'rumour', 'report' (*la calunnia è un venticello!*).

The other set of images is connected with sex. *Feng-liu*, 'Floating in the wind', is a Romeo; 'Wind and rain destroying the blossom' a reference to an all-too-short love affair. If we say that a woman 'loves wind and the moon' we mean she is sexually very active, as the metaphor suggests prolonged love-play during nights together. An undefiled maiden is said not to have 'felt the waves of the wind', while a prostitute is 'a person of wind and dust' (here, dust representing the things of this world, which the Buddhist sees as fleeting and transitory). 'Fighting about the wind' is a quarrel of a jealous nature. 'Wind shoes' are shoes curved like the feathers in a bird's tail – that is to say, women's shoes.

In a third set of images, wind figures as an illness, as 'inner wind' – i.e. a stroke. The word *feng* is connected with the admittedly differently written word *feng* = madness. A 'wind-mirror' (*feng-jian*) is a soothsayer. 'To turn into wind' (*feng-hua*) refers to the practice of taking revenge by leaving the corpses of enemies unburied to rot.

Wine
jiu 酒

Chinese wine is mostly made from grain (→ rice). Wine made from grapes is mentioned in ancient texts, but it does not seem to have appealed to the popular palate. Certainly, far more → tea is drunk. Wine is drunk in company and at receptions in restaurants, wine-shops and brothels. Drunks are a rare sight. Towards the end of the Later Han Dynasty, when all sorts of stimulants were being tried out, 'hard drugs' were added to hot wine. The classical literature records the names of innumerable kinds of wine; today, Mao-tai and Shao-xing wines are particularly popular.

Wine in China never acquired the sacramental significance which it has in the Christian world. When it is poured from a bowl in sacrifice, it is rather as an additive to the → food which is being offered to the god.

Wolf
lang 狼

The wolf, which is found in North China, symbolises cruelty, rapacity and greed. Thus, someone with a 'wolf's heart' is cruel, while a greedy man is 'as greedy as a wolf, with a tiger's eye'. A 'wolf-look' awakens mistrust or fear. Wolf and tiger are connected again in a proverb which says: 'Better to kill ten tigers than one wolf' – because tigers are usually solitary creatures, while wolves hunt in packs and take revenge if one of their number is killed. Among the neighbouring Turkic peoples the wolf is a sacred animal and even ranks as ancestor of their race. The forebears of Chinggis Khan were a grey wolf (*boz kurt*) and a white hind. Turkish tribes carried a banner with a wolf's head on it, or a standard with a wolf's head. In the Ordos area in North China they tell a story about an exposed child which was raised by a wolf, to which the child turns for advice in later life – that is to say, a parallel to the Romulus and Remus myth. It is also said that hunting wolves can imitate the voices of small children, calves and lambs to attract unsuspecting prey.

A 'sex-wolf' (*se lang*) is a lecher.

Wood Oil Tree
tong

Several trees, including Paulownia and Firmiana, are described as *tong*. They are all sources of a valuable oil, obtained from the sap. The word *tong* is phonetically identical with the word *tong* = in common, joint. Pictures showing one or another of these trees coupled with another object express a clear message. For example, a → magpie (*xi*) perched on a *tong* expresses a wish for 'shared (*tong*) joy (*xi*)'.

Wu-tong 梧桐

The *wu-tong* belongs to the Paulownia family of trees and is usually known as *Paulownia imperialis*. Formerly, a material was woven from its flowers and its oil is known as a valuable preservative for all sorts of timber. Its own wood has been widely used for the manufacture of → lutes (*qin*).

The *wu-tong* is native to China and Japan, and is regarded as the tree *par excellence*, favoured by the → phoenix when it wishes to alight. For this reason it often used to be planted in courtyards in the hope that a phoenix would come and bring luck to the whole family.

Magpie on wu-tong *twig:* 'Shared pleasure'

The *wu-tong* symbolises the female element, → *yin*, and is therefore connected with the West. Its counterpart is the → bamboo, which represents the male element, → *yang*, and hence the East. Thus, when a son was burying his mother he carried a ritual mourning staff made of *wu-tong* wood; at the father's funeral this was replaced by a staff of bamboo. Another reason for this distinction in custom may lie in the fact that the *wu-tong* forms knots inwardly, while knots on bamboo grow on the outside: 'inward' is characteristic of the female, 'outward' of the male.

X

Xiao

Filial piety – *xiao* – ranked with loyalty to the ruler as the highest moral duty incumbent on every Chinese. Whole libraries of books and pictures are devoted to illustrating exemplary cases of filial piety: these do not always fit in with our ideas of good moral behaviour, but they are to this day admired and respected by all Chinese. Perhaps the best known series is the so-called 'Twenty-four Examples of Filial Piety' (*Er-shi-si xiao*).

'Donning filial piety' means wearing mourning when parents or other near relatives die. The garments worn on such occasions are called *su* and are made from coarse, undyed cloth which is usually brownish in colour: which does not stop the Chinese from describing it as → white.

Richard Wilhelm has translated the old Chinese work known as the *Xiao-jing* into German as *Das Buch von der kindlichen Ehrfurcht* (1912). He describes the work as 'an extremely interesting attempt to reduce the whole of morality – which includes, as the Chinese see it, the political life of the state – to one all-embracing and unifying principle'.

Xiu-cai

'A blossoming talent' is a man who has passed the first of the state examinations, and who can therefore set about studying for the next grade. For many hopefuls, this was as far as they ever got. The state examination system was abolished in 1904. The title of *xiu-cai* was also given to palace staff who had to be able to read, at least.

Xi-wang-mu 西 王 母

The 'Queen Mother of the West' was the great fairy goddess who dwelt in the legendary Kunlun Mountains. There are many tales about her, summarised here by Marcel Granet: 'The Supreme Ruler is said to dwell in the Kunlun; but the only deity who receives visits there is Xi-wang-mu. She is a man-eater, with a leopard's tail and a tiger's jaws from which comes a tiger-like roar. She spreads plague. Like a witch with wild hair she lives in the depths of a cave. She is a goddess of death, and yet it is from her that one gets the herb of immortality. Sometimes she gives feasts high up on a jade tower.'

Around two thousand years ago, she was supposed to have a male partner – Dong-wang Gong, the King of the East. But in the centuries that followed, this male partner cut less and less of a figure, while Xi-wang-mu herself remained powerful. In outward appearance, however, she changed quite a lot. 'Later art portrays her as a stately Chinese lady, finely balanced between maidenly delicacy and matronly opulence' (Ferdinand Lessing).

In ancient times, so we are told, Xi-wang-mu often exchanged visits with Emperors. When she came from the West (the Gobi Desert is often named) she brought with her valuable gifts, especially fine white → jade, since white is the symbolic colour of the West.

Xi-wang-mu on the phoenix

In the gardens of Xi-wang-mu

Since about the 1st century BC, however, she is supposed to bring a → peach, the symbol of → longevity, which is associated with her to this day. Old descriptions of paradise also associate her with the herb of → immortality. Her palace is 'to the west of the Tortoise Mountains and the Spring Mountains. Her capital contains the Kun-lun Park and the Wide-Wind Garden . . . servants with bright turbans and tiger-striped sashes attend her, while pages wave the feathers of their marvellous fans in the sunlight.' Her birthday was celebrated on the 3rd day of the 3rd month (an ancient feast-day) and her visits to the Emperor took place on the 7th day of the 7th month (a feast-day devoted to women). In many later texts we are told that Xi-wang-mu attained to the Dao, i.e. to the highest insight, by sleeping with men of this world. For the same reason she is of surpassing → beauty, her skin being especially fine.

According to another tradition, as soon as one of the peaches in her park ripened, she invited the gods to a feast of peaches. Great was the disappointment on one occasion, when the → monkey Sun Wu-kong broke into the park and stole all the peaches.

Popular prints show Xi-wang-mu on the jasper terrace of her magic palace; behind her stands a maid with a canopy-shaped fan. Before her stand three gods of → good luck and a → deer.

Y

Yang 陽

The twin concepts of *yin* and *yang* are peculiar to ancient Chinese cosmology. The terms denote two natural principles, one male (*yang*), the other female (*yin*), which were said to have originated from the Primeval One (→ *Tai-ji*); from the union of these two principles arose the five → elements, which then generate the → 'ten thousand things' (a Chinese way of saying 'everything'). *Yin* and *yang* figure in the two oldest books of the Chinese – the *Shi-jing* ('Book of Odes') and the *Yi-jing* ('Book of Changes'). Thus we read in the *Xi-z*, a short treatise appended to the *Yi-jing*: 'Here the shaded, there the sunlit' (*yi yin, yi yang*). The sentence can also be translated in terms of a chronological sequence: 'First the shadow, then the sunlight.' In the language of the *Shi-jing*, *yin* is connected with thoughts of dull, cold weather, *yang* with warmth and sunlight. *Yang* is related to → heaven, the South, → the Emperor, the → dragon; and all uneven numbers are *yang*-numbers.

The word *yang* figures in many compounds, some of which are of specifically sexual significance. Thus the 'Yang-terrace' (*yang-tai*) is the inner part of the vagina; 'Yang-object' (*yang-wu*) is the penis, and *yang-wei* is 'droopy penis' (i.e. after inordinate → sexual activity). *Yang-tuo* is a term denoting an abnormal and painful rigidity of the penis which may develop during intercourse, and which, according to old medical texts, can only be eased if the man sticks a hairpin into the sole of his foot till it bleeds; though he may also try moxibustion, i.e. burning little sticks of incense on his skin. It seems that many prostitutes kept a supply of hairpins ready in their bed-curtains for such contingencies. Should a woman fall into a dangerous state of orgasmic paroxysm, the man should try biting her arm, say the old texts, or sticking needles into her armpit.

Yang-lines are the unbroken lines in the eight → trigrams.

Yarrow (Mugwort)
ai

Yarrow (mugwort) or Artemisia is a strong-smelling plant which provides a green dye and also the pellets used in moxibustion; the pellets are burned on the skin as a cure for gout, rheumatism and various types of paralysis.

The plant should be picked on the 5th day of the 5th month, dried and hung up over the door as a protective screen against poisons. In ancient times, yarrow stalks were used as oracles, presumably because the medicinal properties of the plant have always been highly valued. Yarrow is also one of the → eight emblems of the → scholar.

Yellow
huang

The colour yellow is associated with the metamorphosis or 'state of being' → earth, and with the fifth of the 'heavenly directions', i.e. the → middle. The coupling of 'yellow' and 'middle' (China is the 'Middle Kingdom') is no doubt connected with the annual deposit of loess from the Gobi on the North Chinese plains, which then turn yellow; and this too was the colour of the →

Emperor who ruled the Middle Kingdom.

In sharp contrast with Western ideas, yellow is looked upon very favourably in China, where it is taken as symbolising fame, progress and advancement. The 'Yellow Dragon' is a good sign, and the 'Golden Springs' (*huang quan*) – originally a term denoting the underworld – now means a well-irrigated region, rather than the sulphurous pits of hell.

Huang-di ('Yellow Emperor') was the mythical first Emperor, but it was not until the 6th century AD that yellow was accepted as the fitting colour for the Imperial Majesty; hitherto, → red had been the preferred colour. For many centuries, ordinary citizens were debarred from wearing yellow garments. Buddhist → monks were an exception to this rule, being allowed to wear yellow robes on many occasions. These habits were undecorated. On other occasions the monks wore red robes. In Tibetan Buddhism, a distinction is made between the 'yellow-hats' (*dGe-lugs-pa*) and the 'red-hats' (*bKa-rGyud-pa*), i.e. between the Gelugpa and the Kargyüpa schools.

It is only in the last few decades that the term 'yellow literature' meaning pornography has become current in China. 'Yellow films' have also made their appearance. On the other hand, a 'Yellow-blossom woman' is one who is still a virgin.

Yin   陰

The female principle *yin* is associated with the → earth, with the North and with cold. Originally and properly, the word *yin* means the 'shady side' – that side of a mountain which is not facing the sun. In the ancient *Shi-jing* ('Book of Odes' – 8th–6th century BC) *yin* means 'what is inner', 'inside' (*nei*), and also the cloud-covered heavens. The word was also used to denote the dark, cool room in which ice was stored in summer.

The 'Yin-mountain' is a mountain in the fifth or sixth → hell, peopled by those who have died more sinned against than sinning. In the 'Yin-office' (*yin-si*) sits the Earth-god: he conducts a preliminary hearing, as it were, of dead persons, before handing them over for a more thorough investigation to the 'Judge of Hell' (*yin-cao*).

In any reference to the names of both natural principles, *yin* and *yang*, *yin* always takes precedence, in contrast to the normal order of things in China where woman takes second place to man. Many caves are known where *yin*-stones and *yang*-stones are found; the latter are always dry, the former always wet. In time of drought female stones were beaten with whips; when the rain was too heavy or went on for too long, male stones received the same encouragement. The term 'Yin-rain' refers to rain which, while heavy, is not too violent.

In the eight → trigrams of the *Yi-jing*, the broken lines are known as '*yin*-lines'.

Z

Zhang Guo-lao

張國老

Zhang is one of the eight → Immortals. He is supposed to have been a → bat which turned into a man. In another legend it is said that he is always accompanied by a white ass on whose back he could cover a thousand miles a day. On reaching his destination, he would fold the ass up like a piece of paper and put it in his case. To restore it to normal shape when needed, all Zhang had to do was to spray a little water on it from his mouth.

Zhang is symbolised by a long bamboo cane, the so-called 'Fish Drum' (*yu-gu*). Inside the cane are two rods fitted with hooks, and the whole thing can be used as a means of making a noise. Zhang is also depicted with two drumsticks in his hand; sometimes also with a → phoenix feather or a → peach. He is supposed to have appeared for the first time at the beginning of the 7th century, and to have been a native of Shanxi. A modern fairy-tale makes him out to have been originally a woodcutter. The story goes that, in obedience to a dream, he met → Li Tie-guai on a bridge, who gave him a pill made from mud which had the property of making dead fish come to life again. Other fishermen tried to take the pill away from him, so he swallowed it and became immortal.

Zhang Guo-lao on his ass

Zhong-kui 鍾魁

Zhong-kui is the exorcist *par excellence*. His picture is hung up at the end of the year, or on the 5th day of the 5th month, in order to scare away evil spirits and demons. He is supposed to be connected with the ancient No festivities which were held just before the → New Year. At this feast, men wearing masks representing the various gods drove all evil influences out of the city into the river or the sea. In modern pictures, he is shown with a sword, chasing the five → noxious creatures.

He is a frequent figure on the stage. In one 16th-century drama he

Zhong-kui with his magic sword

Zhong-kui with his bat, conjuring up good fortune

is a scholar who lives with his sister in the mountains of Western China. He is keen to attend the state examination, but lacks the money for the journey. So he goes to a rich benefactor who provides him with enough money and a → sword. On his way, he visits a temple whose monks lay on a feast for his benefactor. Zhong-kui gets drunk, swears at the monks and spoils the feast. If demons can harm men, he says, they should not be honoured with feasts but stamped out. The spirits of starvation in hell then complain to → Guan-yin, the goddess of mercy. She pardons him; but at Buddha's behest he is nevertheless punished, and he falls ill. While an invalid, he is attacked by demons who alter his physical appearance, turn his face black, and give him a comic beard into the bargain. He takes part in an examination and passes; at the ensuing examination, however, he is turned down because of his exceptionally hideous appearance, and he then commits suicide. In → hell, however, he is admired and is given an army of 3,000 soldiers to help him slay demons. He promises his benefactor his sister as wife. Several plays are concerned with the sister's betrothal. In yet another play, Zhong-kui commands 84,000 spirits and is installed as guardian at the bridge leading into the underworld.

Zhong-li Quan

鍾離權

Zhong-li is one of the eight → Immortals. He can be recognised by

Zhong-li Quan with a fan

the → fan he carries, and which he uses to bring the dead back to life. In pictures of him, the fan is often replaced by a feather duster. He is also often portrayed with his stomach bare. According to legend, Zhong-li lived at the time of the Han Dynasty, and discovered 'the great magic of gold-cinnabar' (the philosopher's stone). He could melt mercury and burn lead and turn them into yellow and white silver. And he could fly through the air.

According to one popular novel, he fought for the Song Dynasty (960–1278) against the people of Liao who ruled North China. Another of the eight Immortals, → Lü Dong-bin, took the part of the Liao, but was finally won over by Zhong-li. In one play Zhong-li appears as a judge called upon to decide in litigation again involving Lü Dong-bin. These two Immortals are closely connected with each other.

Zhu-ge Liang

諸葛亮

Zhu-ge Liang (AD 181–234) was China's greatest strategist. He it was who helped Liu Bei to found a dynasty in the state of Shu in Western China (present-day Sichuan). As Liu Bei's faithful adviser he belongs to the heroic figures of the time who have never lost their popularity, either in literature or in popular tradition. His story is told in the famous novel *San-*

guo zhi yan-yi – 'The Chronicle of the Three Kingdoms'. Liu Bei was looking around for a capable adviser and his attention was drawn to Zhu-ge Liang. A scene which was to be repeated in temples over and over again, shows Zhu-ge at the window of his house, which is surrounded by a garden and high walls. Liu arrives with two of his friends to visit him. Twice Zhu-ge pretends not to be at home; and it is only at Liu's third attempt that he is finally admitted to Zhu-ge's presence. The wily strategist wanted to see just how keen to get him Liu Bei really was.

Zodiac
huang-dao　　黄 道

'The Chinese year has a cycle of → twelve signs, to which the daily cycle of twelve two-hour periods corresponds. Each sign – and, accordingly, each two-hour period – is associated with a zodiacal sign. Thus, midnight and the beginning of the annual cycle are associated with the → rat, which is followed in turn by the ox, the tiger, the hare, the dragon, the snake, the horse, the

Zodiac and the annual cycles over a   century

sheep, the monkey, the cock, the dog and the pig (see separate entries). These cyclic symbols should not be confused with the zodiacal symbols as used in Western astronomy' (Richard Wilhelm). In astronomical and → astrological writings especially, the names of the animals are not used, being replaced by the enigmatic horary characters. Formerly time was reckoned in terms of the cycle of twelve, and, as each sign was imbued with the character of the equivalent animal, this had to be taken into account in arranging an engagement, for example; the signs under which the prospective bride and bridegroom had been born had to be compared for compatibility, and, should this be lacking, a planned marriage could be called off.

There are many legends concerning the zodiac – e.g. why the rat beat the ox into first place, and why the cat is absent. During the Middle Ages, the Chinese became acquainted with the zodiac of Western astronomy, but it never made any headway among them.

The → geomantic compass which is still used to locate favourable i.e. lucky sites for dwelling places and graves, gives as many as three readings indicating the cycle of the Twelve Branches, the cycle of the Ten Celestial Stems, and often the cycle of 28 lunar signs (*xiu*).

Bibliography

A-ying, *Zhong-guo nian-hua fa-zhan shi-lue* ('Chinese New Year Pictures: A History of Their Development'), Peking, 1954.

Alekseev, B. M., *Kitaiskaya narodnaya kartina* ('Chinese Folk Pictures'), Moscow, 1966.

Alexander, Mary and Frances, *A Handbook of Chinese Art Symbols*, Austin, Texas, 1972 (Von Boeckmann-Jones Press).

Altizer, Th. J. J., W. A. Beardslee and J. H. Young (eds), *Truth, Myth and Symbol*, Englewood Cliffs, NJ, 1962 (Prentice-Hall).

Bauer, Wolfgang, *China und die Hoffnung auf Glück. Paradiese, Utopien, Idealvorstellungen in der Geistesgeschichte Chinas* ('China and the Hope for Happiness: Paradises, Utopias and Ideals in Chinese Culture'), Munich, 1971.

Bewig, Jutta, *Chinesische Papierschnitte* (Wegweiser zur Volkskunde Nr. 21) ('The Chinese Paper Cut-out': Folklore Manuals No. 21), Hamburg, 1978 (Museum für Völkerkunde).

Burkhardt, V. R., *Chinese Creeds and Customs*, 3 vols, Hong Kong, 1953. Repr. in 1 vol., Taipeh, n.d.

Burrows, D. J., F. R. Lapidus and J. T. Shawcross (eds), *Myths and Motifs in Literature*, New York, 1973 (Free Press).

Cammann, Schuyler, *China's Dragon Robes*, New York, 1952 (Ronald Press).

Cammann, Schuyler, *Substance and Symbol in Chinese Toggles*, Philadelphia, 1962 (University of Pennsylvania Press).

Chavannes, Edouard, *Five Happinesses: Symbolism in Chinese Popular Art*, translated, annotated and illustrated by Elaine S. Atwood, New York, 1973 (Weatherhill Press). (Original in *Journal Asiatique*, Series 9, Vol. 18, 1901.)

Cole, Michael, *Comparative Studies of How People Think*, Cambridge, Mass., 1981 (Harvard University Press).

Day, Clarence B., *Chinese Peasant Cults*, Shanghai, 1940. Repr. Taipeh, 1974 (Cheng-wen Publications).

Doré, Henri, *Recherches sur les superstitions en Chine*, Vols 1–23, Shanghai, 1911–38 (Imprimerie de la Mission Catholique).

Eliasberg, Danielle, *Imagerie populaire chinoise du Nouvel An*, Cahiers publiés par l'Ecole Française d'Extrême-Orient, Vol. 34, 1978.

Fischer, Otto, *Chinesische Landschaftsmalerei* ('Chinese Landscape Painting'), Munich, 1923.

Geertz, C., *The Interpretation of Cultures*, New York, 1975 (Basic Books).

Granet, Marcel, *La pensée chinoise*, Paris, 1924.

Harper, Donald J., *The Wu shih erh ping fang*, Translation and Prolegomena, Ann Arbor, Mich., 1982 (University Microfilm International).

Koehn, A., 'Chinese Flower Symbolism', in *Monumenta Nipponica*, Tokyo, Series 8, 1952, pp. 121 ff.

Leitch, C. B., *Chinese Rugs*, New York, 1928 (Dodd, Mead).

Lessing, Ferdinand, 'Über die Symbolsprache in der chinesischen Kunst' ('On the Language of Symbolism in Chinese Art'), in *Sinica*, Frankfurt, Vol. 9, 1934, pp. 121 ff., 217 ff., 237 ff. Also as off-print, pub. by Erwin Rouselle, Frankfurt, n.d. (China-Institut).

Morgan, Harry T., *Chinese Symbols and Superstitions*, South Pasadena, Calif., 1942 (P. D. and Ione Perkins).

Morris, Desmond, *Gestures, Their Origin and Distribution*, New York, 1979 (Stein and Day).

Nozaki, Seikin, *Kissho zuan kaidai* ('Explanation of Representations of Good Luck Symbols'), 2 vols, Tientsin, 1928. Repr., Taipeh, 1979, under the title *Zhong-guo ji-xiang tu-an* ('Representations of Chinese Good Luck Symbols').

Ostwestliche Symbole und Seelenforschung ('Eastern and Western Symbols and Psychological Investigation'), Eranos Yearbook, 1934, ed. Olga Fröbe-Kapteyn, Zürich, 1935 (Rhein Verlag).

Pommeranz-Liedtke, Gerhard, *Chinesische Neujahrsbilder* ('Chinese New Year Pictures'), Dresden, 1961.

Pommeranz-Liedtke, Gerhard, *Die Weisheit der Kunst. Chinesische Steinabreibungen* ('The Wisdom of Art: Chinese Stone Rubbings'), Leipzig, 1963 (Insel).

Preetorius, Emil, 'Malerei als Schreibkunst' ('Painting as Calligraphy'), in *Kunst des Ostens, Katalog der 'Sammlung Preetorius'* ('Art of the Orient, Catalogue of the Preetorius Collection'), Munich, 1958.

Prunner, Gernot, *Papiergötter aus China* ('Paper Gods from China'), Hamburg, 1973 (Museum für Völkerkunde).

Ripley, M. C., *Collection of Antique Chinese Rugs*, New York, 1908 (Tiffany Studies).

Sälzle, Karl, *Tier und Mensch, Gottheit und Dämon. Das Tier in der Geistesgeschichte der Menschheit* ('Animal and Man, Divinity and Demon: Animals in the Cultural Development of Mankind'), Munich, 1965 (Bayerischer Landwirtschaftsverlag).

San cai tu hui ('Encyclopaedia of the Three Powers: Heaven, Earth, Man'), 1607. Repr. Taipeh, n.d.

Schuster, Carl, 'Some Peasant Embroideries from Western China', in *Embroidery*, Vol. 3, No. 4, pp. 87 ff.

Schuster, Carl, 'Relations of a China Embroidery Design: Eastern Europe and Western Asia, South-East Asia and Melanesia', in *Early*

Chinese Art and Its Possible Influence in the Pacific Basin, New York, 1972, Vol. 2, pp. 243 ff.

Schuster, Carl, 'A Comparative Study of Motives in Chinese Folk Embroideries', in *Monumenta Serica*, 1936, Vol. 2, pp. 21 ff. and 437 ff.

Smith, Arthur H., *Proverbs and Common Sayings from the Chinese*, 1914. Repr. New York, 1965 (Dover Publications).

Sperber, Dan, *Rethinking Symbolism*, translated by A. L. Morton, London, 1975 (Cambridge University Press).

Su yu dian ('Collection of Proverbs'), by Wang Yu-kang *et al.*, Taipeh, 1976 (Wu-chou Publishing Co.).

Tseng, Yu-ho, *Chinese Folk Art in American Collections*, Honolulu, 1977 (University of Hawaii Press).

Walker, Anthony R., *Farmers in the Hills*, Taipeh, 1981 (Asian Folklore and Social Life Monographs, Vol. 105).

Wang, Bo-min, *Zhong-guo ban-hua shi* ('History of Chinese Wood-engraving'), Shanghai, 1961.

Wang, Shu-cun, 'Yang-liu qing chun-nian-hua zi liao ji' ('Spring Pictures by the Masters in Yang-liu Qing'), *Materials*, Peking, 1959.

Wang, Shu-cun, *Zhong-guo de-di nian-hua yan-jiu* ('New Year Pictures from All Parts of China: An Exploratory Study'), Hong Kong, 1976.

Wang, Shu-cun, *Zhong-guo gu-dai pan-hua yan-jiu* ('Ancient Chinese Wood-engraving: An Investigation'), Peking, n.d. (Reprint of newspaper articles).

Weber, V.-F., *Koji Ho-ten. Dictionnaire à l'usage des amateurs et collecteurs d'objets d'art Japonais et Chinois*, 2 vols, Paris, 1923 (privately printed).

Weigand, Jörg, *Fensterblumen* ('Window Flowers'), Rosenheim, 1977 (Rosenheimer Verlag).

Werner, E. T. Chalmers, *Myths and Legends of China*, London, 1922.

Werner, E. T. Chalmers, *A Dictionary of Chinese Mythology*, Shanghai, 1932.

West, Stephan H., *Vaudeville and Narratives: Aspects of Chinese Theatre*, Wiesbaden, 1977 (Steiner).

Wickert, Erwin, *China von innen gesehen* ('China from Inside'), Stuttgart, 1982 (Deutsche Verlags-Anstalt).

Wilhelm, Richard, *Die Seele Chinas* ('The Soul of China'), Berlin, 1926 (Reimar Hobling). Repr., ed. Wolfgang Bauer, Frankfurt, 1980 (Suhrkamp).

Wilhelm, Richard, 'Die chinesische Literatur' ('Chinese Literature'), in *Handbuch der Literaturwissenschaft*, ed. Otto Walzel, Wildpark-Potsdam, 1926 (Athenaion).

Wilhelm, Richard, *Chinesische Volksmärchen* ('Chinese Folktales'), Jena, 1914 (Diederichs).

Williams, C. A. S., *Manual of Chinese Metaphor*, Shanghai, 1920 (Commercial Press).

Williams, C. A. S., *Outlines of Chinese Symbolism and Art Motives*, Shanghai, 1932 (Commercial Press). Repr. under the title *Chinese Symbolism and Art Motives*, New York, 1960 (Julian Press).

Wolfe, Bernard, *The Daily Life of a Chinese Courtesan*, Hong Kong, 1981.

Yang-liu Qing ban-hua ('Wood-engravings by Yang-liu Qing'), Taipeh, 1976.

Yetts, W. Perceval, 'Notes on Chinese Flower Symbolism', *Journal of the Royal Asiatic Society*, January 1941.

Yetts, W. Perceval, 'Symbol in Chinese Art', in *The China Society*, Leiden, 1912 (E. W. Brill).

Zhou, Sou-juan, *Hua-qian xin ji* ('New Remarks on Flowers'), Nanking, 1958.

Zhou, Sou-juan, *Hua-qian hou ji* ('Subsequent Remarks on Flowers'), Nanking, n.d.

Zozayong, *Introduction to Korean Folk Painting*, Seoul, 1977.